Architect of Death
at Auschwitz

ALSO BY JOHN W. PRIMOMO

The Appomattox Generals: The Parallel Lives of Joshua L. Chamberlain, USA, and John B. Gordon, CSA, Commanders at the Surrender Ceremony of April 12, 1865 (McFarland, 2013)

Architect of Death at Auschwitz

A Biography of Rudolf Höss

JOHN W. PRIMOMO

McFarland & Company, Inc., Publishers
Jefferson, North Carolina

Library of Congress Cataloguing-in-Publication Data

Names: Primomo, John W., 1952– author.
Title: Architect of Death at Auschwitz : A Biography of Rudolf Höss / John W. Primomo.
Other titles: Biography of Rudolf Höss
Description: Jefferson, North Carolina : McFarland & Company, Inc., Publishers, 2020 | Includes bibliographical references and index.
Identifiers: LCCN 2020026130 | ISBN 9781476681467 (print : acid free paper) ∞
 ISBN 9781476639420 (ebook)
Subjects: LCSH: Höss, Rudolf, 1900-1947. | Auschwitz (Concentration camp)—Officials and employees—Biography. | Concentration camp commandants—Poland—Oświęcim—Biography. | War criminals—Germany—Biography. | Nazis—Biography. | Auschwitz (Concentration camp)—History. | Höss, Rudolf, 1900-1947. Kommandant in Auschwitz. English
Classification: LCC D805.5.A96 P75 2020 | DDC 940.53/1853862 [B]—dc23
LC record available at https://lccn.loc.gov/2020026130

British Library cataloguing data are available
ISBN (print) 978-1-4766-8146-7
ISBN (ebook) 978-1-4766-3942-0

© 2020 John W. Primomo. All rights reserved

No part of this book may be reproduced or transmitted in any form or by any means, electronic or mechanical, including photocopying or recording, or by any information storage and retrieval system, without permission in writing from the publisher.

Front cover *inset* detail of photograph of SS officers socializing on the grounds of the SS retreat Solahuette outside of Auschwitz, showing Rudolf Höss (United States Holocaust Museum, courtesy of Anonymous Donor); *background* photograph of Auschwitz Block 11 courtyard and Death Wall (Yulia Moiseeva/Shutterstock)

Printed in the United States of America

McFarland & Company, Inc., Publishers
 Box 611, Jefferson, North Carolina 28640
 www.mcfarlandpub.com

To my grandson Wesley Fritz Baird,
whose great grandfather
Colonel Archer Morton Baird
flew in Eager Eagle II, a B-17 Flying Fortress
in the 509th Bombardment Squadron,
351st Bomb Group, 8th Air Force, World War II

Captain Richard E. Hathaway and the crew of B-17 Flying Fortress Eager Eagle II, October 22, 1943. Colonel Archer Morton Baird, far right (courtesy Imperial War Museum).

Acknowledgments

The author wishes to acknowledge with deep and sincere gratitude the extraordinary efforts of Ms. Sandra Lynn Jesse, whose tireless hours of editing these pages proved invaluable. Her keen eye and thoughtful advice provided great assistance in the effort to create effective and informative prose. To the extent this book falls short of scholarly and literary standards, the failure is attributable to the stubbornness of the author, not the wisdom of the editor.

Table of Contents

Acknowledgments vi
Preface 1
Introduction 4

I. Escape and Capture   13
II. Early Years   28
III. The SS   39
IV. Creation of Auschwitz   48
V. The Code of Barbarism   66
VI. Entrance Into Hell   74
VII. Life Within the Wire   85
VIII. Crystal Death   110
IX. Property, Corruption and the Inspectorate   148
X. Justice   157
XI. Responsibility and Atonement   169
XII. Execution   188
XIII. Conclusion   198

Appendix I: Höss Statement of March 14, 1946   205
Appendix II: Höss Affidavit of April 5, 1946   210
Appendix III: Photos of Child Victims   214
Chapter Notes   219
Bibliography   233
Index   237

Preface

In the war crimes trial of SS-Obergruppenführer Oswald Pohl in Nuremberg in 1946, a member of the Tribunal, having heard evidence about the monstrous atrocities at Auschwitz, referred to Rudolf Höss as the greatest mass murderer in history. SS-Reichsführer Heinrich Himmler appointed Höss in 1940 to be the commandant of the newly established Auschwitz concentration camp in Oświęcim, Poland. Then, in 1941, Himmler summoned Höss to Berlin to inform him that Führer Adolf Hitler had chosen Auschwitz for implementation of the Final Solution. As commandant of Auschwitz, the largest and most notorious of Nazi death camps, and later as head of all Nazi concentration camps, Höss methodically and effectively executed Hitler's order to exterminate European Jews. More than 1.1 million men, women and children, mainly Jews and Poles, were put to death at Auschwitz.

Unlike many Nazis in positions of power with affluent backgrounds, Höss came from humble beginnings. At the Nuremberg trial of high-ranking Nazis after the war, Lt. Commander Whitney Harris, an American prosecutor, said Höss reminded him of a "grocery clerk." Though having no more than average intelligence, Höss utilized his own initiative and resourcefulness to build Auschwitz from a few dilapidated Polish Army barracks into the greatest murder factory in the Third Reich. Influenced by Hitler and SS indoctrination, he willingly engaged in genocide to eliminate "enemies of the State"—the Jews. Being a good Nazi and well trained by the SS, Höss followed the Final Solution order without question. As commandant, he possessed the power of life and death over hundreds of thousands of human beings. Höss brutally wielded that power without conscience.

Fleeing to avoid prosecution for the crimes he perpetrated, Höss became a fugitive after the war. He was captured by the British in March 1946. His importance in the chronicle of the Final Solution is magnified in light of the role he played after his arrest. In April 1946, Höss was taken to Nuremberg, where he testified at the trial of Herman Göring, Albert Speer and other major Nazis. Unlike many of his Nazi colleagues, who feigned ignorance or denied participation in the Final Solution, Höss acknowledged his participation at Auschwitz in the gassing of millions of Jews and supplied extensive details concerning the killing operations. His testimony established that Hitler ordered the extermination of the Jews in the Final Solution. The statements he gave at trial and in response to interviews by the prison psychologist and psychiatrist at Nuremberg provide extraordinary insight into the demented Nazi psyche, as well as Höss' own thought process. Apathetically, with no emotion whatsoever, Höss related the process of killing hundreds of thousands of men, women and children in the gas chambers at Auschwitz.

After Nuremberg, Höss was taken to Poland to stand trial for the atrocities he perpetrated at Auschwitz. In his testimony and memoirs, which he wrote while awaiting trial, Höss admitted sending millions of Jews to the gas chambers and reported that hundreds of thousands of persons at Auschwitz died due to starvation and disease. Höss' autobiographical reflections provide a unique perspective on events at Auschwitz, as no other Nazi as close to the killing process was so forthcoming. While admitting to many of the horrors of Auschwitz, Höss attempts to paint his legacy in as favorable a light as possible, omitting many gruesome and horrific details. He claimed that he never mistreated a prisoner and blamed his subordinates for the cruelty imposed on inmates. Höss also said that Hitler and Himmler, not he, were responsible for the calamity of the Final Solution, and that he (Höss) was simply an unknowing "cog in the wheel" of the Nazi extermination machine. Primo Levi, an Auschwitz survivor who wrote the introduction to a publication of Höss' memoirs, stated that "despite his efforts at defending himself, the author comes across as what he is: a coarse, stupid, arrogant, long-winded scoundrel, who sometimes blatantly lies."

This book is both a biography of Höss and a critical analysis of his memoirs. From his loveless, solitary childhood through his service as one of the youngest German soldiers in World War I and his post-war conviction and imprisonment for murder, the author discusses the factors that shaped his future. After entering the Nazi Party, Höss became a farmer, only to forsake his profession when Himmler induced him to join the SS. The book addresses Höss' rise through the ranks and his appointment as the Auschwitz commandant. Höss' creation and supervision of the most infamous and deadly Nazi concentration camp is exposed in excruciating and horrifying detail.

Even in its infancy, when Poles constituted the bulk of prisoners, death was imposed arbitrarily on thousands of inmates in the courtyard of Block 11. Utilizing Auschwitz records, as well as the testimony of numerous survivors and even members of the SS, the book describes the fear and emotional pain of families torn from their homes and the terrifying death in the gas chambers suffered by hundreds of thousands of men, women and children within minutes of arrival at Auschwitz. It details the tortuous and tormented life endured by those found fit to work. Horrendous living conditions, marked by wholly inadequate food, little or no medical care and constant barbaric treatment by SS guards and prisoner functionaries, destroyed the physical and mental well-being of internees. The use of prisoners for slave labor under inhuman conditions further increased the death toll. Jewish inmates were also subjected to painful and often lethal medical experimentation by unscrupulous doctors such as the infamous Josef Mengele. Nuremberg trial records, as well as Höss' own trial proceedings, document the monstrous crimes he committed. The book dispels the impression Höss attempts to create in his memoirs that he was never cruel to or mistreated any prisoners and demonstrates, instead, how he acted with unscrupulous brutality.

Despite the distinct and significant role played by Höss in the torture and killing of human beings on behalf of the Third Reich, little has been written about the commandant of Auschwitz. The version of reality expressed in his autobiography has, for the most part, gone unchallenged. As time passes since the Holocaust, fewer survivors remain to bear witness to the terrible events. The crimes committed at Auschwitz were so horrific and so extensive that many people after World War II, including Jews, did not believe the stories of survivors. Even now, a tendency has arisen to discount the truth of the Holocaust. The sheer magnitude and horror of the tragedy are simply too impossible for some people to believe. Of critical importance is the need to be reminded of the crimes committed by Hitler and ordinary Germans like Rudolf Höss. Anti-Semitism and racial hatred persist. Genocide continues. The painful memory of the Holocaust must be recalled and experienced no matter how many years pass. Simon Weisenthal, a Holocaust survivor who dedicated his life after the war to tracking down and gathering information on fugitive Nazi war criminals, said: "For evil to flourish, it only requires good men to do nothing." Even a "grocery clerk" or farmer can kill millions if given the power.

Introduction

Prior to and during World War II, the Nazis operated numerous labor, concentration and extermination camps in Germany, Poland and other European countries. The largest and most infamous of these camps was Auschwitz, located in southwestern Poland. From its inception in the spring of 1940 until November 1943, Rudolf Franz Ferdinand Höss served as the commandant of Auschwitz. Höss' deadly efficiency led to a promotion in late 1943 to oversee all Nazi concentration camps from the central office near Berlin, a position he held until the end of the war. Owing to his expertise and experience in exterminating European Jews in the gas chambers, he returned to Auschwitz for several months in 1944 to supervise the destruction of almost 400,000 Hungarian Jews.[1]

Auschwitz derives its name from the nearby town of Oświęcim (Auschwitz in German), Poland, about 37 miles west of Krakow. Not initially intended for the mass killing of human beings, Auschwitz began as a transit camp, a stopover for prisoners being transported to other camps and as a camp for Polish political prisoners. Before long, the Third Reich envisioned other purposes. Over time, the concentration camp evolved into Auschwitz I (the original camp near Oświęcim), Auschwitz II (Birkenau, the massive killing center where hundreds of thousands of Jews were sent to the gas chambers) and Auschwitz III (the slave labor camp at Monowitz), as well as numerous satellite camps. The first prisoners—30 common criminals from Germany—arrived on May 20, 1940. By the time the camp was evacuated in 1945, more than a million people had lost their lives there. Though the Nazis tried to destroy evidence of their crimes when they abandoned Auschwitz, the remains of the camp itself, testimony of survivors and documents which have been preserved tell a story of murder, inhuman deprivation and brutal punishment and torture unequaled in the history of mankind.

Rudolf Höss was not the type of person one would expect to be a mass murderer. He was raised in a strict Catholic family. His father, who intended for his son to enter the priesthood, was not alive to influence or direct his son's life choices as an adult, having died while Höss was an adolescent. Following the outbreak of World War I, Höss joined the cavalry and fought as one of the youngest soldiers in the German army, receiving multiple wounds and several decorations. After the war, he joined one of the Freikorps, volunteer militia units of German soldiers that were used as the government or their individual commander saw fit to protect the borders or settle internal political disputes. While in the Freikorps, Höss met Heinrich Himmler, soon to become one of Adolf Hitler's closest confidants and the head of the SS. In the early 1920s, after hearing a speech by Hitler, Höss joined the Nazi Party as one of its earliest members.

In 1924, Höss was convicted of the murder of a fellow Freikorps member and spent several years in prison. Upon his release, he joined the Artaman League, a right-wing, anti–Jewish group dedicated to working the land. In the Artaman League, Höss met and married Hedwig Hensel. In 1933, Höss joined the SS, the elite military unit of the Nazi Party that served as Hitler's bodyguard and special police force. Initially, Höss' role was limited to managing the horse stable on an estate in Pomerania in northern Germany where he worked. In 1934, at Himmler's urging, Höss left the Artamans and became a member of the active SS. His first assignment was the Dachau concentration camp near Munich, one of the first camps established for imprisonment of "enemies of the Reich." Höss rose rapidly through the ranks and, in 1938, was transferred to the Sachsenhausen concentration camp near Berlin. When World War II broke out and a new camp was established in Oświęcim, Poland, Höss was made commandant.

From the beginning, German Führer and dictator Adolf Hitler left no doubt of the contempt he felt for Jews, blaming them for the defeat of Germany in World War I in 1918 and the ills that thereafter befell the German economy. In his 1925 autobiography *Mein Kampf*, Hitler refers to the "Jewish world menace," condemns Jews as parasites and calls for elimination of the existing "Jewish state." He wrote: "…I believe that I am acting in accordance with the will of the Almighty Creator; *by defending myself against the Jew, I am fighting for the work of the Lord.*" Once Hitler led the National Socialist Party to power, German Jews were ostracized, persecuted and forced to flee Germany. Anti-Semitic laws were passed, making it illegal for Jews to vote and own property, prohibiting non–Jews from marrying Jews and depriving Jews of German citizenship. Nazi violence against Jews culminated in *Kristallnacht* on November 9–10, 1938, when German paramilitary forces and German civilians destroyed Jewish-owned stores, buildings and synagogues across the country. In addition to subjugation of Jews, Hitler sought proliferation of the Aryan race and territorial expansion known as *lebensraum*. His invasions of Austria and Czechoslovakia were the first steps in accomplishing these goals.

Meanwhile, contrary to the Treaty of Versailles that formally ended

World War I, Hitler built a powerful German military. Hoping to avoid another world war, European powers sought to placate Hitler rather than challenge his aggression. Hitler assured the world he had no further territorial ambitions after Czechoslovakia and, following the horror of World War I, people wanted to believe him. On January 30, 1939, just prior to his invasion of Czechoslovakia, Hitler delivered a speech in the Reichstag to the German Parliament and the German people in which he prophesied that if war was to break out, it would mean "the annihilation of the Jewish race throughout Europe." Initially, it appeared, Nazi policy meant forced emigration of European Jews. As time passed, however, Hitler's true desire became manifest: extermination of all European Jews.[2]

On September 1, 1939, Germany, in accordance with Hitler's design and without provocation, invaded Poland to the east, inaugurating World War II. The Soviet Union offered no resistance. On August 23, 1939, just one week before Germany's invasion, Germany and the Soviet Union signed a non-aggression agreement, the Molotov-Ribbentrop Pact, in which they agreed, among other things, to divide territory in Poland. From September 1939 until the summer of 1941, Nazis took their assault on Jewry to the east, destroying Polish synagogues while persecuting and imposing numerous restrictions on Jews in Poland, which was home to over three million Jews, the largest Jewish community in Europe. They were forced to live in ghettoes in Warsaw, Krakow, Lodz and other cities in crowded, unsanitary conditions with little food. Large numbers of Polish Jews died. Hitler hated Communism almost as much as he hated Jews. Stalin should have known what was coming. In June 1941, Hitler, in pursuit of more *lebensraum*, attacked his former Soviet Union ally to the east, invading territory previously occupied by the Soviets, which now included eastern Poland and the former eastern European countries of Estonia, Latvia and Lithuania.[3]

As German armies rolled eastward and incorporated more territory into Hitler's sphere of influence, more Jews were subjected to Nazi control. Now, however, persecution took on a more systematic, deadly form. Following the German armies eastward were several *Einsatzgruppen*, SS death squads tasked with murdering the intelligentsia, as well as any elements hostile to the Third Reich, including Jews. On June 17, 1941, the *Einsatzgruppen* officers met with SS-Obergruppenführer Reinhard Heydrich, the chief of the Reich Main Security Office (RSHA), in Berlin, who gave them orders to exterminate Communists and Jews. The *Einsatzgruppen* were aided in their efforts by local police and volunteers motivated by long-standing anti–Semitism and angered by the belief that Jews collaborated with the Communists, who committed numerous atrocities during the recent Soviet occupation. The Wehrmacht—the German Army—also participated in the executions. At first, only men were shot; however, by August 1941, the death squads were instructed it was no longer necessary to discriminate between men and women. Children, too, were murdered. By the end of 1941, the total number of Jewish civilians killed exceeded 500,000 and may have been as high as 800,000.[4]

In January 1942, the Nazis conducted a conference at Wannsee outside Berlin, attended by senior party officials and members of the SS, to discuss the Final Solution to the Jewish problem. The meeting was led by Heydrich, accompanied by SS-Obersturmbannführer Adolf Eichmann. The minutes of the meeting were purposely left vague, but the underlying intent was unmistakable. The transcript shows the participants knew:

> Without a doubt a large number [of Jews] will become natural casualties. It was clear to everyone concerned with this matter about the consequences of this forced deportation.

According to Heydrich, after prior approval by Hitler, the previous policy of emigration of the Jews had been superseded by a policy of "evacuating" the Jews to the East. "Evacuation" meant annihilation by a combination of forced labor and mass murder. The minutes included a list of European countries accompanied by the number of Jews to be "evacuated" from each country, a total of 11 million. The participants discussed the difficulty in shooting millions of people, but did not decide on the means of accomplishing their objective.[5]

Rudolf Höss, the Auschwitz commandant, was not a high-level Nazi and did not merit an invitation to Wannsee. Had he been present, he could have provided Heydrich and the other Nazi officials with a solution to their problem. At Auschwitz, he had already successfully tested, on humans, Zyklon B, a pesticide in the form of crystals that turned to gas at a certain temperature. In September 1941, Höss used Zyklon B to kill large numbers of Soviet prisoners of war. Certainly, the same technology could be used on the Jews. It would be.

By 1942, Höss already knew more about the Final Solution than most of the Wannsee participants. In the summer of 1941, Reichsführer-SS Himmler entrusted him with a "secret Reich matter." Hitler had chosen Auschwitz to implement the Final Solution on account of its easy access by rail and because the extensive site offered space for measures ensuring isolation. Himmler told Höss that if the Nazis did not exterminate the Jews, the Jews would destroy the German people. Eichmann, who was in charge of rounding up and deporting Jews to Auschwitz, knew of the Final Solution and had visited Höss in Auschwitz in September 1941 to coordinate the details. Both Höss and Eichmann were merely waiting for Himmler to issue the necessary orders.

Meanwhile, from time to time, the Jews in the ghettoes were being liquidated. They were told to pack one bag and were transported in cattle cars, sometimes for days, without food and water. Those deported to the east in the spring and early summer of 1942 were often shot upon reaching their destination. Some were herded into gas vans and suffocated with carbon monoxide. Around the same time, deportees were sent to the extermination camps at Chelmno, Belzec and Sobibor in Poland, while work began on another death camp at Treblinka near Warsaw. Jews transported to Auschwitz, who were imprisoned as slave laborers, were subjected to abominable conditions, inflicting death by disease, starvation or physical beatings by the SS. The primary means of extermination, however, was the gas chambers. Throughout the remainder of the war, until the territory occupied by these camps was liberated by Allied forces, the Nazis continued their systematic destruction of Jews, Roma and Sinti gypsies, Soviet prisoners of war, homosexuals, Jehovah's Witnesses and political opponents.[6]

At the end of the war, an International Military Tribunal created by the United States, the United Kingdom, France and the Soviet Union, placed the highest-ranking Nazi officials on trial. The Indictment charged the defendants with (1) Crimes against Peace, (2) War Crimes, including murder, ill-treatment and deportation to slave labor of civilian population, and (3) Crimes against Humanity: namely, murder, extermination, enslavement, deportation and other inhumane acts committed against a civilian population, before or during the war, and persecutions on political, racial or religious grounds. The trial was held in the Palace of Justice in Nuremberg, Germany. Hitler and Himmler had committed suicide, as had Joseph Goebbels, the Nazi propaganda minister. Reichsmarschall Herman Göring, who had been captured by the Allies, was the most notable of the defendants. The trial began in November 1945.[7]

Rudolf Höss eluded capture for almost a year after the end of the war. On March 11, 1946, posing as farmer Franz Lang, he was arrested by British authorities in northern Germany and signed an eight-page statement admitting to atrocities and mass murder at Auschwitz. Based on information from Adolf Eichmann, Höss testified that 2.5 million people had been sent to the gas chambers at Auschwitz and that another half million had died from disease and starvation. In the absence of precise records, the actual figures will never be known. While the true numbers of victims are believed to be lower, they still defy reason. According to the United States Holocaust Memorial Museum, the best estimates of the number of victims at the Auschwitz concentration camp complex, including the killing center at Auschwitz-Birkenau, between 1940 and 1945 are: Jews (1,095,000 deported to Auschwitz, of whom 960,000 died); non-Jewish Poles (140–150,000 deported, of whom 74,000 died); Roma and Sinti gypsies (23,000 deported, of whom 21,000 died); Soviet prisoners of war (15,000 deported and died) and other nationalities (25,000 deported, of whom 12,000 died).[8]

Höss was transported to Nuremberg and called as a witness by defendant Ernst Kaltenbrunner, an SS general and Chief of the RSHA, a position Kaltenbrunner obtained after the assassination of Heydrich in June 1942. On the witness stand, Höss freely acknowledged his involvement in the mass extermination of Jews at Auschwitz. Parts of an affidavit, signed by Höss on April 5, 1946, were submitted into evidence, providing more details as to Hitler's decision to destroy the Jews, the process of selecting those who were fit to work and those who would be sent directly to the gas chambers, the operation of the gas chambers and the disposal of bodies. Both Höss' testimony and his affidavit would be presented at later trials of other Nazis. The evidence provided by Höss at Nuremberg regarding the Final Solution and his part in its implementation proved to be a dagger to the heart of the case of the defendants on trial. Lt. Commander Harris said later that Höss' testimony was integral in establishing the Final Solution and the Nazi atrocities.[9]

While awaiting his own trial before a Polish tribunal in 1947, Höss wrote an autobiography covering his childhood, military experience in World War I, imprisonment for murder, entry into the Nazi Party and experiences at the Dachau and Sachsenhausen concentration camps. He also wrote about Auschwitz and his job as director of all Nazi concentration camps, as well as his efforts to avoid capture by the Allies. Finally, his memoirs include his thoughts about various SS personnel with whom he interacted. Höss' recollections were written between October 1946 and April 1947 at the suggestion of Jan Sehn, the prosecuting attorney for the Polish War Crimes Commission in Warsaw. The statements of Höss provide extraordinary insight, not only into the mechanics of the Nazi killing machine, but also the mind of an individual who willingly, without question, followed Hitler's order to kill hundreds of thousands of innocent men, women and children. Many Nazis denied knowing of the Final Solution, while others admitted awareness but denied involvement. Only Höss, whether from pride in his achievement or resolution to his fate, admitted that he superintended the destruction of more than a million human beings. As noted by prosecutor Harris, there could be no doubt about the Holocaust after Höss testified.[10]

Without emotion, and as a matter of fact, Höss explained his reasons for implementing Hitler's plan of eliminating an entire race of people from Europe. According to Höss, "Every German had to subordinate himself unquestionably and uncritically to the leaders of the State, who alone were in a position to understand the real needs of the people and to direct them along the right path." When reproached after his arrest for not refusing to obey the extermination order, Höss pointed out that he was a soldier and an officer and compared himself to a pilot who refused to drop his bombs on a target with no military significance, knowing that women and children would be killed.[11]

Some historians have challenged the accuracy of parts of Höss' testimony as to certain dates, numbers and names. According to Höss, the eight-page statement he gave to the British after his arrest was obtained by beating and while he was in a state of forced intoxication. However, his affidavit of April 5, 1946, his Nuremberg testimony and his autobiography were not coerced and are consistent in all material respects with each other and with the statement obtained by the British. His accounts also substantially agree with reports by surviving prisoners and Nazi guards. If Höss made factual misstatements, they are, in all likelihood, simple errors not intended to mislead. As noted by Primo Levi, an Auschwitz survivor, Höss' autobiography is "substantially truthful." If there is deception, it occurs in his attempts to convince posterity he pitied the victims and was helpless to control his subordinates in the barbaric treatment of Auschwitz prisoners. Höss also omits a great deal of the atrocities imposed on Auschwitz inmates. He attempts to avoid responsibility on the ground, rejected by the Tribunal that judged him, that he was simply following orders.[12]

Throughout his memoirs, Höss repeats that he was not a sadist, was not cruel and never mistreated a prisoner. Auschwitz survivors and even testimony from SS who worked under Höss' command portray him in a far more nefarious light. Höss' directives, beginning at Sachsenhausen and continuing at Auschwitz, brand him not as the mild-mannered commandant he would appear from his memoirs, but as a brutal SS disciplinarian who did not consider prisoners to be people. Höss blamed others for the evils of Auschwitz and claimed he always pitied the victims whose lives were extinguished. Yet the example he set for his subordinates and his lifelong allegiance to National Socialism belie his effort to escape culpability.

Ironically, at the end of his autobiography, Höss states, "I could never have brought myself to have made this confession of my most secret thoughts and feelings, had I not been approached with a disarming humanity and understanding [by his Polish jailers] that I never dared to expect." As the commandant of Auschwitz, Höss demonstrated neither humanity nor understanding for fear it would be taken as a sign of weakness by the prisoners. At the end of his life, the unexpected compassion he received softened his heart, to a degree. In a final statement, Höss asked for forgiveness from the Polish people for his "enormous crimes against humanity," but he did not apologize for killing one million Jews in the gas chambers.

After time for deliberation, Höss conceded in his memoirs that extermination of the Jews was fundamentally wrong. Yet, incredibly, he did not reach this conclusion on moral grounds but because it brought the wrath of the world down on Germany and led the Jews closer to their "ultimate objective." Nazis systematically killed six million Jews and millions of other individuals during World War II. The statements of Rudolf Höss establish that he proudly and efficiently built and operated the Auschwitz extermination camp, sending more than 1.1 million men, women and children to their deaths. By his testimony, Höss provides a unique internal perspective to the most deliberate, evil and catastrophic horrors ever perpetrated by human beings upon one another.[13]

I

Escape and Capture

In the fall of 1944, most objective observers knew Germany would lose the war. The Americans and British were advancing north through Italy and closing in on Berlin from the west while the Soviet army was approaching from the east. Reichsführer-SS Heinrich Himmler knew the end was coming and what it meant. While many in the outside world had heard about the Final Solution and the horrors of Nazi concentration camps, some did not believe the stories. Others thought they were exaggerated: "No such places could possibly exist. Germans are decent, honorable, cultured people. Even the Nazis could not murder millions of men, women and children simply because they are Jewish." Himmler knew that as the Allies took more and more territory, especially in the east, they would liberate the extermination camps, and the Nazis would be unable to hide the abomination they had perpetrated.

In November 1944, Rudolf Franz Ferdinand Höss was the head of Amtsgruppe DI in the Inspectorate of the Concentration Camps, part of the SS Economic-Administrative Main Office (WVHA), overseeing all Nazi concentration camps. In Budapest, Hungary, he met with SS-Obersturmbannführer Adolf Eichmann, who was responsible for rounding up Jews in their native countries and deporting them to the extermination camps. According to Eichmann, negotiations were ongoing between Himmler and Jewish representatives in Switzerland through various middlemen. Eichmann told Höss that Himmler had directed that all exterminations must stop immediately. On November 25, 1944, Himmler ordered that the gas chambers and crematoria at Auschwitz be demolished. His purpose was unmistakable: destroy the most obvious evidence that the Nazis had been systematically killing European Jews.[1]

In the short span of mid–May to early July 1944, under Höss' direct supervision, Auschwitz gas chambers had exterminated almost 400,000 Hungarian Jews, more than at any other comparable time period. The Nazis killed and burned almost 10,000 human beings per day using five gas chambers, crematoria and outdoor pits. After July 1944, gassing significantly diminished. Now, in compliance with Himmler's order, workers began dismantling crematorium II by removing the furnace, chimneys and roof. Openings were made to place dynamite charges. In December 1944, crematorium III was disassembled. A squad of 50 women was formed to remove ashes from the incineration pits, fill them in, and cover them with turf. Crematorium IV, which was damaged during a prisoner revolt in October 1944, and Bunker II, which served as a gas chamber, were also taken apart. A barracks used as an undressing room for victims before entering Bunker II was torn down. On January 20, 1945, crematoria II and III were blown up with dynamite. Crematorium V was destroyed January 26, 1945.[2]

In the summer of 1944, the SS moved about half of the population of Auschwitz (then a total of about 130,000 inmates) to other camps. On January 18, 1945, the SS marched the remaining Auschwitz prisoners who were able to walk, approximately 56,000 inmates, including those of the Auschwitz satellite camps, west, away from the advancing Soviet Army. On January 27, 1945, the Soviets liberated Auschwitz and found about 7,000 prisoners, the total combined from Auschwitz I (the original camp), Auschwitz II (Birkenau) and Monowitz (the slave labor camp), who had been left behind because they were too weak to be removed on January 18. The fact that the Nazis left anyone alive was truly fortunate.

Remains of Crematorium II at Auschwitz II-Birkenau (author photograph).

I. Escape and Capture

The Soviets also found the remnants of Adolf Hitler's Final Solution. Despite the blasting of crematoria II and III, the walls, floors, underground dressing rooms and gas chambers were clearly visible. Parts of the furnace of crematorium V remained. Other metal furnace parts were located on the grounds of Bunker II. The Nazis had burned down 29 of 35 storehouses where property stolen from incoming Jews was collected. In the warehouses that remained, the liberators found about 370,000 men's suits and 837,000 women's coats and dresses. Some 44,000 pairs of shoes were left, along with prostheses, household goods and other personal items. Perhaps most disturbing was the 7.7 tons of human hair, packed and ready for transport, which would be used to create yarn for garments for German workers and soldiers. According to estimates, the hair was shaved off about 140,000 female prisoners.[3]

While attempting to destroy evidence of the Final Solution, Himmler engaged in secret diplomacy with the Western Allies in the fantastic hope he would be chosen to lead Germany into peace after the war. Himmler proposed releasing tens of thousands of Jews as a good faith gesture to jump-start the negotiations. At the end of World War I, Hitler claimed (and World War I veterans like Höss believed) that Germany lost the war not due to any failure of German soldiers on the battlefield, but because Jews, among others, stabbed Germany in the back. Ironically, near the end of World War II, it would be Himmler, one of Hitler's closest confidants, who would betray him,

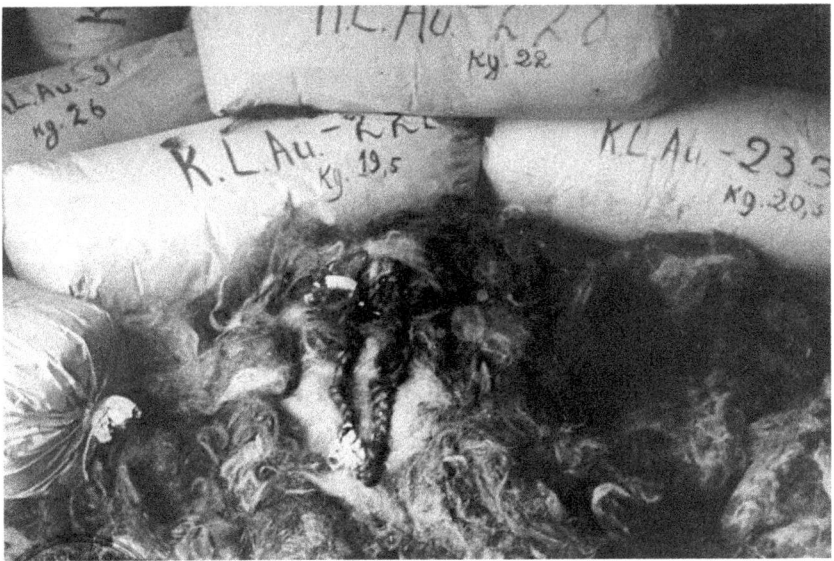

Bales of hair of female prisoners found in Auschwitz warehouses after liberation (courtesy U.S. Holocaust Memorial Museum, Washington, D.C.).

and he proposed using Jews to do it. Meanwhile, in January 1945, Himmler had given the order for the complete evacuation of all the camps in the east. According to several testimonies, he warned camp commanders: "The Führer holds you personally responsible for … making sure that not a single prisoner from the concentration camps falls alive into the hands of the enemy." No matter what he did about the Jews without Hitler's knowledge, Himmler knew he could not openly defy Hitler without facing certain death.[4]

In addition to keeping witnesses out of the hands of the Allies, Himmler also, incredibly, wanted the camp prisoners to continue their slave labor on behalf on the German war effort. The retreat from Auschwitz in January 1945 was properly called a Death March. It was the middle of winter. Auschwitz prisoners, already severely compromised physically by conditions at the camp, were forced to march through the falling snow in intense cold. Some of the prisoners headed northwest toward Germany while others marched due west toward Austria. They had little or nothing to eat; thirst was their worst enemy. Inmates were forced to sleep wherever they stopped—pig sties or barns or sometimes in the open. Many stumbled to the ground due to lack of strength. Without the assistance of a friend or relative or other prisoner to get them back on their feet, an SS guard would simply shoot them to keep the march moving. Corpses lined the roads. Open rail cars at Gleiwitz, 50 kilometers from Auschwitz, and Wodzislaw, 65 kilometers away, carried them the rest of the journey, if they could make it that far. Prisoners even died while riding in the open freight cars, only to be tossed out along the tracks to make room for the remaining inmates and guards.[5]

As the war now progressed toward its inevitable end, communications were breaking down. SS-Obergruppenführer Oswald Pohl, the head of the WVHA, received no reports from Richard Baer, the Auschwitz commandant, regarding the location of the prisoners removed from Auschwitz. Pohl decided to send Höss in search of the Auschwitz prisoners. He found Baer at the Gross-Rosen concentration camp near Swidnica in western Poland making preparations for the arrival of the Auschwitz inmates. However, Baer had no idea where the 50,000 Auschwitz inmates might be. Although the original plan called for the Auschwitz prisoners to relocate to Gross-Rosen, that course was no longer feasible because of the Soviet advance. Höss drove on, hoping to reach Auschwitz in time to assure that the order for the destruction of everything important had been properly carried out. He could get no farther than the Oder River, near Raciborz, Poland, 85 kilometers west of Auschwitz; Soviet armored spearheads were already fanning out on the far side of the river.[6]

There, Höss met up with the Auschwitz prisoners:

> On all the roads and tracks in Upper Silesia west of the Oder I now met columns of prisoners, struggling through the deep snow. They had no food. Most of the

> non-commissioned officers in charge of these stumbling columns of corpses had no idea where they were supposed to be going. They only knew that their final destination was Gross-Rosen. But how to get there was a mystery. On their own authority they requisitioned food from the villages through which they passed, rested for a few hours, then trudged on again. There was no question of spending the night in barns or schools, since these were all crammed with refugees. The route taken by these miserable columns was easy to follow, since every few hundred yards lay the bodies of prisoners who had collapsed or been shot. I directed all the columns I could reach to go westwards, into the Sudetenland, so as to avoid the incredibly chaotic bottle-neck near Neisse.[7]

According to Höss, he gave strict orders to the men in charge of the columns of prisoners that they were to no longer shoot prisoners incapable of further marching. Instead, they were to hand them over in the villages to the Volkssturm or home guard. When he met officers from Auschwitz who had managed to obtain a vehicle, he posted them at crossroads to collect the wandering columns of prisoners and move them westward, eventually by train if possible. As evidence of his further attempt to restore order, Höss related that near Głubczyce he came upon a German Air Force officer in the act of stopping his motorcycle and intending to shoot a prisoner leaning against a tree. When Höss shouted at him and asked what harm the prisoner had done him, the officer laughed impertinently in Höss' face, so Höss drew his pistol and shot him—the officer. Höss' efforts on behalf of the prisoners is unverified.[8]

The recollection of one Auschwitz survivor concerning Höss' actions on the Death March was quite different. George Klein stated that, as he hid inside a straw wagon, he heard the sound of a machine gun. He looked out and recognized Höss on a horse. According to Klein, Höss ordered 500–1,000 women to lie down in a field. Their heads were covered. At Höss' command, a German machine gun on a wagon opened fire, killing all of the women.[9]

Höss recalled "open coal trucks, loaded with frozen corpses, whole trainloads of prisoners who had been shunted on to open sidings and left there without food or shelter." Roads were blocked by retreating military columns, as well as crowds of refugees. Höss even saw groups of prisoners, often without guards, who had escaped or whose guards had simply vanished. They, too, were making their way westward. The snow was deep, and it was very cold. Having witnessed the chaotic mass of suffering humanity, Höss went to General Heinrich Schmauser in Breslau to urge him to stop the evacuation. Schmauser advised Höss of Himmler's directive that made him responsible for assuring that not a single healthy prisoner remained in any camp under his authority.[10]

Near the end of 1944, Höss' family moved to the immediate vicinity of the Ravensbrück concentration camp, 90 kilometers north of Berlin. When the WVHA offices in Berlin were bombed by the Allies on April 16, 1945, the WVHA was moved north to Darss in Pomerania on the Baltic

Sea. Höss and his family went with the Inspectorate of the Concentration Camps, headed by SS-Gruppenführer Richard Glücks, to Darss, then west to Schleswig-Holstein. In addition to his own family, Höss was responsible for the wife of Theodor Eicke, her daughter and children and several other families, and was instructed to keep them out of enemy hands. Eicke had been instrumental in establishing the Nazi concentration camps and was the first chief of the Inspectorate of the Concentration Camps. He had been shot down and killed during a reconnaissance flight in 1942. The Inspectorate group traveled by night in trucks, without lights, along crowded roads. Glücks and SS-Standartenführer Gerhard Maurer, the head of Amtsgruppe DII, the Labor Department, took a route different from Höss. In Rostock, two of the large trucks carrying the wireless equipment broke down, and by the time they were repaired, the trucks were captured by enemy tanks. On the way, the group learned that Hitler committed suicide on April 30, 1945.[11]

For too many Germans, Hitler was more than a leader—he was a Godhead. Höss and his wife Hedwig were simultaneously struck by the same thought: "Now we, too, must go." Höss said:

> With the Führer gone, our world had gone. Was there any point in going on living? We would be pursued and persecuted wherever we went. We wanted to take poison. I had obtained some for my wife, lest she and the children fall alive into the hands of the Russians in the event of their making an unexpected advance.

The same thought had occurred to Hitler's propaganda minister Joseph Goebbels. Tragically, he and his wife Magda murdered each of their six children by poison before killing themselves. Höss and Hedwig decided against that course:

> Nevertheless, because of the children, we did not do this. For their sake we wanted to take on our own shoulders all that was coming. But we should have done it. I have always regretted it since. We would all have been spared a great deal, especially my wife and the children. How much more suffering will they have to endure? We were bound and fettered to that other world, and we should have disappeared with it.[12]

After fleeing from Auschwitz, Frau Thomsen, the governess for the children of Höss and Hedwig, had gone to live with her mother at St. Michaelisdonn in Holstein. Höss took his family there. Himmler and other members of the government retreated to Flensburg, 110 kilometers north of St. Michaelisdonn, one of the last areas of Germany not in the hands of the Allies. Höss took his oldest son, Klaus, and drove to Flensburg, expecting to receive new orders. Hitler was dead, but perhaps all was not lost if Himmler could lead them forward. Höss believed he still had some role to play in the Third Reich.[13]

Höss was stunned by the scene. While the world had "crumbled beneath our feet," Himmler was "beaming and in the best of spirits. There was no more talk of fighting." He said: "Well, gentlemen, this is the end. You know what you now have to do." Höss initially thought Himmler meant that, in accordance with what he had been preaching to the SS for years, each of them must make the ultimate sacrifice. Instead, Himmler instructed them to "hide in the Army." Every man for himself was the order of the day. Supremely disappointed, Höss thought, "Such was our farewell message from the man to whom I had looked up so respectfully, in whom I had had such implicit trust, whose orders and utterances had been gospel to me." Maurer and Höss looked at each other in "dumb astonishment." These were not the inspiring words from the Reichsführer-SS that the veteran Nazis had expected. Höss felt betrayed. Himmler's message was hardly consistent with the SS ideals for which he had served so many years. Höss claimed that, had he been alone, he would have committed some act of despair. But now, he had his department chiefs, the officers and men of his staff and his family to look after.[14]

Glücks was taken, half dead, to the naval hospital and admitted under another name. Höss contacted a well-known submarine commander. He and the rest of the departmental staff dressed as sailors and were issued false papers as naval personnel. Höss became boatswain's mate Franz Lang and went to the island of Sylt with orders to report to the Naval Intelligence School. He knew enough about naval life to make himself inconspicuous. Höss sent Klaus back to Hedwig, along with his driver and car. With little work to do, Höss had time to ponder deeply what had happened.[15]

Meanwhile, Himmler wandered about in the vicinity of Flensburg until May 21, when he set out with 11 SS officers hoping to pass through British and American lines to his native Bavaria. In an effort to disguise himself, he had gone so far as to shave off his moustache, wear a black patch over his left eye and, perhaps most degrading of all for him, don an enlisted man's uniform. The group was stopped the first day at a British control point where, after questioning, Himmler confessed his identity. He was taken to British Army headquarters at Lüneberg where he was strip-searched and made to change into a British Army uniform to avoid any possibility that he might be concealing poison in his clothes. Unknown to his initial captor, Himmler kept his vial of potassium cyanide concealed in a cavity of his gums. When a second British intelligence officer arrived and instructed a medical officer to examine Himmler's mouth, he bit on the vial and was dead in 12 minutes, despite frantic efforts to keep him alive. When Höss learned of Himmler's death, he again contemplated his own fate. Höss, too, had a vial of poison, but chose to "wait on events" before using it.[16]

As Höss began his new life as Franz Lang, hoping to elude capture by the Allies, the soldier who would eventually capture him was starting his assignment as a Nazi hunter. At the end of April 1945, Lieutenant Howard Hervey Alexander, a British officer, received orders to report to British headquarters in Brussels, Belgium. He had been chosen to serve as a member of the war crimes investigation team. As it happened, Lt. Alexander was uniquely qualified for this special task. He was born Hanns Hermann Alexander in Berlin on May 6, 1917, 15 minutes before his twin brother Paul. They were the children of Dr. Alfred Alexander and his wife Henny. The Alexanders were Jewish, but generally attended synagogue on only the most holy of days.[17]

On January 30, 1933, Adolf Hitler became Chancellor of Germany. Two months later, on April 1, 1933, the National Socialists called for a boycott of Jewish businesses. The Alexanders watched as SA (*Sturmabteilung*) storm troopers—Nazi street thugs—marched down their street and blocked the door to the office where Dr. Alexander maintained his medical practice. Only the intervention of Colonel Otto Meyer, under whom Dr. Alexander served in World War I, prompted the Brownshirts to disperse.[18]

The atmosphere of Jewish hatred was too much for Hanns' sister, Bella. She moved to London with her English fiancé. Anti-Jewish laws forced Hanns and Paul to change schools and outlawed Dr. Alexander's ability to be reimbursed for treating patients from public health insurance, a significant part of his income. Nazi anti–Semitism was affecting more and more of the Alexanders' daily lives. Late in 1934, Hanns heard a sermon by a rabbi who warned that all Jews should leave Germany. In early 1936, while Dr. Alexander was in London visiting Bella, the decision was made to move the family to England. He stayed and told the rest of his family to come as soon as they could. Henny worked on selling Dr. Alexander's practice in Berlin and then joined the family. In May 1936, Hanns traveled to Switzerland and met up with Paul, who had gone there previously with Henny's parents. He took the train south to Munich then west to Switzerland, passing through the town of Baden-Baden, the birthplace of Rudolf Höss.[19]

Hanns flew to London in June 1936. By September 1936, the entire family was together in England. Hanns studied English, and the family made the best of their new life. They watched as the situation for Jews in Germany worsened. They listened in shock as, on November 9, 1938, *Kristallnacht*, 250 synagogues and 7,000 Jewish-owned stores and businesses were attacked. Many who stood, watched and did nothing had been their non–Jewish neighbors and friends. Then on September 1, 1939, Hitler invaded Poland, and England declared war on Germany. Hanns decided to enlist, not to fight for the country of his birth, but in the Royal Air Force.[20]

In May 1940, Hanns and his unit arrived in France as part of the British Expeditionary Force. As the Germans overwhelmed the Netherlands and Belgium and pushed into France, Hanns was among 300,000 British and Allied forces trapped at Dunkirk between the Germans and the English Channel. His outfit was one of the last to be picked up on the French shore and returned to Great Britain. Once back in England, he asked his commanding officer if he could change his name in his military papers to something sounding less German—hence Howard Hervey Alexander. In 1943, both Hanns and his twin brother Paul, also a member of the Royal Air Force, applied and were accepted for officer's candidate school. In July 1944, following the successful D-Day invasion at Normandy, Lt. Alexander returned to France. He arrived in Brussels for his new assignment as part of the war crimes investigation team on May 8, 1945.[21]

Hanns' first assignment was to interrogate SS officers at a concentration camp in northern Germany—Bergen-Belsen—300 kilometers west of Berlin. He and his driver arrived on May 12, almost a month after the camp had been liberated by the British on April 15. Inside the camp, Hanns beheld the true horror of the thousand-year Reich. Liberating British forces found not just dead inmates, but piles of corpses. Health concerns required immediate burial of the dead by bulldozer in mass graves. The living were emaciated and barely alive. Typhus was a continuing threat. The camp had no water, food or medicine, and little shelter. The journey of approximately 20,000 of the inmates forced to march out of Auschwitz on January 18 had ended at Bergen-Belsen. Present-day visitors to Bergen-Belsen will find numerous mass graves, each containing the remains of between 500 and 2,000 human beings.[22]

While the British soldiers were deeply affected by Bergen-Belsen, the experience touched Hanns' soul. Hanns was German and this atrocity occurred in Germany. And he was Jewish. If he and his family had not gone to England, the fate of any of these poor wretched human beings could have been his fate or his family's. Hanns was outraged. On May 16, Lt. Col. Leo Genn received a telegram at Bergen-Belsen instructing him to take command of the team of investigators and interpreters assembled at the camp. The unit was called Number 1 War Crimes Investigation Team or "1 WCIT." Hanns worked as an interpreter for the unit. They had a list of 165 high-profile war criminals. On the list was Rudolf Höss, the former commandant of Auschwitz, though his name was misspelled and his birth date, height and weight were wrong.[23]

On May 17, Hanns and one of the team investigators, Captain Fox, drove 27 kilometers south to Celle where they interviewed their first witness, SS-Obersturmführer Franz Hössler, who had been assigned to Auschwitz. Hanns asked Hössler what he knew about the gas chambers. Hössler responded that everyone knew about the gas chambers, but he was not involved in the selection of prisoners—that was done by the doctors. Hössler claimed he made many complaints to the commandant, Höss, about people being sent to the gas chambers, but was told it was none of his business.[24]

As Nazi hunters would learn, the SS minimized their own involvement and tended to blame others for the barbaric acts that were committed. Hanns and Captain Fox had no way of knowing that, in fact, Hössler was one of Höss' most ruthless and cold-blooded killers. On September 16, 1940, Hössler traveled with Höss to the Chelmno extermination camp for an inspection of its body-burning facilities. On July 28, 1941, 575 Auschwitz I inmates were adjudged to be invalids, cripples or chronically ill prisoners and selected for termination. Hössler accompanied the group to the Sonnenstein Euthanasia Center in eastern Germany on the pretext of taking them to another camp where the work would be easier. At Sonnenstein, they were gassed in a bathhouse with carbon monoxide delivered through the showers as part of the Aktion 14f13 program. Hössler supervised the first extermination of Jews at the Auschwitz I crematorium on February 15, 1942.

On June 10, 1942, about 50 prisoners from an Auschwitz penal company attempted to escape while at work. During the pursuit 13 were killed, while nine managed to escape. The next morning after roll call, Camp Commander Hans Aumeier demanded the names of the organizers of the breakout from the remaining 320 prisoners. When no one answered, Aumeier called 20 prisoners from the ranks and personally shot 17, while Hössler shot three. That evening the entire penal company was gassed in Bunker I. In October 1943, Hössler, pretending to be a representative of the Foreign Ministry, instructed a group of incoming Jews, who believed they were being transported to Switzerland, that they must undress and be disinfected before continuing their journey. Hössler was very polite and reassuring, when, in fact, the group was being ushered into one of the Auschwitz gas chambers. On May 25, 1944, several hundred persons from a Hungarian transport fled into the woods to avoid gassing. Hössler took charge of the operation to recover the group and, once the Hungarians were cornered in a floodlit area, directed that all those who had tried to escape be shot.[25]

After interviewing Hössler, Captain Fox and Hanns drove 32 kilometers west to Schwarmstedt, where they interviewed Fritz Klein, one of the doctors who Hössler identified as being responsible for making selections of prisoners for the gas chamber. He acknowledged he had overseen many of the selections. He said he acted on orders of Dr. Eduard Wirths, the chief camp physician, and that the commandant of the camp was Rudolf Höss. The next day, back at Celle, Hanns and Captain Fox interviewed Elizabeth Volkenrath, a senior women's guard at Auschwitz. When asked, she said Rudolf Höss was responsible for the events at Auschwitz.[26]

The sights at Bergen-Belsen and the statements of the perpetrators set Hanns in motion. He vowed to hunt down Nazi war criminals, in particular Höss. Hanns asked Lt. Col. Genn to set out on his own. Genn refused. Hanns went anyway on his own time. Although he interviewed hundreds of German soldiers and civilians in the summer of 1945, few provided information of any value. The commandant of Bergen-Belsen at the end of the war was SS-Hauptsturmführer Josef Kramer, formerly one of Höss' adjutants at Auschwitz. At Genn's request, Hanns reinterviewed Kramer on September 1 to correct his original statement that he knew nothing about the gas chambers at Auschwitz. Kramer related that Höss advised him that, even though the gas chamber and crematorium were situated in his part of the camp, Kramer had no jurisdiction. In all likelihood, the conversation between Höss and Kramer took place between May and July 1944, when Kramer was the commandant of Birkenau and Höss returned to Auschwitz for the sole purpose of supervising the extermination of Hungarian Jews. At that point, Hanns and Genn realized that Höss' testimony could establish the existence of the Holocaust.[27]

Several weeks after Himmler's death on May 23, 1945, the Sylt Naval Intelligence School, where Höss was serving as boatswain's mate Franz Lang, surrendered to the British and was removed to the internment district between the Kiel Canal and the Schlei. Höss was transported to a prison in Heide, a small town located 100 miles south of Flensburg. There, Höss was close to his family, whom he was able to see quite often. Klaus visited him every few days. Höss petitioned for release, asserting that he was Franz Lang, a farmer, and wished to work on a local estate. He was released and obtained a job through the Labor Department. On July 5, 1945, Höss arrived at Gottrupel, six miles west of Flensburg. He slept in a barn at the edge of the village and began farming land.[28]

The first war crimes trial did not take place in Nuremberg. Instead, it began on September 17, 1945, in the German city of Lüneberg, against Josef Kramer and 44 other defendants associated with the Bergen-Belsen concentration camp. Kramer testified that Höss was responsible for the deaths of millions of people in the Auschwitz gas chambers. The trial ended November 17, three days before the Nuremberg trial began. Kramer, Klein, Hössler, Volkenrath and Irma Grese, a guard at Auschwitz who refused to cooperate with investigators, were convicted and executed. As the trial neared its end, Hanns again sought permission to hunt fugitive war criminals. This time Genn agreed. Hanns was given access to war criminal files, a car and driver and the power to arrest. He was also promoted to captain.[29]

Following his successful capture of Gustav Simon, the Gauleiter of Luxembourg, and a trip to London to become engaged, Hanns returned with orders to focus on a new mission: capturing the men who ran the Concentration Camp Inspectorate, Amtsgruppe D. SS-Standartenführer Dr. Enno Lolling, the head of Amtsgruppe DIII, committed suicide in May 1945, and SS-Sturmbannführer Wilhelm Max Burger, the head of Amtsgruppe DIV, was in Polish custody. That left Glücks, Höss and Maurer. At the end of January 1946, Hanns and Major Caola, another investigator, drove to Hanns' hometown of Berlin. They then drove to the Concentration Camp Inspectorate in Oranienberg, 35 kilometers north of Berlin. All documents had been destroyed, so they sought out former Inspectorate staff members. They learned that Glücks, Maurer and Höss, along with their families, had fled north toward the Danish border.[30]

Twice while Höss worked at Gottrupel he traveled the 116 kilometers to St. Michaelisdonn to see Hedwig. They met briefly outside of town to avoid being seen by British patrols. Shortly after Christmas 1945, Hedwig's brother, Fritz Hensel, who worked in Flensburg, met with Höss to give him a letter and clothes from Hedwig. Fritz told him he was in grave danger, as the British Field Security Police were watching Hedwig and the children. They had also repeatedly searched their house. Direct communication with them was no longer possible. Höss could only contact them through Fritz. In early March 1946, Fritz visited Höss with news about his family and to talk about their future. They discussed smuggling everyone out of the country. Höss knew they could not all go together; it was too risky. He decided the family should leave Germany. He would go first, and his family would follow.[31]

In pursuit of the remaining three Inspectorate leaders, Hanns drove to Flensburg to interview Glücks' wife. She confirmed that she and her husband left Berlin with Höss at the end of April 1945, ten months earlier. Although she said her husband had committed suicide, Hanns was doubtful. Unable to obtain confirmation about Glücks' fate, Hanns focused on Höss. On March 8, 1946, Hanns went to the headquarters of the British Field Security Section 92 at Heide. There, he met Captain William Victor Cross, who told Hanns they had been monitoring Höss' wife and children and recently intercepted a letter from Höss. Coincidentally, Hedwig had been brought in for questioning the day before and was being held in nearby Lunden prison.[32]

No doubt surprised and pleased, Hanns immediately drove to the prison and sat down in a cell with Hedwig Höss. Hanns told her who he was and his purpose. Hedwig, continuing to display Nazi arrogance and spousal loyalty, refused to give him any information. The next day, March 9, he drove 43 kilometers south to her home at St. Michaelisdonn, where he confronted the four oldest children while Hedwig remained in custody. Hanns asked them where their father was living. He went to each child separately, beginning with Klaus. Hanns screamed the question into Klaus' face and banged his fist on the table, but it was no use. He even threatened to kill Hedwig. The children would not betray their father. Hanns was determined not to leave empty-handed. He took 15-year-old Klaus with him.[33]

When they arrived at Lunden prison, Hanns led Klaus to Hedwig's cell. Though surprised to see her son in the jail, her demeanor did not change. When Hanns asked Hedwig where Höss was living, she again said she did not know. The next day, March 10, Hanns questioned Klaus further. He said he had not seen his father since the last days of the war. Angry at the attack on her child, Hedwig said she and Klaus would go on a hunger strike. Hanns then placed them in separate cells. The next time he asked Hedwig for Höss' location, she said he was dead.[34]

On the evening of March 11, 1946, a noisy steam engine was pulled behind the prison. Hanns burst into Hedwig's cell and told her Klaus would be on the train and headed for Siberia; she would never see her oldest son again. Hedwig could save Klaus only by divulging her husband's location and alias. Hanns left a pencil and paper on her bed. Hedwig was broken; she could not take the chance the British captain was bluffing. When Hanns returned to Hedwig's cell 10 minutes later, he retrieved a piece of paper on which Hedwig had indicated Höss was living at the Hans Peter Hansen farm in Gottrupel under the name Franz Lang.[35]

Hanns and Captain Cross decided to arrest Höss as soon as possible. Gottrupel is only an hour's drive northeast of Lunden. The men of the Field Security Section 92 were organized and briefed on the mission. Like Hanns, many of them were German Jews who had been forced from Germany and who had lost loved ones in Auschwitz. Anticipating that Höss would be injured, Hanns took a doctor. At 11 p.m. the group of 25 men arrived at Gottrupel. Hanns and the doctor approached the barn at the Hans Peter Hansen farm and knocked loudly. Höss, awakened from sleep, thought he was being robbed.[36]

Höss opened the door. Before him was a large group of British soldiers with guns drawn. Hanns stuck a pistol into his mouth and searched Höss for cyanide pills. According to Höss, his vial of poison had broken two days before. When Hanns asked to see identification papers, Höss produced the false Franz Lang ID. Hanns knew it was fake. He told Höss he believed he was the commandant of Auschwitz. Höss denied it. Hanns compared a photograph of Rudolf Höss to the man who stood before him and knew it was Höss. He continued to insist his name was Franz Lang. Höss did not yet know Hedwig had given up his false name and hiding place. He could only hope that he could convince Hanns of his false identity and be given the chance to flee the country as he had planned.[37]

Hanns noticed Höss was wearing his wedding ring. "Give it to me," he said. "I can't," replied Höss, "it has been stuck for years." "No problem," Hanns said, "I'll just cut off your finger." When Höss realized Hanns intended to carry through with his threat, he handed him the ring. On the inside was inscribed the names "Rudolf" and "Hedwig." Hanns was aware his men hated Höss, as did he. Willing to face the consequences, he gave them the chance to take their "pound of flesh" from the commandant of Auschwitz. They almost literally did so. Hanns told the men, "In ten minutes, I want to have Höss in my car—undamaged," and left. The soldiers dragged Höss to one of the barn's slaughter tables, ripped off his pajamas and beat him with axe handles. Höss screamed. After a short time, the doctor told Hanns, "Call them off unless you want to take back a corpse." The beating ended, and Höss was carried out of the barn covered only with a blanket.[38]

On the drive back to Heide, Höss confirmed to Hanns he was the commandant of Auschwitz and that he was "personally responsible for the deaths of 10,000 people." Once in Heide, Hanns removed the blanket from Höss' shoulders and made him walk naked to the prison. He was back in the barracks from which he was released by the British eight months before. Hanns and a sergeant began interrogating Höss while forcing him to drink alcohol and beating him with a whip taken from Höss. Believing Höss had used the whip to flog prisoners, his interrogators turned it on him. Throughout the questioning, Höss was handcuffed. He would complain later to Dr. Leon Goldensohn, the psychiatrist at Nuremberg, that without shoes or socks he suffered from frostbite in the cold cell.[39]

On March 15, Höss was driven to Camp Tomato in Minden near Hanover, where he was subjected to additional interrogation. Höss said he received "further rough treatment" at the hands of the English prosecutor, and the conditions in the prison accorded with that behavior. Following questioning, Höss provided a statement, eight pages in length, which was typed and signed on or about March 15, 1946. The statement (see Appendix I) provides background of his early days with the SS and his concentration camp experience at Dachau and Sachsenhausen before starting the camp at Auschwitz. Höss states that Himmler ordered him to Berlin in June 1941, where he was told that Hitler had directed the Final Solution of the Jewish question. Höss indicates that other extermination camps—Belzec, Treblinka and Wolzek near Lublin (Sobibor)—could not be expanded to handle mass exterminations as could Auschwitz. Himmler directed him to contact SS-Obersturmbannführer Eichmann concerning the sequence of incoming transports.[40]

Höss following capture by the British (courtesy Yad Vashem—the Holocaust Heroes' and Martyrs' Remembrance Authority).

I. Escape and Capture

In his statement, Höss explained that the first transports of Jews came from Slovakia and Upper Silesia in 1941, and that people were deceived into believing they were being deloused as they were led to the gas chambers. They were killed with Zyklon B within 3–10 minutes. Before they were cremated, gold teeth were removed. Until the crematoria were built, the bodies were burned in pits. Remaining bones were pulverized, and ashes were dispersed in the river. Höss also explained the selection process at the train platform to determine who was fit to work and the extermination and cremation process after the large crematoria were built. He described how the clothing and property of prisoners were sorted by a work party of prisoners. Valuables were sent to Berlin. Höss also discussed the medical experiments conducted on prisoners at Auschwitz.

The capture of Rudolf Höss was noteworthy, especially to the prosecutors at the ongoing trial of Nazi war criminals in Nuremberg. By late March 1946, the prosecution had presented its evidence and most of the prosecutors had gone home. Lieutenant Commander Whitney R. Harris, U.S.N.R., a member of the United States prosecution team, remained in Nuremberg. When he learned that Höss was in British custody in northern Germany, he asked the British to send him to Nuremberg. The British had their statement and promptly obliged. After three weeks of British captivity, for the first time since his arrest, Höss' handcuffs were removed. He was shaved, given a haircut and allowed to wash. Höss was on his way to Nuremberg.[41]

Of his first statement given to the British, Höss said, "I do not know what is in the record, although I signed it." Höss had been roughly handled by his British captors, motivated as much by retribution as to gain a confession. That document, standing alone, would constitute a poor foundation on which to base proof from Höss of the existence of the Holocaust. However, for reasons known only to Höss, he chose to speak on multiple occasions of the atrocities perpetrated at Auschwitz. He provided an affidavit at Nuremberg on April 5, 1946. Höss then testified before the Tribunal at Nuremberg on April 15, 1946. As he awaited his own trial in Poland, he wrote an autobiography encompassing the events at Auschwitz while he was commandant until 1943 and when he returned to oversee the extermination of Hungarian Jews in 1944. Finally, at his own trial in 1947, Höss admitted, for the most part, the allegations of the charges against him. Höss never complained that mistreatment affected any statement or testimony he gave after March 15, 1946. Comparison of Höss' statement of March 15, his affidavit of April 5, his testimony of April 15 at Nuremberg and his memoirs indicates that the substance of the facts he relates about Auschwitz is in all material aspects the same. Whatever might be said of the British treatment of Höss after his capture, it had no impact on the truth of his admissions.[42]

II

Early Years

The future Auschwitz commandant was born to Franz Xaver and Lina Höss on November 25, 1901, in the spa community of Baden-Baden situated in southwestern Germany. They christened their son Rudolf Franz Ferdinand Höss. Baden-Baden lies at the northwestern border of the Black Forest mountains, six miles east of the Rhine River, Germany's border with France. In Höss' youth, the population of Baden-Baden hovered around 16,000, but as many as 70,000 visitors overwhelmed the town each year to enjoy the hot springs for which Baden-Baden was known. The Höss family grew with the births of Maria Luise in 1904 and Margarete in 1906. Their home was situated on the outskirts of Baden-Baden in a neighborhood consisting of scattered and isolated farmhouses. Höss had few playmates his age, but that was fine with him. He enjoyed the solitude of the woods and the time he spent with animals, particularly the horses of nearby farmers. He was happier alone.[1]

When Höss was six years old, his family moved an hour northeast to the much larger city of Mannheim. For two years, he was instructed by a private tutor, and then enrolled in elementary school. Höss greatly missed the company of animals, so, on his seventh birthday, his parents gave him a coal-black pony, which he named Hans. Höss was ecstatic. The pony went everywhere with him, even into the house when his parents were away. In Mannheim, Höss did not lack for other children his age to play with, but time with Hans was his greatest pleasure. The person who would be Höss' undoing near the end of his life, Captain Hanns Hermann Alexander, bore the same name. The coincidence could not have escaped Höss' notice.[2]

While living in Baden-Baden, Höss saw little of his father, who spent much of his time traveling on business. In Mannheim, Franz Xaver took a more active role in his son's life, checking his schoolwork and discussing his future. Franz Xaver was a devout Catholic and was determined that Höss should become a priest. He took his son on pilgrimages to all of Germany's holy sites. Höss prayed fervently, took his religious duties seriously and treated adults respectfully. Franz Xaver fascinated Höss with stories of his military service in East Africa and the work performed by missionaries in African jungles. Though Höss said he was determined, one day, to perform the same charitable work as the African missionaries, his father's tales of military service had a greater impact on him.

Not surprisingly, Franz Xaver raised his son with strict military discipline. Höss learned that great evils almost always spring from small, apparently insignificant misdeeds. Franz Xaver taught him that no matter how strong one's opposition might be to the laws and decrees of the State, unconditional obedience was required. When Höss joined the SS, this dogma was reinforced. Hitler and the Nazis took this lesson even farther. In the Third Reich, failure to fully support the State or the Führer constituted treason. Eventually, Höss would completely shutter his morality and responsibility to think for himself.[3]

At Nuremberg, after a lifetime of favoring the ideals of the National Socialist Party over those of the Catholic Church, Höss told Dr. G. M. Gilbert, the prison psychologist, that his strict father was a bigot and fanatical. Dr. Gilbert asked if Franz Xaver ever beat Höss. "No," said Höss. "I was only punished by prayer if I teased my sister, or tried to lie, or any little thing like that. The thing that made me so stubborn and probably made me later on cut off from people was his way of making me feel that I had wronged him personally, and that, since I was spiritually a minor, he was responsible to God for my sins, and I could only pray to expiate my sins. My father was a kind of higher being that I could never approach, and so I crawled back into myself and I could not express myself to others. I feel that this bigoted upbringing is responsible for my becoming so withdrawn. My mother also lived in the shadow of this fanatic piety." Considering the principles of the man Höss chose to follow and to regard as God on earth—Adolf Hitler—the harsh judgment of his father seems misdirected.[4]

Höss described the relationship between his parents as one of loving respect and mutual understanding. He saw no display of tenderness between them and, perhaps as a result, Höss showed no tenderness to anyone. He respected his parents, but could not say he loved them, and he could not turn to either of them as a confidant. If Höss had a problem, he worked it out for himself as best he could. Unlike Höss, his sisters, Maria Luise and Margarete, were quite affectionate with their mother. They were also devoted to Höss and perpetually sought to establish a loving relationship with their brother. Höss wanted nothing to do with them. When he was forced to interact with his sisters, he would nag them until they cried. Even as he wrote his autobiography at the end of his life, Höss described them as strangers.[5]

The extent to which Höss' parents or the communities in which he lived may have influenced his later views about Jews and his eventual willingness to implement the Final Solution cannot be ascertained from his autobiography. Höss states that nothing much of importance happened during his early school years. He told Dr. Gilbert that he attributed his anti–Semitic beliefs to the early writings and speeches of Hitler and Joseph Goebbels, the Nazi propaganda minister. Nevertheless, the hatred and violence indicative of Hitler and the Nazi Party that Höss joined made their presence felt in both of his hometowns. On *Kristallnacht*, November 9–10, 1938, the Nazis rounded up the Jewish men in Baden-Baden, marched them to the synagogue and forced them to read from Hitler's autobiography, *Mein Kampf*. Failure to read loudly enough prompted blows from the Nazis. Eventually the synagogue was burned while the Jews were made to stand and watch. "If it had been my decision," one of the SS men told the Jewish congregation, "you would have perished in that fire." The Jews of the state of Baden were among the first to be deported from Germany. In Mannheim, the synagogue was set on fire on the morning of November 10. "The brownshirts of the SA had taken out the prayer books, the prayer shawls, the Torah scrolls, everything they could get their hands on. They'd dumped them in a pile on the street, and, laughing boisterously, were trampling them, enjoying themselves… 'Burn the Jews!' they kept chanting. 'Burn the Jews!'"[6]

As Höss entered adolescence, Catholicism and soldiering were the most prominent influences on the young man. A seemingly innocuous event occurred at school which would significantly impact the direction of his life and affect him even more than the subsequent death of his parents. Despite his religious fervor and his desire to perform missionary work, Höss was not particularly well-behaved and engaged in plenty of mischief with his Mannheim friends. During one of the usual scuffles at the entrance to the school gymnasium, he unintentionally pushed one of his classmates down the stairs, causing him to break his ankle. Many students had fallen down those stairs before, including Höss, without consequence. This boy was just unlucky. The school punished Höss, who confessed his error at church, but he delayed in telling his parents.[7]

That evening, the priest to whom Höss confessed and who was a friend of his father, came to their house for dinner. The next morning, Franz Xaver confronted Höss about the incident at school and Höss' failure to tell him. Naturally, he was punished. Höss was very upset, not because of his father's punishment, but because the priest to whom he had confessed had violated the sanctity of the confessional. In the Roman Catholic Church, the Seal of the Confessional is the absolute duty of priests not to disclose any information they learn from penitents in the course of the Sacrament of Penance. According to Roman Catholic canon law, "The sacramental seal is inviolable; therefore, it is absolutely forbidden for a confessor to betray in any way a penitent in words or in any manner and for any reason."[8]

Höss knew that his father could only have learned of the incident from the priest. He described the violation of the confessional's seal of secrecy as "monstrous." He had been betrayed not only by the priest, but by his father, who used the secret information against him. Höss' faith in the sacred priesthood was destroyed. He never again went to confession and no longer considered the priesthood worthy of his trust. The next year, Franz Xaver died. In writing his memoirs, Höss stated, "I cannot remember that I was very much affected by this."[9]

More significantly in the life of Rudolf Höss, World War I broke out. In the summer of 1914, Höss was only 12 years old, too young to fight, but he was fascinated by the events. He convinced his mother to let him join the auxiliary of the Red Cross. As he wrote his autobiography, Höss remembered the uniforms of both German and French soldiers stained with blood and mud and still heard the stifled groans. He stated that when he was not in school, "...I spent my whole time in the hospitals, or the barracks, or at the railway station meeting the troop transports and hospital trains and helping with the distribution of the food and comforts." In the hospitals, he saw the critically wounded soldiers, many who were dying or dead. He listened, spellbound, to the soldiers in the barracks talk about life and death at the front. Höss said, "The soldier's blood that ran in my veins responded." He wanted to serve as a soldier as his father and grandfather had before him. He often hid on troop trains, only to be taken home by military police due to his tender age. Despite his mother's efforts to dissuade him from the military, neither school nor religion attracted his attention any longer.[10]

In 1916, while working in the hospital, Höss, now 14, met a cavalry captain in the 21st Baden Regiment of Dragoons, the same regiment in which his father and grandfather had served. With the help of the captain, Höss joined the Dragoons. His mother was opposed to his plan to become a soldier, so Höss joined without her knowledge. "At the end of the school term in early summer, I pretended to be going to visit my grandparents in the Black Forest. That was the usual thing for me to do during the summer vacations, and so my [mother] did not become suspicious. But that year, instead of visiting my grandparents, I actually went to the garrison of the captain of cavalry. He was organizing a unit to be sent to Turkey—the Asiatic Corps. I was trained hurriedly and two weeks later left for Turkey. It was only after my departure that I wrote my mother of my whereabouts, because I was afraid if they knew where I was in Germany, they would have me returned." Höss would not see his mother again. Höss and the Dragoons were sent by train and horseback to Kut, in present-day Iraq, 100 miles south of Baghdad.[11]

Höss and the Dragoons arrived at the Iraqi front in December 1916. He had just turned 15. His cavalry unit was attached to a division of Ottoman Turks. Beginning in December 1916, a force of 50,000 British Indian soldiers advanced towards Baghdad and engaged the Turks in February 1917 in the Second Battle of Kut. Before Höss' training could be completed, a force of British, New Zealanders and Indians attacked the German-Turk force. When the fighting became intense, the Turkish troops fled, leaving the Germans isolated among the stones and the ruins. To make matters worse, they were running out of ammunition. The enemies' fire became more intense and more accurate. Höss called to the man beside him. When he received no answer, Höss turned and saw that he was dead, shot through the head.[12]

Höss became terrified. Then, he noticed his captain, behind a rock, methodically firing back at the enemy. That was enough to calm Höss, who realized he, too, needed to start shooting. The Indian troops came nearer. Suddenly, one of them rose from behind some rocks and advanced. Höss momentarily hesitated, then pulled the trigger. The Indian fell dead. Höss was no longer afraid and continued shooting. The Turks rejoined the Germans, and together they launched a counterattack. Höss advanced forward and looked at the man he killed as he passed his body: "…I did not feel very happy about it at all."[13]

His captain expressed amazement at Höss' coolness under fire for the first time. When Höss told him how he really felt, his captain laughed and said all soldiers feel the same. Höss and his captain became very close—like father and son. He looked out for Höss and expressed pride when Höss was decorated or promoted. The difference between his captain and his father was significant. Höss' own father dispensed criticism and punishment, not praise. The captain was killed in the spring of 1918. Höss was profoundly affected by his captain's death, far more than by the loss of his father.[14]

In early 1917, Höss' unit was transferred to Palestine in the Holy Land. He was wounded in the knee and sent to a hospital in Wilhelma, a German settlement between Jerusalem and Jaffa. Two things of significance happened while he was there. First, he learned that Jerusalem monasteries cheated pilgrims and visitors to the Holy Land by selling, at a high price, moss with red spots claiming the red spots were the blood of Christ. Most of his friends were indifferent, feeling that anyone who would believe such nonsense deserved to be swindled. Höss, instead, was angry. He believed it was sinful for the Church to prey upon the deep religious convictions of pilgrims, many of whom had spent their life savings to visit the Holy Land. Added to the previous breach of the seal of confessional secrecy by his Mannheim priest, Höss would eventually lose all faith in the Catholic Church and renounce his religious beliefs altogether.[15]

The second memorable event for Höss was a brief love affair with a young German nurse who took particularly good care of him. "Not even my mother could have looked after me better than did this nurse," said Höss. Initially, he was distressed by her tenderness and the way in which she would hold him longer than was necessary. He had not been comfortable with the gentle hand of his mother. Eventually, the female affection that made him uneasy to this point in his life became acceptable. Höss and his first love consummated their relationship, though they would never see each other again after his discharge from the hospital.[16]

Höss was wounded twice more before the end of the war in November 1918. He was shot in the thigh in November 1917 and suffered wounds to his hands and knees in February 1918. For his service, Höss was awarded the Iron Cross, First and Second Class, and the Iron Crescent and the Baden Service Medal. Since the spring of 1918, the teenage veteran commanded an independent cavalry troop. He and his men were in Damascus when Germany surrendered. Rather than be interned, the now 17-year-old cavalry commander led his soldiers, men in their 30s, across the Black Sea through Bulgaria and Rumania over the Transylvanian Alps to Hungary, Austria and finally home to Germany. Höss learned that "the ability to lead men depends not on rank, but on skill, and that in difficult situations it is icy calm and unshakeable imperturbability that are decisive in a commanding officer." He would repeatedly exhibit that demeanor as the commandant of Auschwitz.[17]

While Höss was away at war, his mother died. As when his father died, Höss was emotionally unaffected. Upon her death, his sisters had been sent to a convent. In her last letter to her son, Lina Höss urged him to fulfill his father's desire to become a priest. Showing little respect for the man he had become and his own wishes, his relatives badgered Höss to go at once to a training college for priests. Höss' uncle, his guardian, had sold the worldly possessions of the Höss family and retained enough money to send his sisters to the convent and Höss to the priesthood.[18]

Höss was indignant. He now realized for the first time the full significance of his mother's death. He had nothing—no family, no belongings, no future in Mannheim. Already disenchanted by the priest's breach of confessional secrecy and the deception perpetrated by the monasteries on the Holy Land pilgrims, Höss decided against becoming a priest, and he told his uncle so. Knowing the wishes of Höss' parents, his uncle refused to give him money for any profession other than the priesthood. The significant events of his life drove Höss to make a momentous decision away from the Catholic Church and towards the company of his army comrades. He renounced his inheritance and left Mannheim for East Prussia to join the Freikorps. Höss needed the kinship of brothers-in-arms. "Oddly enough it was I, the lone wolf, always keeping my thoughts and my feelings to myself, who felt continually drawn towards that comradeship which enables a man to rely on others in time of need and of danger."[19]

In the wake of World War I, a belief took hold among German war veterans that Germany had not lost the war, but was forced to surrender solely because it had been "stabbed in the back" by civilian revolutionaries who overthrew the monarchy. The German soldiers wanted to believe that the army had never been defeated. In fact, as the tide of the war turned, it was the German Supreme Army Command, led by General Erich Friedrich Wilhelm Ludendorff, who beseeched the civilian government to make peace. As revolution forced Russia out of World War I in 1917, Germany was undergoing a revolution of its own. The constitutional monarchy would ultimately be replaced with a democratic parliamentary republic which later became known as the Weimar Republic.[20]

Life in Germany under the fledgling republic was anything but stable. The Freikorps were volunteer units of German soldiers used as the government or their individual commander saw fit to protect German borders or settle internal political disputes. Reichsmarschall Hermann Göring later described them as "fighters who could not become de-brutalized." In the Freikorps, Höss and other former German soldiers found comradeship, understanding, economic security and a continuation of the military life they had learned to love. The Freikorps were used to violently put down a perceived Communist takeover in January 1919 in Berlin. Efforts by the Left to establish extremist governments in other parts of the country were likewise repressed.[21]

Höss belonged to Freikorps Rossbach, led by Gerhard Rossbach, which first fought in Latvia. Although ostensibly fighting the spread of Communism, Rossbach's men sought to serve German interests only: to secure land for Germany on the Baltic Sea. Höss recalled, "Officially the Freikorps was not paid for by the government, but unofficially it was financed by the government and by industry. The Rossbach Freikorps consisted of 3,000 men. There were innumerable Freikorps, from company to regimental strengths." Höss described the fighting as "more savage and more bitter than any I had experienced … in the World War." For the first time, he saw the horrors of war inflicted on the civilian population. Latvian nationalists who sought independence fought the Freikorps and the Russians and took revenge on their own people, who offered aid to either German or Russian soldiers. Höss saw houses where the occupants—women and children—were burned to death. At the time, he believed he was witnessing the "height of man's destructive madness."[22]

After fighting in the Baltic States, the Freikorps Rossbach served in Mecklenburg, the Ruhr and Upper Silesia. Höss said it was the nature of the Freikorps that they acted in the government's interest, but not with the government's express blessing. The Freikorps often administered justice according to the ancient Germanic pattern of *Vehmgericht*, medieval courts that passed sentence in secret. When the Freikorps was no longer useful to the government, they were disowned, as were their heavy-handed methods.

Nevertheless, they often refused to disband. Höss remained associated with the Freikorps until 1921. At that time, he became an apprentice agriculturalist on an estate in Silesia and Schleswig-Holstein, the northernmost state of Germany.[23]

Höss became more and more alienated from religion until he finally broke with the Catholic Church completely in 1922. Not surprisingly, his allegiance turned to the men and the philosophy that made him a man. In November 1922, Höss attended a reunion of Freikorps Rossbach veterans in Munich, where he heard Adolf Hitler speak for the first time. Höss was so sufficiently impressed that he immediately joined the National Socialist German Workers' Party (NSDAP), the Nazis, as member 3,240. Nazism became his religion. The Freikorps is considered a forerunner of the Nazi movement in Germany.

As did Höss, Rossbach joined the Nazi Party early on. Rossbach and other Freikorps members marched with Hitler during the failed Beer Hall Putsch in Munich in 1923. Rossbach was also active in the *Sturmabteilung* (SA), the original paramilitary wing of the Nazi party also known as the "Brownshirts," in the 1930s. In his singular and thorough analysis of the Freikorps movement, Robert G. L. Waite states in *Vanguard of Nazism* that the real importance of the movement lies in the "brutality of spirit and in that exaltation of power which the men of the Free Corps (Freikorps) bequeathed to the Third Reich."[24]

The Freikorps acted outside the law with little fear of repercussions. As Höss noted, rarely were the "executioners" of justice caught and brought to trial. Höss would be one of the exceptions. In response to a French invasion of the Ruhr in western Germany, Lt. Albert Leo Schlageter, a Freikorps leader, blew up a railway bridge near Calkum. He was captured by the French, tried by a French military court and, on May 26, 1923, executed by a French firing squad. Immediately, he became a martyr to German freedom.[25]

Convinced that Schlageter had been betrayed, the Freikorps and Höss, who had fought with Schlageter in the Baltic and the Ruhr, sought justice against the traitor. On May 31, 1923, Höss and other former Freikorps members, including Martin Bormann, who later became Hitler's private secretary, abducted Walter Kadow, a former Freikorps soldier who they believed had betrayed Schlageter. He was driven into the woods where he was beaten, his throat was cut and he was shot. Höss acknowledged he was present. While not admitting the part he played in Kadow's death, Höss said, "I was in complete agreement with the sentence of death being carried out on the traitor."[26]

Within a few days, one of the participants told the story of the murder to a newspaper. Höss was arrested on June 28, 1923, and spent nine months in jail awaiting trial. The political situation in Germany was unstable, and he anticipated he would be set free. While his defense attorneys told him that he could expect a lengthy term of imprisonment, Höss was not concerned: "I firmly believed that my trial would probably never take place and that even if it did I would certainly be acquitted." Even after he was convicted and sentenced on March 15, 1924, to 10 years at hard labor, Höss remained optimistic.[27]

Bitter reality set in when he was transferred from Leipzig to a Prussian prison at Brandenburg. Höss noted, "Every aspect of life was strictly regulated down to the smallest details. Discipline was on severe, military lines." Notwithstanding his murder conviction, Höss never really saw himself as a criminal, believing that the imposition of death on Kadow was justified. As a political prisoner, he was kept in solitary confinement. Although at first unhappy about this arrangement, Höss learned to prefer solitary as it allowed him to avoid the merciless bullying practiced by the "real criminals" in the larger cells. Despite being segregated, Höss came into daily contact with other prisoners during exercise in the courtyard or on the way to the washhouse or prison administration. He also heard them talk from his window. Höss recalled, "I got a fairly good insight into the minds and souls of these people and an abyss of human aberrations, depravities and passions was opened before my eyes."[28]

Höss observed and listened to murderers, professional thieves and sex offenders. He noted that prison was a "regular school for criminals," with the young eager to learn from the older inmates. Favors were paid by sexual services. He categorized the prisoners with him in solitary confinement, claiming he obtained a "deep insight into the psyche of these condemned men." He observed that "[a] lengthy term of imprisonment makes even the best man irritable, unsociable, and lacking in consideration." Perhaps most significant was his realization that the psychological effect of punishment on serious-minded prisoners was far greater than that caused by physical hardship. Höss would not forget the lessons he learned.[29]

Höss himself suffered emotionally from his imprisonment. Two years into his sentence, he was suddenly overcome by a change in mood. Höss became very irritable, nervous and excited. He could not eat or sleep, paced up and down in his cell and found it difficult to concentrate. His nervous agitation persisted until he was taken to the prison doctor, who diagnosed prison psychosis. Höss was told he would get over it and was given an injection. After several days of sedatives, Höss was returned, at his request, to his cell. His depression began to alleviate.[30]

As might be expected from someone who was raised in a rigid home, Höss was a model prisoner. He obeyed all the rules and kept his cell clean and neat. He even taught himself some English. While he otherwise would have qualified for early release, Höss was told that, as a political prisoner, he must serve his entire sentence. Unexpectedly, a majority was created in the

Reichstag, the German Parliament, by a coalition between the extremists on the right wing and the extremists on the left wing, both of whom wanted their political prisoners to be released. As a consequence of this unlikely arrangement, Höss was set free on July 14, 1928, after serving five years of his 10-year sentence.[31]

Being out of prison on his own in Berlin so suddenly, it was as if the 26-year-old Höss was in a dream. He stayed with a friendly Berlin family while deciding what to do with his future. His friends wanted him to leave Germany and avoid further political involvement with the extreme right. His old comrades encouraged Höss to join ranks with the Nazis. Initially, Höss had other ideas. "Although I had been a Party member since 1922 and was in firm agreement with the Party's aims, I had nevertheless emphatically objected to their use of mass propaganda, their bargaining for the goodwill of the people, the way they appealed to the lowest instincts of the masses, and indeed their tone." In time, personal ambition and SS indoctrination would cause him to ignore the sensible first impressions he formed of Hitler and the Nazis.[32]

Höss wanted a farm and a large, healthy family. In the brief time between his service in the Freikorps and his imprisonment, Höss developed a passion for farming. After his release from prison, he established contact with the Artaman League, an agrarian movement which he described as a "community of young people of both sexes who had the interests of their country at heart." According to Höss, they were "people who all, at one time or another, had wanted to escape from the unhealthy, dissolute and superficial life of the towns and especially of the large cities, and to discover for themselves a healthy and tough but natural way of life on the land."[33]

In truth, the Artaman League was no ordinary, backyard-variety garden club. No doubt it was an agrarian movement intended to induce people to abandon city life and get back to the *Blut und Boden*—"blood and soil." The group was also undeniably right-wing, anti–Slavic and anti–Jew. As the Freikorps is considered a forerunner of the Nazi movement, many future Nazis also first followed the Artaman path. Members were expected to adhere to a strict moral code, which included abstinence from alcohol and tobacco. During this time, Höss became further acquainted with his future boss, Heinrich Himmler, who he first met while in the Freikorps. As courier for his own Freikorps, Höss frequented the home of General Ludendorff. Himmler also had business there as a representative of his Bavarian Freikorps. General Ludendorff was the protector and secret head of the nationalist movements, with their disguised military or semi-military organizations, which were forbidden by the Treaty of Versailles that formally ended World War I.[34]

Within the Artaman League, Höss also met Hedwig Hensel. They were perfectly suited for one another and shared the same ideals and outlook on life. They married on August 17, 1929. Over the next five years, Höss and Hedwig were happy, worked hard and had three children: Klaus, born February 6, 1930, Heidetraut, born April 9, 1932, and Inge-Brigitt, born August 18, 1933. Höss had found the very woman for whom, during all his years of loneliness, he had longed. For Hedwig, he felt the love he had never felt for his family.

Unfortunately, not even with Hedwig could Höss share his deepest feelings. The emotional solitude that pervaded his childhood continued into his marriage. At Nuremberg, Höss told Dr. Gilbert, "Yes—I was always alone. Of course, I loved my wife, but a real spiritual union—that was lacking." Hedwig noticed the distance he kept and thought Höss was not satisfied with her. He told her that was just his nature, and she must be reconciled to it. Later, at Auschwitz, despite the close proximity of the Höss villa to the Auschwitz I crematorium, Höss tried to prevent Hedwig from learning about the Final Solution. She stood by him even after discovering that, as commandant of Auschwitz, he was sending thousands of men, women and children to their deaths in the gas chambers. Höss would find his inability to share his innermost thoughts with Hedwig to be a source of perpetual sorrow.[35]

III

The SS

After the failed Beer Hall Putsch in Munich in November 1923 and his subsequent imprisonment for treason, Hitler realized that power must come *through* the constitutional system in Germany, not by *overthrowing* it. The parliamentary election of 1928 was not encouraging to him. The NSDAP received 810,000 votes, giving them only 12 seats in the Reichstag. Hitler was a dynamic and formidable speaker, but his inflammatory oratory and radical ideas tended to fall on deaf ears. Life in Germany had stabilized since World War I and prosperity prevailed. Hitler was confident it would not last. He was right. Germany had borrowed a great deal of money, particularly from American investors, to pay war reparations required by the Treaty of Versailles and to increase its vast social services. On October 24, 1929, the stock market on Wall Street crashed. Suddenly, Germany could get no more money from the United States and was unable to repay its outstanding loans. As German exports dropped precipitously, millions of German workers became unemployed, and the German economy tumbled.[1]

Hitler used the crisis to his full advantage. He promised to make Germany strong again. He would do this, he said, by refusing to pay the unpopular war reparations, repudiating the humiliating Treaty of Versailles, stamping out corruption, making the money barons accountable (especially if they were Jewish) and assuring that every German would have a job and bread. He told Germans exactly what they wanted to hear. New parliamentary elections were called for on September 1930. Hitler hoped his campaign promises would garner enough votes to increase the number of Nazi seats from 12 to 50. Instead, the NSDAP recorded 6,409,000 votes, entitling the party to 107 Reichstag seats.[2]

Hitler was surprised and elated. The NSDAP ballooned from the smallest political party in Parliament to the second largest, behind only the Social Democrats. As Germans continued to struggle, Nazi fortunes rose. In the July 1932 election, the Nazis secured 230 seats, making them the largest party in the Reichstag. On January 30, 1933, because no party had secured a majority, President Paul von Hindenburg reluctantly appointed Hitler Chancellor of Germany. Shortly after Hindenburg died on August 2, 1934, the offices of Chancellor and President were combined, effectively granting Hitler the President's powers. Hitler was now dictator of Germany. Thereafter, every member of the German armed forces took the following oath:

> I swear by God this sacred oath, that I will render unconditional obedience to Adolf Hitler, the Fuehrer of the German Reich and people, Supreme Commander of the Armed Forces, and will be ready as a brave soldier to risk my life at any time for this oath.[3]

To aid them in their rise to power in their early days, the Nazis gathered men into a paramilitary force to be used as muscle when necessary to strong-arm their opposition. This group was called the *Sturmabteilung*—the SA or Brownshirts. The SA grew into an armed band of several hundred thousand men who protected Nazi meetings, broke up gatherings of others and generally terrorized anyone who opposed Hitler. They were, in effect, a group of street thugs. As a more dependable, more elite force, Hitler created the *Schutzstaffel*, or SS. In 1929, Hitler named Heinrich Himmler, formerly a chicken farmer and Höss' Artaman League acquaintance, to head the SS. When Himmler took charge, the SS consisted of no more than 300 members. By 1933, membership had grown to more than 50,000. The SS would eventually be charged with the responsibility of administering the concentration, labor and extermination camps of the Third Reich.[4]

From its inception, the SS operated as a military organization, and its members considered themselves to be soldiers of both the party and the state. They wore distinctive black uniforms and tall black boots with dual lightning bolts, signifying "SS" on a collar patch. The *Totenkopf* (death head's skull) was prominently displayed on the front of SS headgear, no doubt to impress and intimidate. The SS served as the ideological vanguard of the Nazi movement; purity of blood was critical. For the most part, they were not men of thought. Johannes Hassebroeck, who like Höss served as a concentration camp commandant, stated, "I was full of gratitude to the SS for the intellectual guidance it gave me. We were all thankful. Many of us had been so bewildered before joining the organization. We did not understand what was happening around us, everything was so mixed up. The SS offered us a series of simple ideas that we could understand, and we believed in them."[5]

The Nazi idea of racial purity was incompatible with Christian humanism. The SS promoted faith in God, but its members could no longer identify themselves as Catholic or Protestant. The SS sought to substitute primitive nature rituals for the religious customs and holidays which its members enjoyed prior to joining the SS. As noted by Tom Segev in *Soldiers of Evil*, "the

III. The SS

more the rift grew between the SS man and his past and the values his family held, the greater became his isolation and his dependence on the organization." Höss' alienation from his family and the Catholic Church made him "just the man" for which the SS was looking. His strict upbringing also provided a good foundation for SS life. SS training was geared towards hardening its men. Discipline was harsh. It was believed that toughness towards others would derive from toughness towards oneself. The difficulty tended to create solidarity and a feeling of comradeship among the members of the SS.[6]

The owner of the estate in Pomerania in northern Germany for which Höss worked wanted to establish an SS horse stable, and Höss' service in the cavalry in World War I gave him the necessary experience. On August 18, 1933, another daughter, Inge-Brigitt, was born to Höss and Hedwig. A month later, on September 20, 1933, Höss applied to become a member of the SS to manage the stable. His status was initially that of SS-Anwärter. Over the next six months, Höss was on probation. Basic instruction in the SS included ideological indoctrination along with physical education and military training. Once accepted, SS men received a tattoo in the armpit of the left arm showing the soldier's blood type. Many SS soldiers who sustained serious injuries or wounds during the war were saved by this tattoo. A nearby comrade with the same blood type could readily be found and used for an immediate transfusion. These blood-type tattoos were only compulsory in the SS. After the war, Allied soldiers hunting the SS for war crimes would use the tattoo as a means of identifying their prey, many of whom tried to disguise themselves as ordinary soldiers. On April 1, 1934, Höss was accepted into the SS, and his status changed to SS-Mann; on April 20, 1934, Höss was promoted to SS-Sturmann.[7]

In June 1934, Himmler approached Höss about joining the ranks of the active SS. He felt comfortable and secure with his farming life. Höss recalled, "I was unable to come to a decision for a long, long time ... [but in the end the] temptation of being a soldier again was ... too strong." Hedwig doubted that Höss would find complete fulfillment and inner satisfaction in the SS. In the SS, Höss saw a reasonably certain prospect of rapid promotion with the accompanying financial benefits. He assumed he could always return to farming after he retired. Höss' first assignment was the concentration camp at Dachau.[8]

In March 1933, less than two months after Hitler came to power, the Dachau concentration camp opened nine miles north of Munich. Most of the initial inmates were political opponents of the Nazi regime, such as Communists and Social Democrats. Soon enough, criminals, homosexuals, Gypsies, clergy, Jehovah's Witnesses and, of course, Jews, were imprisoned there. In June 1933, Himmler appointed SS-Oberführer Theodor Eicke as commandant of Dachau. At the end of November 1934, Höss was promoted to SS-Unterscharführer (corporal) and joined the Guard Unit

Upper Bavaria formed by Eicke as part of the General-SS. Höss described Eicke as the founder of most concentration camps and the one person who gave them their form and shape. Eicke had ingratiated himself to Hitler in July 1934 on the Night of the Long Knives by participating in the execution of Ernst Röhm, the head of the SA, after he became a threat to Hitler. As Tom Segev noted in *Soldiers of Evil*, "Theodor Eicke ... did not excel as an ideologist or theorist; his strength was in molding the SS mentality in daily life."[9]

By 1936, the SS was composed of three parts: the General SS (Allgemeine SS), the Militarized Formations (later the Waffen SS) and the Death's Head Formations. Guards and administrative personnel in concentration camps were members of the Death's Head Formations. The first Death's Head unit was set up in 1933 in Dachau immediately after Eicke received command of the camp. The Guard Unit Upper Bavaria of which Höss was a member was incorporated into the Death's Head Formations. Within a short time after arriving at Dachau, Eicke removed most of the police and the SA. He sought more stable individuals who were younger, more motivated and more idealistic. Until 1937, to qualify for acceptance into the Death's Head Formations, a person had to be: 16 to 23 years of age, a minimum height of 5 feet 8 inches and a German citizen with no police record. Thereafter, the age limit was 22. Finally, an applicant must be able to demonstrate more than 100 years of racial purity.[10]

Eicke was an inflexible Nazi of the old school. Tom Segev stated, "In his mind, he and the Nazi movement were one." Through Eicke, Höss learned that "...the prisoners were sworn enemies of the state, who were to be treated with great severity and destroyed if they showed resistance." Prisoners were flogged for the slightest offense. Eicke emphasized the need of the guards to be tough and warned them that prisoners would take advantage of any sign of weakness. He said it would be unworthy of any SS-man to feel pity for an enemy of the State. According to Höss, Eicke succeeded in "engendering in simple-natured men a hatred and antipathy for the prisoners which an outsider will find hard to imagine." It was Eicke's intention that his SS-men should be basically ill-disposed towards the prisoners and to treat them roughly. This influence spread throughout all the concentration camps. Höss attributed all the torture and ill-treatment inflicted upon the prisoners in the camps to this "hate indoctrination."[11]

Most of Eicke's men loved him and called him "Papa Eicke." He made it a habit of talking to them outside the presence of their superior officers. Eicke instilled pride in his men: "There are no fighters in the SS better than we are. There are none more daring and none harder than we are. Germany could not hold on for a single day without us." To maintain the high level of performance, Eicke assured his men that to serve under his command was a great privilege. He warned that anyone who fell short of the required level of achievement would be dismissed from the Death's Head Formations, a humiliating failure. Höss recalled that four SS guards who had engaged in a racket with prisoners at Dachau were paraded in front of the entire guard unit, stripped of their badges of rank and SS insignia by Eicke, then marched past each company.[12]

Höss' toughness at Dachau was tested early. Two prisoners who had stolen cigarettes from the canteen were sentenced to twenty-five lashes each. The SS troops were formed in an open square with the prisoners in the middle. The first prisoner was made to lie across the flogging block, while two soldiers held his head and hands. After his sentence was read, two block leaders delivered alternate strokes. The process was repeated with the second prisoner. The first prisoner made no sound, but the second man screamed throughout the flogging and attempted to break free. Höss was in the front rank and was compelled to watch everything. The flogging and the screaming made him shudder. Höss stated, "Later on, at the beginning of the war, I attended my first execution, but it did not affect me nearly so much as witnessing this corporal punishment."[13]

After his first experience, Höss made sure he was in the back row for the prisoner floggings. Even later, as a block leader, he avoided them whenever possible. He knew many block leaders who seemed to relish these scenes. Höss described them as "sly, rough, violent and often common creatures. They did not regard prisoners as human beings at all." He noted that some of these men even chose to hang themselves rather than be held accountable for the brutality they inflicted. In his autobiography, Höss made no attempt to explain why he was so disgusted by the flogging of prisoners yet was able to supervise the murder of more than one million people.[14]

Höss rose rapidly through the ranks. On March 1, 1935, he became a block leader in the protective custody camp and was promoted to SS-Scharführer (sergeant) on April 1, 1935. Höss claims he did not seek promotion to block leader and did not want the position. By this time, Eicke had been named chief of the Inspectorate of Concentration Camps near Berlin. When Eicke visited Dachau, Höss requested and was granted an interview. He told Eicke he had joined the active SS because he wanted to be a soldier, and he asked to be sent back to his unit. Eicke knew Höss' history and felt that his time in prison made him eminently suitable to take charge of prisoners himself. In fact, he felt no one was better qualified than Höss for duty in the protective custody camp. His path could not be changed. According to Höss, he now regretted leaving the simple farming life where he and Hedwig had been happy and content.[15]

On July 1, 1935, Höss was promoted to SS-Oberscharführer (staff sergeant), then to SS-Hauptscharführer (master sergeant) on March 1, 1936.

From April 1, 1936, until September 1936, Höss served as Rapportführer at Dachau. In that capacity, he was required to oversee discipline and be present during the floggings he detested. In June 1936, Himmler and Bormann, Höss' Freikorps and Kadow murder associate, visited Dachau. Then-commandant Hans Loritz and Eicke recommended Höss for another promotion. On September 13, 1936, Höss became a member of the SS officer corps as SS-Untersturmführer (second lieutenant). From September 1936 until May 1938, Höss was responsible for the administration of stores and prisoners' property. During this time, another boy, Hans-Jurgen, was born to Höss and Hedwig on May 1, 1937.[16]

Despite his personal experiences as a prisoner, Höss claimed he did not feel comfortable supervising concentration camp prisoners. He recognized the enormous differences between the prisoners with whom he shared time at the Brandenburg prison and those in the concentration camp. While there were criminals in Dachau, there were also political prisoners and inmates with antisocial tendencies, such as homosexuals, Gypsies, Jehovah's Witnesses and Jews. They were subject to the arbitrary powers of SS men and of prisoner leaders, harsh camp discipline, years of living as a member of a crowd and the monotony of the daily routine. However, Höss recognized that the worst aspect of concentration camp life was the uncertainty of the term of imprisonment, which had a significant psychological effect on the prisoners. After studying the political prisoners in Dachau he was directed to supervise, Höss made the interesting observation that three fourths of them could have been released without any harm to the Third Reich.[17]

On August 1, 1938, Höss was transferred to the Sachsenhausen concentration camp at Oranienburg, 22 miles north of Berlin. The commandant was SS-Standartenführer Hermann Baranowski, with whom Höss had served at Dachau. Despite the fact that Eicke's office was nearby, the atmosphere in Sachsenhausen was less brutal than at Dachau. Baranowski was strict and severe, but maintained a sense of justice. Höss said he hoped to emulate Baranowski. In September 1938, Höss was promoted to SS-Obersturmführer (first lieutenant), and two months later to SS-Hauptsturmführer (captain). Within a year, the life of Höss and his family and eventually much of the world would turn upside down at the whim of Germany's duly elected dictator.[18]

Following his occupations of the Rhineland, Austria and Czechoslovakia, it was only a matter of time before Hitler took another country. All attempts by peace-minded nations in Europe to appease him had proved futile. Hitler was ready for war, and his military chiefs made plans for the invasion of Poland. On August 31, 1939, they initiated Operation Himmler. Hitler directed that 150 Polish uniforms and Polish small arms be delivered to Reichsführer-SS Himmler and SS-Obergruppenführer Reinhard Heydrich, the chief of the Reich Main Security Office. Led by SS-man Alfred Helmut

III. The SS

Naujocks, a group of SS soldiers dressed in Polish uniforms attacked the German radio station at Gleiwitz near the Polish border. A speech was broadcast condemning Germany and inciting war. Concentration camp prisoners from Dachau, also in Polish uniforms, were shot and laid around the station. Of course, a response by Germany to this affront was necessary. On September 1, 1939, Germany attacked Poland on the land, in the air and from the sea, inaugurating World War II.[19]

At the beginning of the war, all the frontline Deaths Head units in the camps were replaced by reservists from the General SS. Höss recalled that on the very day the war started, Eicke delivered an address to the officers of the reserve formations which had relieved the regular SS units in the camps. While regular SS were sent to the front, senior camp officers such as Höss were barred by Himmler from serving lest they be captured. Eicke emphasized to Höss and those who remained at the camps that the harsh laws of war now prevailed. Every order must be regarded as sacrosanct and carried out without hesitation, no matter how harsh and severe it may appear. The main task of the SS was to protect Hitler's State from every kind of peril and especially against internal dangers. Eicke demanded an inflexible harshness towards the prisoners. He referred to their intensive training and pointed out that the SS were the only ones who could protect the National Socialist State from internal danger.[20]

The first day of the war also required Höss to oversee an execution at Sachsenhausen. A Communist refused to perform ARP (air raid precautions) work at the Junkers factory at Dressau. Junkers was a major German aircraft and aircraft engine manufacturer. The factory authority reported the man to the police, who took him to the Gestapo in Berlin. After reviewing the report, Himmler ordered that he be shot. The condemned man was taken to Sachsenhausen for execution. As adjutant, Höss headed the commandant's staff and bore responsibility for carrying out the order. Höss gathered three of his more reliable junior officers and instructed them in the matter of procedure. When the man arrived, Höss led him to a post erected for the execution. Höss stepped back and gave the command to fire. After the man collapsed, Höss shot him once in the head. Höss remarked that no one thought that Eicke's words from earlier in the day would become reality so quickly. He recalled that all of those who witnessed the execution, many of whom were World War I veterans, were deeply affected by the event. Yet the flogging he watched at Dachau was more disturbing than the execution in which he participated at Sachsenhausen. The Eicke mentality was taking hold.[21]

Once war broke out, it became dangerous even to question the harshness of the penalties the SS were ordered to impose. If anyone in the SS, even those of senior rank, dared to express an opinion that severe punishment soiled the black uniform of the SS, it would be reported to Eicke. The freethinker would be called before Eicke, who would tell him that, despite his long service with the SS, he has not yet understood the function of the SS. He emphasized that the most important task assigned to the SS is to protect the new State by any and every means. Eicke stressed that every opponent of the State, according to the danger he represents, must either be kept in custody or be destroyed. He pointed out that the destruction of internal enemies of the State is just as much a duty as is the destruction of the enemy from beyond the frontiers, and such action can therefore never be regarded as dishonorable. Eicke would inform the man that the reported remarks are a sign of weakness and sentimentality, emotions which are not only unworthy of an SS leader, but which might become dangerous. For this reason, it was his (Eicke's) duty to report the persons concerned to the Reichsführer-SS (Himmler) with a view to punishment. Eicke only had use for men who were unconditionally tough, and who also understood the meaning of the death's head, the skull and crossbones, which they wore on their uniforms as a special badge of honor.[22]

Executions became a regular duty for Höss. Most of the men put to death either refused to perform war service or were saboteurs. However, on one occasion, Höss was faced with the execution of a fellow SS leader. The SS man had been ordered to arrest a Communist party official. He had known the Communist a long time and, acting out of kindness, allowed the man to visit his home and say goodbye to his wife. As the SS waited in the sitting room, the arrestee made his escape. When the SS man reported the incident, Himmler, in accordance with the policy of showing no mercy, ordered that the SS man be shot. Only the day before, the condemned man and Höss had been discussing executions. Now, Höss led him to the post, stepped back and gave the order to fire. As before, Höss administered the last shot to the head. Höss was evolving, "At the time I believed that this was asking too much of human nature, and yet Eicke was insisting on ever greater harshness. An SS-man must be able to destroy even his closest dependants should they commit an offense against the State or the ideals of Adolf Hitler." Höss would always recall this execution to remind himself of the need "to exercise perpetual self-mastery and unbending severity." Höss was becoming mindless.[23]

In December 1939, Höss became commandant of the protective custody camp at Sachsenhausen. The next month, Commandant Loritz was transferred from Dachau to replace Baranowski, after his death, as commandant at Sachsenhausen. Loritz, who previously worked well with Höss and recommended him for promotion, made life difficult. Loritz hated Baranowski and thought Höss had asked for a transfer out of Dachau in 1938 when, in fact, it was Commandant Baranowski who had requested that Höss be transferred to Sachsenhausen. Loritz was tough on the SS men and the prisoners. Fortunately for Höss, his unpleasant service under Loritz would not last long. He would soon be given the opportunity for his own command.[24]

Commandants of Nazi concentration camps, like Baranowski and Loritz, fell in the middle of the rank hierarchy, usually majors (Sturmbannführer) or lieutenant colonels (Obersturmbannführer). They were subordinate to the Inspectorate of the Concentration Camps led by Eicke early in the war and the WVHA later in the war. Rules and regulations intended to govern SS personnel and inmates emanated from this central location. As a practical matter, especially after war broke out, commandants often acted without rules, exercising unlimited power over life and death. The widow of Amon Göth, the commandant at the Plazsow concentration camp in Krakow, said "the camp was a kingdom to its commandant, and within it he was its king." Until the start of the war, at least, some measure of accountability was imposed on commandants who abused their authority by mistreating prisoners in their care. Two concentration camp commandants, Adam Grünewald and Karl Chmielewski, were tried and found guilty of the deaths of prisoners as a result of brutality in their camps. As will be seen, standard rules did not apply at Auschwitz. Camps were divided into departments, and various officers assisted the commandant to run the functions of the camp. Generally, the primary duty of the commandant was to assure the internal security of the camp. At Auschwitz, the commandant's role extended much farther.[25]

In *Soldiers of Evil*, Tom Segev wrote about camp commandants:

> They were mediocre people, without imagination, without courage, without initiative. From the personnel files, most of them seem to have had shallow personalities. Their grayness seems to have camouflaged them within the system in which they worked, allowing them to function somewhere around the middle management level; they did not frame ideology and did not establish policy. Most of the orders they sent to their subordinates came to them from their superiors. The system obviously did not require managers of any higher level. But their mediocrity is misleading: they were not Germans like all the Germans and not even Nazis like all the Nazis. It is not the banality of evil that characterizes them, but rather inner identification with evil.

In general, Segev is describing Höss. However, Auschwitz would make something of Höss that no other camp would do to any other commandant. On the other hand, Höss made Auschwitz into a camp like no other.[26]

IV

Creation of Auschwitz

As Hitler imposed his authority over Germany and the annexed territories, larger numbers of political opponents and "undesirables" were imprisoned. The invasion of Poland in the fall of 1939 significantly increased the geographical area controlled by the Nazis and the number of people over whom they exercised dominion. As mass arrests continued, existing camps and jails were unable to meet the ever-growing demand, so the SS was required to establish additional facilities. The idea of establishing a concentration camp at Oświęcim, Poland, or, as it was called in Germany, Auschwitz, originated with SS-Gruppenführer Erich von dem Bach-Zelewski, the Higher SS and Police Leader Southeast. At Bach-Zelewski's suggestion, the head of the Inspectorate of Concentration Camps, SS-Oberführer Richard Glücks, sent a commission headed by SS-Obersturmführer Walter Eisfeld in early 1940 to investigate the feasibility of creating a large concentration camp at Oświęcim in Upper Silesia, near the confluence of the Vistula and Sola rivers. The prospective location had served as Polish Army barracks and consisted of eight two-story and 14 one-story brick buildings. Eisfeld advised against the site; the buildings were run down and located on swampy ground.[1]

The report of a second commission assigned to evaluate the suitability of the barracks at Auschwitz was more favorable. Finally, a third commission led by Höss was sent to examine the location. He had been told that the camp would be used as a regional prison for opponents of the Reich and to temporarily house Polish prisoners prior to transportation west as slave laborers. Höss was not unfamiliar with Upper Silesia, having served there as a member of the Freikorps. In an interview in 1946 with Dr. Leon Goldensohn, the Nuremberg prison psychiatrist, Höss recalled, "Auschwitz was originally thought of as a quarantine camp for Poles from the General Government. Poles were originally scheduled to come to a concentration camp in the Reich itself, and Auschwitz was originally meant to be only a transient quarantine station where prisoners would be held for a few weeks to determine whether they had illnesses which were contagious, such as typhus or fleck fever."[2]

IV. Creation of Auschwitz

At Sachsenhausen, Höss labored under the heavy hand of Commandant Loritz who wanted to replace him with someone more to his liking. Also, Höss was anxious to advance his career and saw, in his review of the Polish site, an opportunity to demonstrate his initiative and concentration camp expertise. Another negative report about the camp would not accomplish his goals. After his inspection, Höss reported that the barracks could be utilized for the intended purposes. Glücks relayed the positive report to Himmler. Based upon Höss' recommendations, Himmler issued an order on April 27, 1940, that established Konzentrationsläger (KZ or KL) Auschwitz with a capacity of about 10,000 prisoners.[3]

Höss was reassigned from the Sachsenhausen concentration camp to Auschwitz. Five other SS men, including SS-Hauptscharführer Gerhard Palitzsch, were sent with him to begin work on the camp, along with 30 Sachsenhausen internees picked by Palitzsch. The group first adversely affected by the building of the camp were 1,200 unemployed Polish refugees expelled from their homes near the site. More residents of the area would later be forced to leave. On May 1, 1940, Höss was appointed commandant of Auschwitz. His adjutant was SS-Obersturmführer Josef Kramer, who later became the commandant at the Bergen-Belsen concentration camp, and Höss' camp commander was SS-Obersturmführer Karl Fritzsch. In his memoirs, Höss stated that he intended that everything done wrong at Dachau and Sachsenhausen would be done differently at Auschwitz, though he never specified exactly what that was. He immediately went to work, though he did not have much to work with. As Höss observed, "My task was not an easy one. In the shortest possible time I had to construct a transit camp for ten thousand prisoners, using the existing complex which, though well-constructed, had been completely neglected, and were swarming with vermin."[4]

At least initially, Höss received no support of any kind from the Inspectorate of Concentration Camps. If he needed "bread or meat or potatoes," Höss had to find them on his own. He would also "organize" (the concentration camp term for steal, barter or exchange) trucks and fuel. He drove as far as 60 miles to get cooking pots, bed frames and straw mattresses. Unable to acquire barbed wire, Höss directed his laborers to strip old field fortifications and an abandoned Polish prisoner of war camp. The original camp became known as the Stammlager or just Lager or eventually, Auschwitz I. Prisoners who entered the camp passed through a steel gate under a sign that read "ARBEIT MACHT FREI," meaning "work sets you free."[5]

In his autobiography, Höss attempted to explain this infamous message that greeted and tormented all who entered Auschwitz I:

> All my life I have thoroughly enjoyed working. I have done plenty of hard, physical work, under the severest conditions, in the coal mines, in oil refineries and in brickyards. I have felled timber, cut sleepers and stacked peat....

ARBEIT MACHT FREI signage over entrance to Auschwitz I (author photograph).

> I myself derive no real satisfaction from my labors unless I have completed a good job of work thoroughly....
> During my subsequent imprisonment, where choice was possible, I chose work that required a certain amount of attention and was not purely mechanical.
> Such employment spared me hours of useless and enervating self-pity. In the evening I had the satisfactory feeling that not only had I put another day behind me, but also that I had done a useful job of work....
> I have discussed this question of work with many of my fellow prisoners in the penitentiary and also with many of those detained in the concentration camps, especially at Dachau. All of them were convinced that in the long run life behind bars or behind wire would be unbearable without work, and that to be without work would be the worst imaginable punishment.
> Work in prison is not merely an efficient corrective, in the best sense of the word, in that it encourages the prisoners to discipline themselves and thus makes them better able to withstand the demoralizing effect of their confinement. It is also a means of training for those prisoners who are fundamentally unstable and who need to learn the meaning of endurance and perseverance. The beneficent influence of work can draw many prisoners away from a life of crime.

Höss acknowledged that his statements only applied when "conditions are normal."[6]

According to Höss, it was Eicke's firm intention that no matter what category, those prisoners whose steady and zealous work differentiated them from the others should in due course be released, regardless of what the Gestapo and the Criminal Police Office might think to the contrary. A concentration camp prisoner was, by Hoss' account, "occasionally" released, until the war started. Work at Auschwitz, which was not established until after the war started, meant slave labor under inhuman conditions with no chance of discharge—unless one considers death a liberation from the agony and torment imposed by the barbaric conditions under which Auschwitz prisoners lived and worked.[7]

The first transport of Poles, a total of 728 men, arrived at Auschwitz on June 14, 1940. In addition to stealing barbed wire, prisoners were employed in the construction and renovation of the new camp. They surveyed the camp, drafted technical plans for new buildings and laid out sites for future buildings and streets. All the inmates worked at building the camp except for those who took care of the SS and the prisoners, for example in the camp kitchen, the prisoners' infirmary, the SS kitchen, the SS sick bay and in the SS departmental offices, such as the Admissions Office of the Political Department. In 1940, the hardest work the inmates endured involved leveling the roll call area, paving the streets, working the gravel pits, demolishing the houses and farms of the residents evacuated from a nearby town and transporting construction material. No equipment or machines were provided. The prisoners were required to perform these back-breaking jobs with the tools at hand. While doing this work, which was beyond their strength, the underfed and utterly exhausted prisoners were beaten, abused, and killed. New transports arrived daily to replace the dead workers and to increase the size of the workforce.[8]

In the fall of 1940, the Reich Main Administration and Economic Office (WVHA) began to see the worth of Auschwitz in a different light. SS-Obergruppenführer Oswald Pohl, the head of the WVHA, visited the camp in September 1940 and determined that Auschwitz could serve a vital economic purpose. He foresaw the building of a German Earth and Stone Works (DESt) factory where slave labor would utilize sand and gravel from nearby pits to make concrete. Pohl ordered Höss to double the capacity of the camp by adding a second story to the 14 one-story buildings. Himmler, too, envisioned a greater purpose for Auschwitz. In November 1940, Höss submitted a verbal progress report of work at Auschwitz to the Reichsführer-SS. Himmler, recalling his days with the Artaman League, determined that Auschwitz would provide great value as an agricultural research station. According to Höss, he complained to Himmler about the problems he was addressing at Auschwitz, particularly regarding hygiene, and requested help. He would receive none. Himmler scoffed, reminding Höss Germany was at war and telling him he was too pessimistic.[9]

Auschwitz was a Class I concentration camp according to Nazi standards, intended for "less serious prisoners definitely capable of improvement." However, the measures taken to secure the camp gave the impression the inmates were high risk. SS-Unterscharführer Pery Broad, who worked in the Political Department at Auschwitz, indicated that the Stammlager was secured by two barbed wire and electric fences, which reached four meters in height. At night, the fence was brightly lit by a close chain of lamps. Large flood lights were placed in the watch towers, which could cover the entire camp. Behind the inner fence was a strip of gravel three meters in width. Anyone who crossed into this area was shot.[10]

Each of the buildings in the Stammlager was assigned a number. Block 9 was the infirmary while Block 20 was used to quarantine prisoners with contagious diseases. The most feared and notorious building at the camp was Block 11, a two-story structure at the southern corner of the compound. It was a prison within a prison. Nearly all the windows were completely bricked up with the exception of a narrow strip to allow a sliver of daylight into the building. Even the cellar windows were heavily barred. In the basement were small, dark cells along narrow corridors. In addition to ordinary cells, which provided little air and light, Block 11 added a new dimension of punishment—four standing cells. Intended for one individual, these cells were often crammed with up to four prisoners at a time. Broad observed,

Auschwitz I security (author photograph).

IV. Creation of Auschwitz

"…[M]any prisoners were doomed to spend there, naturally without one ray of light, terrible hours, weeks even. It was out of the question to sit down there. The prisoners cowered down in the darkness. When the cold in the winter was severe, it was impossible to get warm by moving about." Even for minor offenses, prisoners could be committed to a standing cell for days without food or water.[11]

Wieslaw Kielar was one of the 728 men who arrived in Auschwitz with the first transport of Poles on June 14, 1940. He was committed to a standing cell as punishment for some offense. He later described what he endured:

> On my hands and my feet—otherwise I would not have been able to get in—I crawled into the black opening of the standing cell. The Blockführer helped me with my clumsy stumping into the tiny cell, which stank of excrement, by hitting my stretched buttocks with all his power. "Faster, faster, you dog!" he urged me impatiently.… In the pitch dark I felt the used breath of three fellow victims on my face. One of them had great difficulty breathing and whimpered weakly from time to time, "Water! Food! Water!" He hung against me with his whole weight seeking support and warmth. I felt his emaciated body shaking from cold and exhaustion, and he stank terribly. Compared to his stench the vapor of the worst phlegm or diarrhea seemed like the smell of sweetest perfume. The other two were in slightly better condition. They told me that they had already stood in this cell without food or water for two days. They complained that I had been sent to their cell. There was only one hope left: that this other one would die before the next day. Then there would be three again, and it would be possible to change one's position, move one's feet, and stretch one's arms.

Before the night ended, their wish was granted: the weakest man died.[12]

Block 11 was most infamous not as much for what happened inside as for what took place outside in the courtyard between Block 11 and Block 10 next door. High stone walls connected the fronts of both buildings, while a massive wooden gate barred the entrance to the courtyard. No one outside the courtyard could see what happened inside. SS-Untersturmführer Maximilian Grabner, who led the Political Department, Pery or other members of the Political Department would periodically go to Block 11 for the purpose of "dusting out" the cellars; in other words, selecting prisoners to be shot—usually on the weekends.[13]

Grabner was a member of the SD or Sicherheitsdienst, the security service of the SS, and was a criminal investigator of the Gestapo. No one in the Political Department of a concentration camp was a "boy scout." However, even Broad described Grabner as having "unscrupulous brutality" and "morbid ambition." He was not satisfied unless his officers produced enough criminal reports against prisoners and requests for executions. His subordinates dared not contradict him. Broad noted that Höss was Grabner's equal in sadistic cruelty and unscrupulousness, but even Höss avoided confrontation with Grabner whenever possible. Hermann Langbein, an Auschwitz survivor, wrote at length of his experiences in *People in Auschwitz*. He expressed the opinion that Grabner was the most vigorous exterminator of human beings, surpassed only by Höss himself. At the postwar trial of SS-Obergruppenführer Oswald Pohl, the head of the WVHA, Auschwitz survivor Jerry Bielski testified everyone was afraid of Grabner and Höss.[14]

On November 22, 1940, 40 Polish prisoners were shot in retaliation for violence in Kattowitz, Poland. Such killings, in small groups or large numbers, would become regular occurrences at the Death Wall or Black Wall in the courtyard between Block 11 and Block 10. The condemned were forced to undress in a room adjacent to the courtyard, then were taken to the courtyard. Other prisoners were often required to hold the inmate against the wall. SS-Hauptscharführer Gerhard Palitzsch, who came with Höss from Sachsenhausen, regularly served as executioner. Inmates loaded the corpses onto stretchers and placed them in a pile at the courtyard gate.

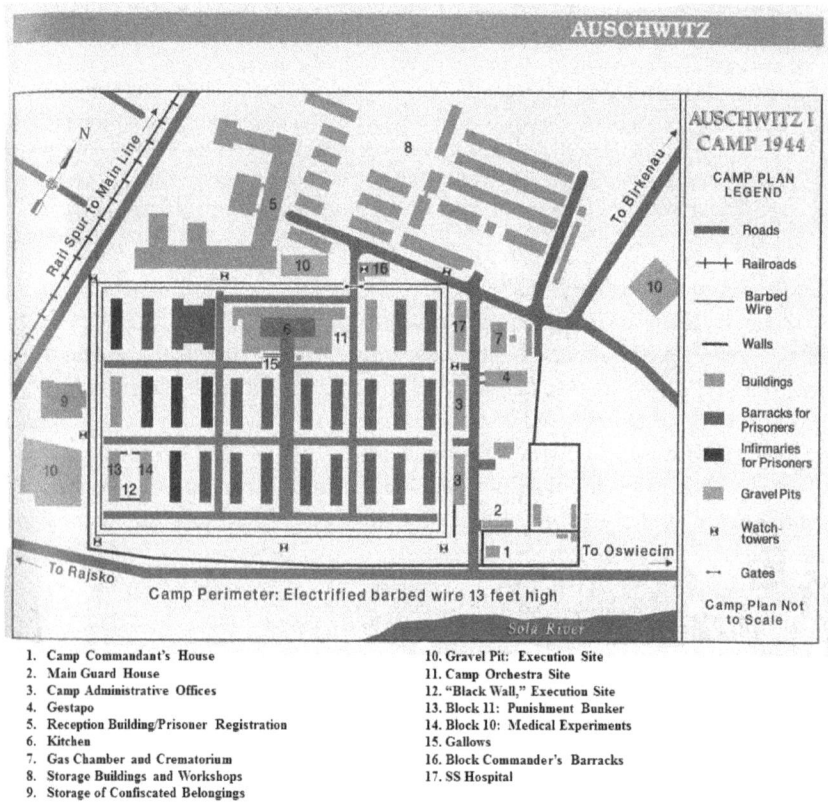

1. Camp Commandant's House
2. Main Guard House
3. Camp Administrative Offices
4. Gestapo
5. Reception Building/Prisoner Registration
6. Kitchen
7. Gas Chamber and Crematorium
8. Storage Buildings and Workshops
9. Storage of Confiscated Belongings
10. Gravel Pit: Execution Site
11. Camp Orchestra Site
12. "Black Wall," Execution Site
13. Block 11: Punishment Bunker
14. Block 10: Medical Experiments
15. Gallows
16. Block Commander's Barracks
17. SS Hospital

Map of Auschwitz I (courtesy U.S. Holocaust Memorial Museum, Washington, D.C.).

When the executions were completed, the bodies were taken by cart to the crematorium for burning.[15]

On November 11, 1941, the first executions by small caliber weapons were performed at the Death Wall by Palitzsch. Höss and a camp doctor were present. The condemned were led to the wall, naked, one by one, with their hands tied behind their backs. Before execution, the prisoner's number was written on his chest if he was to be shot in the back of the neck or on his leg if he was to be shot by a firing squad. In his *Reminiscences of an SS Man*, Broad described in detail the excruciating mental terror and death inflicted on thousands of Auschwitz inmates taken from the cellar of Block 11 to the Death Wall in the courtyard:

> A prison warder opened the first cell door with a key selected from a large key-ring. Then two iron bolts were pulled out. Escape from this prison was impossible, particularly as it was situated in the middle of the camp with its live wire fences. A choking stench issued from the crowded, narrow cell. One prisoner shouted, "Achtung!" and, their faces apathetic, the emaciated men clad in dirty, white and blue rags, stood up in a line. One could see that some of them were barely able to stand erect. They accepted with apathy the procedure which might decide upon their lives or deaths and which they had, with better luck perhaps, already gone through with. It was the apathy of men whose will to survive had been destroyed. [SS-Hauptsturmführer] Aumeier held against the door the list of men who would be tried that day. The first prisoner gave his name and stated how long he had been in prison. The camp leader briefly questioned the reporting officer as to the cause of his arrest. Should the prisoner have been arrested by Section II, which was usually the case with recaptured fugitives, then the matter was within Grabner's competence. Both camp dignitaries then took their decision—either penal report 1 or penal report 2. Prisoners of either group left the cell and formed ranks in two groups in the corridor. The rest remained "in prison pending the investigation." The "criminal activities" of prisoners from group 1 amounted to having somewhere stolen a few potatoes, having got one undergarment too much or having smoked a cigarette during work, not to mention other trifles of this sort. They were lucky if they escaped with flogging or a term in a penal company, which meant excessively hard work. But the unlucky ones, whose further fate was decided by the code word "penal report 2" would fare much worse. Aumeier drew with his blue pencil a thick cross at every name, putting small lines round the corners of the cross, and everybody could see it. It was no secret what "penal report 2" meant. The group of the less important cases, whose lives were saved once more, were led into the camp where they would get their punishment. Large common cells on the ground floor and on the first floor, in which more than a hundred people were sometimes crowded together, were then emptied, if their windows were on the yard. The prisoners and detained civilians, both sexes separately, were conducted into cells on the other side of the corridor. Those who had been sentenced to death were led into the lavatory on the ground-floor. Prisoners whose function in Block 11 it was to act as clerks and to clean the premises, covered up the windows and made their fellow-sufferers undress. The victims seemed to have already said good-bye to the world and it was perhaps a relief to them to know that in a few minutes they would

be freed from their torturers and from their sufferings. The helpers wrote with indelible pencils the prisoners' numbers upon the naked bodies of the victims to make the identification of the bodies in the mortuary or in the crematorium later on possible. Aumeier, Grabner and some of the SS men had meanwhile gone into the yard. But the majority of the SS men had already left. Nobody cared to be in Grabner's company; it was dangerous to be constantly reproached with slackness by a Gestapo man. And among Grabner's subordinates there was a majority of fanatics, who could hardly be accused of being soft.

    A black wall was situated at the stone wall of Block 11. This wall, constructed of black isolation plates, had become the journey's end for thousands of guiltless people. Among them were patriots who would not betray the country they loved for pecuniary benefit, men who had managed to escape from the hell of Auschwitz and who had had the bitter misfortune to be recaptured, men and women, conscious of their nationality, from all the countries then occupied by the Germans. The shooting of the condemned was done by the reporting officer or by a prison warder. Not to arouse the attention of passers-by who might then be walking along the road leading not far behind the stone wall, the weapon used was a small calibre gun with 10 or 15 cartridges. Aumeier, Grabner and the actual executioner, holding his gun ready to fire behind his back, took their positions, fully enjoying their feeling of omnipotence. In the background several frightened carriers were ready with their stretchers to fulfill their gruesome task. They were unable to hide the horror clearly visible in their faces. A prisoner was standing near the black wall with a spade in his hand. One prisoner, belonging to the cleaning squad and specially chosen for his strength, was approaching at a run, quickly propelling the first two victims forward. He kept a fast hold on their arms and then pressed their faces to the wall. "Preste" (straight) was the command should one of them turn his head to the side. Some of those walking skeletons had spent months in the stinking cells, where animals would hardly be kept, and they could barely manage to stand straight. And yet, many of them shouted at that last moment, "Long live Poland," or "Long live freedom." The executioner was then in a particular hurry to shoot them in the back of their heads, or he tried to silence them with brutal blows. Fully conscious of their power, the SS men nervously laughed in such cases, but they did not like to hear such cries which were an evidence that national pride and love of freedom could not be broken, not even by the utmost terror. Thus did the Poles die and the Jews too, as to whom the Nazi propaganda maintained that they were base slaves, whining for mercy, and that they had no right at all to live, only the Germans had that right! The SS men had almost always the same spectacle before them—men and women, young and old, all those people managed to gather their last resources in order to die honourably. There was no abject pleading for mercy, often instead a last look of abysmal contempt, which made those primitive thugs fly into a sadistic rage. Shot after shot was fired with hardly any noise. The victims fell down with a groan. The executioner made sure that the shots he had fired from a distance of a few centimeters were effective. He stepped upon the forehead of the man lying on the ground, pulled the eyelids back and thus ascertained that the victim was dead. If a rattle was still heard, one of the SS leaders gave the order—"That one must get one more!" A shot in the temple or in the eye finally put an end to a wretched life. The carriers ran to and fro in the quickest tempo. They loaded the corpses on the stretchers and carried them to a heap at the other end of the yard. More and more blood-stained bodies lay there. Blood kept running in a thin streamlet from the wound at the back of the head and down the back for several minutes after shooting. Silently and outwardly unmoved, the prisoner with the spade stepped nearer, whenever the two bodies were taken away and covered up the puddles of foaming blood with sand. The executioner mechanically reloaded his gun again and again, and one execution incessantly followed another. Should a pause in his work be necessary, he would put down the gun, whistle a tune or talk with the men around him about quite indifferent things. By that cynical attitude he wanted to show that it did not affect him at all to be "finishing off that rabble"; he wanted to boast how "tough" he was. He was quite proud of the fact that his conscience did not trouble him when he was murdering the guiltless victims. If one of them did not hold his head still, he would press the muzzle of his gun into his neck and put his face directly to the wall. This happened above all when he heard the patriotic outcries. SS men were aware that prisoners behind the wall, listening to the last demonstrations of the fanatic faith of the martyred men, were morally uplifted and strengthened in their own patriotic feelings by them. The last seconds of the men standing in front of the black wall were often drawn out in a cruel way. They felt the cold, bloody muzzle of the gun against their necks, they heard the pulling of the trigger ... the gun was blocked! The bored executioner then put the gun away, slowly tried to fix it, telling his companions it was high time to get a new gun. Nobody cared that the victim suffered unbearably during the protracted execution. The iron grip on his arms never relaxed. The gun was finally set right and it functioned properly that time, but further blocks would occur again. The whole indescribably gruesome show was over after an hour or so. Grabner had "dusted out" the bunker and could enjoy a substantial breakfast. The yard of Block 11 was again deserted. The sand in front of the black wall, which stood there with such indifference, was freshly raked. A swarm of flies was buzzing above some big, black-red spots at the other end of the yard. A wide, dark track led through the camp, beginning at the massive wooden gate with the judas, the gate which barred entrance to the yard. The track led towards the exit from the camp in the direction of the crematorium.[16]

Although Höss and the Nazis sought to hide their atrocities by destroying documentary evidence, some paperwork survived. Records reflect the following murders committed at Block 11 in one three-month period—March 19 through June 25, 1942:

> March 19—144 women are brought to Block 11 where Camp Commander Aumeier and Roll Call Leader Palitzsch are present. The women are stripped naked and shot.
> April 3—eleven Polish prisoners are shot at the execution wall of Block 11.
> May 12—in the courtyard of Block 11, four Polish prisoners are shot at the execution wall.
> May 27—168 prisoners are shot at the execution wall in the courtyard of Block 11.
> June 4—twelve Polish prisoners shot at the execution wall of Block 11.
> June 6—eleven Polish prisoners shot at the execution wall of Block 11.
> June 12—sixty Polish prisoners shot at the execution wall of Block 11.

> June 14—more than 200 Polish prisoners shot at the execution wall of Block 11.
> June 17—120 Polish prisoners shot at the execution wall of Block 11.
> June 19—fifty Polish prisoners shot at the execution wall of Block 11.
> June 25—forty prisoners shot at the execution wall of Block 11.[17]

Polish prisoners accused of being part of the resistance were included among those shot in the courtyard of Block 11. Once or twice a month, the Police Summary Court of the State Police Office of Kattowitz held its sessions at Auschwitz. The "court" was led by SS-Obersturmbannführer Rudolf Mildner. Pery Broad described him as "one of the most blood-thirsty butchers that existed in the Third Reich." The Reich Main Security Office (RSHA) issued an order to the Gestapo to carry out sentences within concentration camps. Prisoners were brought to Auschwitz from local jails for sentence and execution. Most of the accused had already been interrogated and incriminated themselves, though, on occasion, inquiries were conducted at Auschwitz. Often, the prisoners were forced to carry "mysterious wooden structures" used to torture them into admitting their guilt. If the screams became too loud, a gas mask would be placed on the victim's head. Eventually, in most cases, the "confession" was signed.[18]

Mildner, who led the Police Summary Court between 1941 and 1943, came to Auschwitz to pronounce sentence, almost always death, and to gleefully witness the executions. According to Höss, about 60 to 70 persons were shot each month. Höss estimated about 1,500 men were sentenced to death by Mildner's court. Broad recalled a 16-year-old boy who stole food from a shop because of unbearable hunger. Mildner sentenced him to death. The sentence itself was not enough to satisfy the sadistic Mildner, who asked the boy, "Are you afraid to die?" The youth stood silent, trembling slightly. In an effort to raise the boy's fear to terror, Mildner declared, trying to give his voice the full, fateful significance, "You will be shot today." Broad said Mildner could not hide the satisfaction he felt in having power over life and death.[19]

Brief mention must be made of the organizational structure at Auschwitz. Concentration camps were initially under the auspices of the Reich Main Security Office (RSHA). In March 1942, Reichsführer-SS Himmler incorporated the Inspectorate for Concentration Camps, headed by Theodor Eicke until the start of the war then by SS-Gruppenführer Richard Glücks, into the SS Economic-Administrative Main Office (WVHA). By doing so, Himmler placed Glücks under the supervision of his own economic expert in the WVHA, Oswald Pohl. Auschwitz consisted of seven departments—the commandant's office, the Political Department, camp administration, prisoner labor, administration-economic, camp SS medical service and SS unit welfare and training. Camp administration and the Political Department

IV. Creation of Auschwitz

played the leading role in the terror and extermination system. The officials in the Political Department were employees of the Gestapo or the Kripo (criminal police). The head of the Political Department reported to the camp commandant and to the Reich Main Security Office (RSHA) and carried out orders from both the commandant and the RSHA. The heads of the Political Department were Grabner until 1943 and his successor, SS-Unterstumführer Hans Schurz. The camp director and the head of the Political Department jointly made decisions on placing prisoners in the camp jail and shooting prisoners at the Death Wall.[20]

Undoubtedly inconvenient, the crematorium was located at the opposite end of camp from Block 11. In June 1940, a double muffle incinerator was installed in the crematorium by Topf & Sons at the Stammlager. It consisted of two openings, so that multiple corpses could be burned at a time. Up to 70 corpses could be consumed in a 24-hour period. Although sufficient when Auschwitz opened, within a few months a greater burning capacity was needed. Höss requested a second incinerator due to the number of bodies being burned. A third incinerator would be sought in the fall of 1941 because of the ever-increasing death rate, particularly due to political prisoners and Soviet prisoners of war who were being shot by the Gestapo.[21]

Reichsführer-SS Himmler had bigger plans for Auschwitz beyond service as an internment camp. He envisioned transforming the area into a model of German settlement in the East. In January 1941, I. G. Farben selected a site near Auschwitz for the construction of four Buna factories to manufacture 30,000 tons of synthetic rubber a year. The confluence of three rivers and

Block 11 courtyard and Death Wall at Auschwitz I (Photo Archives, Auschwitz-Birkenau State Museum, www.auschwitz.org).

necessary raw materials made the region favorable for such a project. While a ready slave labor force could be provided by the camp, I. G. Farben was more interested in deriving its workforce from incoming ethnic Germans. Soon, plans for the German town of Auschwitz were being developed with a proposed population of 40,000 Reich citizens. Already, Reichsmarschall Hermann Göring and Himmler were ordering "evacuation" of Jews from Auschwitz and the surrounding area to free up living space for workers to be employed in the construction of the Buna factory.[22]

Himmler made his first visit to Auschwitz in March 1941. He was delighted with the progress Höss had made and directed that the Stammlager be expanded to accommodate 30,000 prisoners. He also stated that he wanted to build another camp nearby at the Polish village of Brzezinka, known as Birkenau to the Germans—a much larger camp, one that would house 100,000 inmates for expected prisoners of war. Concerns and objections by local authorities to the feasibility of a camp that size, based upon sewage issues, among others, were dismissed outright by Himmler, who said, "Gentlemen, this project will be completed; my reasons for this are more important than your objections!" Himmler also directed that 10,000 prisoners be made available to I. G. Farben for construction of their industrial plant.[23]

Höss recalled, "The intention of the Reichsführer was that Auschwitz

Crematorium at Auschwitz I (author photograph).

IV. Creation of Auschwitz

Himmler and Höss (courtesy Ghetto Fighters' House Museum, Israel/Photo Archive).

should become one immense prisoner-cum-munitions-center. What he said during his visit in March of 1941 made this perfectly plain. The camp for 100,000 prisoners of war, the enlargement of the old camp to hold 10,000 prisoners, the ear-marking of 10,000 prisoners for the synthetic rubber factory, all this emphasized his point." Höss had his orders and intended to follow them. "Then I was ordered to dry out the swamps and erect model farms and build up agriculture as much as possible. I was ordered to construct a prisoner-of-war camp to accommodate 100,000 in a neighborhood three kilometers from the original camp, called Birkenau. The population in that

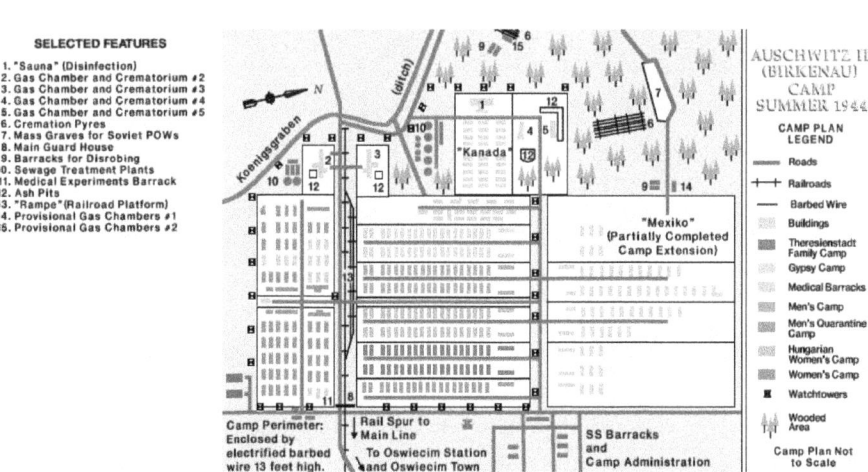

Map of Auschwitz II–Birkenau (courtesy U.S. Holocaust Memorial Museum, Washington, D.C.).

territory, consisting of about seven villages, was evacuated and sent to the town of Auschwitz. Those that could be employed in factories or the railroad stayed in Auschwitz, but the others, who were only farmers, went to work for the General Government elsewhere." Himmler was clearly impressed with the work Höss was doing. In April 1941, Höss was awarded the War Service Cross Second Class with Swords, a decoration usually reserved for frontline combatants.[24]

Despite Himmler's pronouncement for expansion of Auschwitz, work did not begin on Birkenau until October 1941. Höss was given 10,000 Russian POWs to build the new camp. They were the first Auschwitz inmates to have prison numbers tattooed on their bodies. Although Himmler had directed that the strongest prisoners be sent to Höss, the poor treatment of Russian

Barracks at Auschwitz II–Birkenau after liberation (Photo Archives, Auschwitz-Birkenau State Museum, www.auschwitz.org).

IV. Creation of Auschwitz   63

POWs by the Nazis had taken its toll. According to Höss many of the Russian prisoners, supposedly the best available, could hardly stand when they arrived in October 1941. By October 8, demolition of farms and construction on Birkenau had begun. The work and the weakened condition of the Russians killed many of them. By February 1942, most of the Russian POWs had died of typhus, undernourishment and other ailments. Höss observed that "cases of cannibalism were not rare in Birkenau." Auschwitz records indicate that some Russian POWs were killed by phenol injections to the heart and some were beaten to death by the SS. Of the 10,000 Russian POWs who provided the main labor force for Birkenau, only a few hundred were still alive by the summer of 1942.[25]

Design of the huge Birkenau camp was placed into the hands of German architect and engineer, SS-Sturmbannführer Karl Bischoff. He was assisted by Fritz Ertl, who proposed a two-part camp for a projected 97,000 inmates. The original plan was modified by Bischoff, who changed the camp's capacity from 97,000 to 125,000 inmates. The increase was accomplished, not by more construction, but by forcing more inmates into the same space. The original plan provided that each barracks would house 550 prisoners. Bischoff struck through "550" and replaced it with "744." Living space for three was now living space for four. Plans called for construction of 174 barracks, each with

Barracks at Auschwitz II–Birkenau, present day (author photograph).

62 bays. Each bay had three levels. Birkenau was built for the large influx of Russian prisoners of war that the Nazis anticipated would arrive after initiation of Operation Barbarossa, the German invasion of the Soviet Union. Like the Jews, Soviet prisoners were viewed as *untermensch*—subhuman—by the Germans. At Auschwitz, the "private" space provided to a Soviet prisoner was the size of a coffin. Once the German advance eastward stalled and the massive Soviet POW population failed to materialize, Birkenau became a slave labor camp for Jews, non–Jewish Poles and others.[26]

Bischoff and Ertl provided one wash barrack for each 7,800 inmates and one latrine for each 7,000 inmates. The latrine meant to serve 7,000 inmates consisted of a shed with one concrete open sewer serviced by little water, no seats and, of course, no walls for privacy. Gisella Perl, an inmate of section BIa after it became the women's camp of Birkenau, described the grotesque and humiliating situation imposed on the prisoners: "There was one latrine for thirty to thirty-two thousand women and we were permitted to use it only at certain hours of the day. We stood in line to get into this tiny building, knee-deep in human excrement. As we all suffered from dysentery, we could rarely wait until our turn came, and soiled our ragged clothes, which never came off our bodies, thus adding to the horror of our existence by the terrible smell which surrounded us like a cloud." The construction itself was wholly

Latrine at Auschwitz II–Birkenau after liberation (Photo Archives, Auschwitz-Birkenau State Museum, www.auschwitz.org).

inadequate. Perl continued, "The latrine consisted of a deep ditch with planks thrown across it at certain intervals. We squatted on these planks like birds perched on a telegraph wire, so close together that we could not help soiling one another." Undoubtedly, the unsanitary conditions contributed to the spread of various diseases which ran rampant through the camp and which led to the death of untold numbers of prisoners. The time and effort which Bischoff failed to expend on the latrines was, instead, directed towards the crematoria.[27]

V

The Code of Barbarism

When Rudolf Höss testified at Nuremberg on April 15, 1946, the trial of the high-ranking Nazi war criminals had been ongoing for five months. A great deal of evidence had been introduced, mainly in the form of documents generated by the Nazi government and captured by the Allies after the war. The monotony of document production and speeches by lawyers was interrupted by a film of Nazi concentration camps as they appeared when liberated by the Allies. The motion picture shown to the Tribunal, the defendants and the spectators was filmed at various camps including Buchenwald, Dachau, Mauthausen, Nordhausen, Ohrdruf and Bergen-Belsen. It made little difference which concentration camp was depicted. No one could forget the shocking and revolting images described by one who saw the film:

> The impression we get is an endless river of white bodies flowing across the screen, bodies with ribs sticking out through the chests, with pipe-stem legs and battered skulls and eyeless faces and grotesque thin arms reaching for the sky.... On the screen there is no end to the bodies, tumbling bodies and bodies in mounds and single bodies with holes between the eyes and bodies being shoved over cliffs into common graves and bodies pushed like dirt by giant bulldozers, and bodies that are not bodies at all but charred bits of bone and flesh lying upon a crematory grate made of bits of steel rail laid upon blackened wood ties.[1]

When the film ended, the courtroom was totally silent. Spectators sat in stunned disbelief. Even the defendants, who knew about the existence of the camps, were shocked by the images.

Madame Marie Claude Vaillant-Couturier provided the Tribunal with an eyewitness account as a survivor of life inside Auschwitz. She stated:

> It is difficult to convey an exact idea of the concentration camps to anybody, unless one has been in the camp oneself, since one can only quote examples of horror.... If asked what was the worst of all, it is impossible to answer, since everything was atrocious. It is atrocious to die of hunger, to die of thirst, to be ill, to see all one's companions dying around one and being unable to help them. It is atrocious to think of one's children, of one's country which one will never see again, and there were times when we asked whether our life was not a living nightmare, so unreal did this life appear in

all its horror. For months, for years we had one wish only: The wish that some of us would escape alive, in order to tell the world what the Nazi convict prisons were like everywhere, at Auschwitz as at Ravensbruck. And the comrades from the other camps told the same tale; there was the systematic and implacable urge to use human beings as slaves and to kill them when they could work no more.[2]

The cruelty and barbarism that became the trademark of Auschwitz were not confined to the gas chambers and emanated from, or at the very least were fully acquiesced, by Rudolf Höss. Höss' memoirs do not read like *Mein Kampf* or the writings of Joseph Goebbels. His tone is not vitriolic, and he uses none of the malevolent language condemning the Jews which spewed from the mouths of Hitler, Goebbels and others. Primo Levi, who wrote the introduction to Höss' autobiography, *Commandant of Auschwitz*, said Höss was not a sadist; he did not enjoy inflicting pain. The prison psychologist and psychiatrist at Nuremberg noted that Höss talked about mass murder as a matter of fact and apathetically. He showed no emotion. Perhaps that is what made him so dangerous. He supervised several thousand SS officers and enlisted personnel and was responsible for tens of thousands of prisoners in a camp where "everything was atrocious" and life was a "living nightmare."[3]

Höss' mindset—his matter-of-fact manner of discussing life and death at Auschwitz—shocked his interrogators and the Tribunal. As regards the living conditions of inmates, he stated that, in general, when the war started, concentration camp prisoners "were on the same basis as those of other prisoners under legal administration." He testified that the mass influx of prisoners after the war changed things. While the need for additional living space could be accommodated during the first years of the war, lack of building material precluded additional construction as the war progressed. Also, according to Höss, "rations for the internees were again and again severely curtailed by the provincial economic administration offices." As a result, "…internees in the camps no longer had the *staying* power to resist the now gradually growing epidemics" (emphasis added). By this, Höss meant they were dying faster. He knew it was the will of Himmler, as early as 1941, that the concentration camps were to become armaments plants to further the German war effort. At that point, Höss said, "I had to become harder, colder and even more merciless in my attitude towards the needs of the prisoners."[4]

Höss knew that conditions in the camp were deplorable. Auschwitz was overcrowded with insufficient food, lack of sanitation and wholly inadequate medical care. Höss claimed he sought assistance from Berlin and received none. Himmler told him it was his responsibility as commandant to solve the problems he encountered, yet Höss did nothing to relieve these conditions himself. Also, food deprivation and hard labor served a penological purpose: Höss' need and desire to maintain control over his large population. The prisoners in their severely weakened state were less likely to attempt to revolt or to resist Nazi authority. If they died due to the conditions, no matter; they were replaced with more prisoners. Höss was answerable to no one for the loss of life.

While Höss attested at Nuremberg to much that was true, he also lied outright and by omission. Höss was asked about the ill-treatment and torture of inmates and testified:

> These so-called ill-treatments and this torturing in concentration camps, stories of which were spread everywhere among the people, and later by the prisoners that were liberated by the occupying armies, were not, as assumed, inflicted methodically, but were excesses committed by individual leaders, subleaders, and men who laid violent hands on internees.[5]

In his memoirs, Höss was more honest and admitted he was aware prisoners were "ill-treated" by the SS. In fact, mistreatment of prisoners by the SS at Auschwitz was persistent, brutal and often lethal. When asked to give her observations of the SS, a well-educated German Jewish woman, forced to constantly look down in submission to her captors, said, "To me they were all the same. If you ask me what they looked like, I can only say that all of them wore boots." In *People in Auschwitz*, survivor Hermann Langbein noted that "[f]or the nameless inmate who was tortured daily and did not dare raise his eyes, cudgels and boots were a substitute for his tormentors' faces."[6]

Professor Robert Waitz, an inmate physician in Monowitz, the Auschwitz labor camp, stated, "All SS officers regard themselves as outstanding, almost as supermen. All SS noncommissioned officers are crude fellows, sadists, and thieves who try to 'organize' as much as possible for themselves. They are all really convinced that inmates are not human beings but personifications of the evil of this world. To them an inmate is a species of animal that must be punished and ought to be made to suffer by every means and as much as possible before it is finally exterminated. Generally speaking, feelings of compassion or human mercy are completely unknown to them."[7]

Waitz accurately describes the model SS-man as envisioned by SS-Oberführer Theodor Eicke, the father of Nazi concentration camps, enhanced with Höss' hand of cruelty. Eicke taught Höss that prisoners are "sworn enemies of the state, who were to be treated with great severity and destroyed if they showed resistance." Eicke warned against any show of pity. According to Höss, Eicke instilled "a hatred and antipathy for the prisoners which an outsider will find hard to imagine." Höss attributed all the torture and ill-treatment inflicted upon the prisoners in the camps to this "hate indoctrination." Yet Höss himself was far more brutal than Eicke in the penalties he imposed, and he expected similar severity from his SS inferiors.[8]

In his memoirs, Höss claims he never mistreated prisoners and "was never cruel" and "never maltreated anyone, even in a fit of temper," and he

V. The Code of Barbarism 69

instructed his subordinates that Eicke's views about inmates should be abandoned. Not only did Höss himself continuously follow Eicke's mandate to treat prisoners as the enemy, he punished prisoners with greater barbarity than Eicke would have ever permitted. Höss refused to show pity when sympathy would pour from the heart of any normal human being. It was Höss who remained, throughout his tenure at Auschwitz, "ill-disposed towards the prisoners." Kazimierz Smolen stated that "Höss would watch the beatings and hangings as if he were watching a movie, but with no reaction showing in his face." Höss says he never hated the Jews. Whether or not he felt Hitler's loathing of Jews, his actions and inactions caused their perpetual suffering just the same. Höss taught the SS, by his example, how cruelly the inmates should be treated. In turn, the SS instructed prisoner functionaries—kapos and block elders—to be equally mean and merciless to inmates.[9]

An incident that took place at the Sachsenhausen concentration camp shortly after the war began is indicative of the type of brutality Höss would sanction as commandant of Auschwitz. Because the event is clearly inconsistent with his assertion that he was never cruel and never mistreated a prisoner, Höss omits it from his autobiography. At Sachsenhausen on January 18, 1940, when Höss was commandant of the protective custody camp, he ordered that the inmates who were not working due to the frost remain standing outside after roll call. He told SS-Hauptscharführer Gerhard Palitzsch, who was one of his subordinates that day, that he wanted the inmates to freeze for a while. Despite the deteriorated condition of many of the inmates, he dismissed concern about their exposure to the elements, indicating that the "sluggards" could well suffer one day in the cold when the others would be cold outside [the camp]. The temperature was -26 degrees Celsius (-15 degrees Fahrenheit). After the working kommandos (work groups) were gone, 800 people remained on the roll call ground, most of them without coats or gloves. Hour after hour, they stood in place, subjected to an icy wind. After a short while, several were dragged to the infirmary barracks by the block elder.[10]

Upset that his intent to inflict some misery on the nonworking prisoners was being thwarted, Höss stopped the elders from taking the inmates to the infirmary. More and more prisoners collapsed—some dying, some dead. A number of inmates crawled towards the infirmary barracks. Höss ordered the doors to be closed. After a while he appeared himself at the closed door, where a heap of desperate and crawling human beings was accumulating. As Höss left the infirmary, he stepped over the people who were lying on the ground. They seized the legs of his pants and the hem of his coat, begging him for help. Höss ignored them and walked away. One of the men cried: "Murderer! Murderer!" When a camp elder implored him to let the people go inside, Höss replied, "Those are not people, they are inmates." On that day 78 people died, and during the night of January 19 another 67 died. Many others lived only a few days or weeks longer.[11]

Höss had no legitimate reason for making the prisoners stand in the cold for as long as he did. Consistent with his training, Höss treated them as inmates, not as people—he said so himself. Höss raised his hand to no one, shot no one and beat no one. He knowingly and willfully subjected prisoners who were already physically compromised to bitter, freezing, bone-chilling cold for no valid punitive reason. His actions that day resulted in the deaths of more than 150 prisoners.

Höss demonstrated to the SS and the prisoner functionaries the acceptability of treating inmates in inhuman ways. If the commandant was willing to be cruel, they could and should be cruel. Palitzsch served with Höss at Sachsenhausen during the deadly roll call on January 18, 1940, and came with Höss to Auschwitz. Palitzsch became an especially notorious and bloodthirsty executioner in the courtyard of Block 11. Höss had set the example for him to follow. Punishments employed by SS men such as Palitzsch were imposed not only with the acquiescence of Höss, but also at his direction.

SS-Unterscharführer Pery Broad, who worked with SS-Untersturmführer Maximilian Grabner, the head of the Auschwitz Political Department, in executing prisoners in Block 11, noted that Höss was Grabner's equal in sadistic cruelty and unscrupulousness. Until early 1942, the largest single group of prisoners in Auschwitz were Poles. With regularity, they were shot in large groups for unspecified reasons. As for Höss, who proclaimed he never mistreated anyone, Auschwitz records show that on several occasions, he implemented extraordinarily cruel punishment on prisoners who had committed no offense of any kind.[12]

Höss mentioned that escape from Auschwitz was not difficult, but such attempts risked reprisal, including the arrest of family members and the liquidation of other inmates. On one occasion, Höss ordered that the parents of a man who had escaped be arrested. They were forced to wear placards announcing they would remain in Auschwitz until their son returned. On March 10, 1943, Bronislaw Staszkiewicz escaped from Auschwitz. Höss ordered that his mother, Barbara Staszkiewicz, be brought to Auschwitz from another camp. She was placed on a podium with a sign indicating she had been brought there in place of her son. Höss hoped to deter others from escaping. Bronislaw Staszkiewicz was never captured. His mother died at Auschwitz in November 1943.[13]

Lethal action was also taken by Höss against innocent inmates simply to deter escape. Pery Broad wrote that if an inmate escaped, other prisoners from his work squad would be punished by extended roll call through the night or by placement by Höss in a cell until they starved to death. On April 23, 1941, Höss, with the cooperation of camp commander SS-Obersturmführer Karl

V. The Code of Barbarism

Fritzsch, chose 10 prisoners and condemned them to starve to death in retaliation for the escape of a prisoner. They were locked in a cell in the basement of Block 11 and given nothing to eat or drink. All of them died by May 26, 1941. One of the victims was an older man who voluntarily took the place of a 16-year-old boy so paralyzed with fear he could not step out of the line when called. On June 17, 1941, Höss again chose 10 prisoners and condemned them to starve to death in retaliation for the escape of a prisoner. They died between June 19 and June 27 *even though the prisoner who escaped had been caught June 20*. On June 24, 1941, Höss once more chose 10 prisoners and condemned them to starve to death in retaliation for the escape of a prisoner. They died by June 30. Later, in July 1941, Fritzsch, having learned this punishment method from Höss, sentenced 15 prisoners to death by starvation in retaliation for the escape of a prisoner.[14]

Not even Eicke, who Höss accused of instilling the SS with a "hate indoctrination," approved of such an inhumane method of retaliation or punishment. If an escaped prisoner was recaptured when Eicke was in charge, Eicke would require that he be led past other prisoners with a sign, "I am back," while beating a large drum around his neck. Then, the prisoner would be given 25 lashes as punish for escaping. If an escapee was captured alive during Höss' tenure at Auschwitz, he was publicly hanged in the camp. If he was shot in the pursuit, his corpse was displayed next to the camp entrance for all to see with a sign, "I am back." Nevertheless, the escapes and attempted escapes continued. Apparently, SS-Gruppenführer and Generalleutnant of the Waffen-SS, Richard Glücks, the Concentration Camps Inspector and Höss' superior in the WVHA, wanted to replace Höss because of the unprecedented high number of escapes at Auschwitz. Himmler, who was also frustrated with the number of escapes from Auschwitz, authorized Höss to use any means necessary to anticipate and prevent escapes. Höss, who found flogging so objectionable at Dachau, spoke of no hesitation in his memoirs in implementing the death penalty for every person who attempted to escape.[15]

It made no difference to Höss that the killing of innocent prisoners to deter escape was wholly ineffective. In Auschwitz, one's own survival was paramount. Inmates knew they were likely to die, so escape by anyone with the means and a plan made perfect sense. On June 20, 1942, four Polish prisoners working in the garage of the troop's supply depot took their chance. Three of them wore SS uniforms and the fourth posed as a prisoner in chains. They stole a car and succeeded in making their escape. They later sent Höss a letter sarcastically apologizing for stealing the car.[16]

The cruelty which Höss permitted was also meted out by prisoner functionaries—inmates with supervisory authority over other inmates. On a Sunday in May 1942, Filip Müller, a prisoner confined to Block 11, rested in the yard with several hundred other inmates when Vacek began barking orders. Vacek was a professional criminal and came from Sachsenhausen with Höss and Palitzsch. He had been appointed by the SS as a Funktionschäftling, a prisoner entrusted with special duties. Vacek had been trained at Sachsenhausen in brutal methods to be used against inmates and brought to Auschwitz. He was part of a particularly privileged group that exercised the absolute power of life and death over their fellow prisoners. Müller related that, on that day, Vacek had no purpose except to kill:

> From [his] vantage point he was able to survey every corner of the yard below and bellow out his commands: "Shun! Caps on! Caps off! Get a move on!"
> With eagle eyes he watched to see that his orders were carried out meticulously. At the command "Caps off!" we whipped our flat caps from our shaven heads and slapped them against our right thighs with the flat of our hands. Unless this produced the whip-cracking sound envisaged by Vacek, the exercise would be repeated until he was satisfied. On this occasion it had already been repeated more than a hundred times. At first glance this tedious drill, not unlike the drilling of army recruits, might appear to be perfectly harmless and nothing out of the ordinary. In fact, it merely served to provide Vacek with the desired pretext for putting prisoners to death.
> On this particular Sunday his first victim was a father of four whose right hand was paralyzed. Before he became an inmate of Auschwitz he had scraped a living by reciting the Kaddish, the prayer for the dead, in the synagogue of his native town. It was, of course, quite ludicrous to expect a man with his handicap to execute the "Caps off! Caps on!" drill correctly. Vacek flung himself on the disabled man and dragged him across the yard. There he stood him with his face to the wall. His next victim was a deaf tailor who had been a fraction of a second late in snapping to attention. The drill continued.... Anything trivial that displeased or irritated him, such as a man's long nose, a pair of spectacles with thick lenses, an ill-fitting cap, was sufficient reason for him to pounce on one unfortunate prisoner after another and line him up against the wall.
>
> ...
>
> By now thirty unfortunates had been stood against the wall. Vacek and his underlings ordered them to line up in ranks of five. And now, behind our backs, began what in Auschwitz went under the name of *sport*. "At the double! Lie Down! Get up! Lie down! Crawl! Get up! Jump! At the double! About turn!" Like hunted animals the wretched prisoners were harried and chased across the yard. They flung themselves on the ground; crawled on their bellies; leapt up; jumped with arms held out in front; ran about panting and pushing each other in a vain attempt to avoid the blows which were hailing down on them non-stop. They were flushed with exertion, sweat mixed with blood streaming down their faces and necks. Anyone who failed to get up was lost. A blow from a truncheon, followed by several more if necessary, finished him off. Many had already given up: more than half the prisoners were lying motionless on the ground although only twenty minutes had gone by. "At the double! Lie down! Get up! Jump! Lie down! Get up! Crawl!" Remorselessly command followed command. On the point of complete exhaustion, the remaining prisoners still tried to carry out the orders shouted at them. But before long they too lay still in their zebra-striped uniforms; and were then bludgeoned to death with truncheons. Vacek's bloodthirsty gaze surveyed his harvest of death. Then he wiped the sweat from his forehead, his face distorted by a terrible sneer, his eyes still flashing menacingly. He

was visibly pleased with his achievement. No doubt he would have enjoyed finishing off the rest of us in the same way.

Meanwhile the dead bodies had been collected and laid on their backs side by side. Their hands were crossed on their chests and their unseeing eyes seemed to stare questioningly up into the sky. Vacek and his block orderlies turned away, their job well done.[17]

Bruno Schlage, the SS-Rottenführer on duty, watched to assure Vacek did his work properly. Suddenly, a prisoner spoke up, a lawyer and an authority on Jewish writing, protesting that prisoners were beating prisoners. He was sure the authorities in charge were unaware of what was happening. He stepped forward directly in front of Schlage and insisted that he file a report and have the matter investigated. That was a mistake. Schlage became livid and told Vacek to give the man what he deserved. Vacek picked up his truncheon and beat the man to death.[18]

Auschwitz was an enormous camp, larger than any other. There were not enough SS to guard all the prisoners, so Höss needed the kapos and block elders to help maintain control and discipline. He could not stop the escape attempts; he could only try to limit them. Various resistance movements existed in Auschwitz, and Höss was undoubtedly aware of these efforts. Physical weakness through food deprivation and hard labor contributed to keeping the prisoners subjugated, but the strong, firm hand of the SS and the prisoner functionaries was considered absolutely necessary. The fact that no general uprising ever occurred in a camp where at one time the population equaled 140,000 is testament to the success of Höss' severe discipline.[19]

On the day the war started, Eicke told Höss and other members of the SS in the concentration camps that it was necessary to display an inflexible harshness towards prisoners. Rather than abandon Eicke's ways, as Höss claimed, his methods at Sachsenhausen and Auschwitz perpetuated this philosophy in even more inhuman and barbaric ways. From its creation until the end of 1941, Poles predominated at Auschwitz and suffered the most. As of early 1942, when Jews became the largest population, the emphasis was on the Final Solution. From that point on, according to Höss, "[t]hey [the Jews] knew, without exception, that they were condemned to death, that they would live only so long as they could work." The hardships of captivity made survival unlikely. As commandant of Auschwitz, Höss furthered the dual Nazi goals of work and murder.[20]

VI

Entrance Into Hell

Unlike Treblinka, Sobibor, Belzec and Chelmno, camps also situated in Poland, Auschwitz was not intended strictly for extermination. Until 1942, prisoners taken to Auschwitz could expect incarceration. Thereafter, when the Final Solution became the policy of the Third Reich, it was a different story. Even then, while most deportees arriving on transports were taken directly from the train to the gas chambers, some prisoners escaped immediate death and were utilized as laborers to advance the German war effort. However, eluding the gas chambers was far from a guarantee of survival. Höss knew this. It was part of the Nazi plan that unlivable conditions in Auschwitz together with unforgiving daily work would result in a significant death toll. More inmates were always available to fill the workforce. Through the use of the gas chambers and intolerably harsh daily living and work conditions for incarcerated prisoners, the Nazis would accomplish their goal of exterminating European Jews. Auschwitz was the only facility which could satisfy the dual Nazi goals of work and murder.[1]

Most prisoners arrived at Auschwitz by rail. The first unloading ramp was located adjacent to the main camp, the Stammlager, and was used throughout the time the camp was in operation, mainly serving Auschwitz I. The second ramp, known as the "Alte Judenrampe," became operational in 1942. It was located on the grounds of the Oświęcim freight station, between the Auschwitz I and Birkenau camps. The majority of the mass transports of Jews that arrived between 1942 and May 1944, as well as the mass transports of Gypsies who were imprisoned in the Birkenau camp beginning in February 1943, unloaded at this ramp. The third ramp was built inside the Birkenau camp, and went into operation in May 1944 in connection with the anticipated arrival of transports of Hungarian Jews. The railroad spur along this ramp ran as far as the gas chambers and crematoria II and III.[2]

The tragic story of how families and human lives were destroyed at Auschwitz is all too similar. Uprooted from their homes—fathers, mothers, children, grandparents—followed by forced residence for months or years in

VI. Entrance Into Hell

squalid ghettos, they were herded onto trains for "resettlement." Henri Landwirth, an Auschwitz survivor, recalled:

> Imagine that one day you are asleep in your bed. Your father is asleep in his bed. Your mother is asleep in her bed. Your sister is asleep in her bed. Everything is okay. You can sit up in bed and feel safe. Your family is there around you. Together, you protect each other. If you want, you can walk around the house and look at everybody sleeping. Then one morning you wake up and everything has changed. There are no more beds, no more house. There is no more father asleep nearby watching over you. Where there was once peace and quiet and safety, there is now danger, noise and constant threats. Imagine how you would see this if you were a child. Imagine how frightened you would be.[3]

Being forcibly taken from the safety of their homes without any semblance of legal authority was itself monstrous; now the families would be deported to unknown destinations. Until the latter part of the war, most victims would not have been aware of a camp called Auschwitz or what awaited them there. People were crowded into cattle cars—sometimes 70, sometimes 80, sometimes 100 persons in each one. There was no room to sit down, so they took turns. Rarely was food provided; you ate what you brought with you. Each car was given one bucket as a toilet. The stench from urine and excrement was nauseating. Sometimes another bucket with water was included. The air was stale, and there was little light. The trip lasted for several days.[4]

Arrival at Auschwitz brought relief from the cramped and unsanitary boxcar, but thrust the families into a macabre world no one could have imagined. The door would be thrown open and the order "Raus! Raus! Schnell! Schnell!" ("Out! Out! Hurry! Hurry!") would be shouted in German and other languages. Barking ferociously, dogs strained at their leashes while figures in striped uniforms—kapos or prisoner functionaries as they were known to the Germans—yelled at the confused and frightened people, directing them where to go. If someone did not move quickly enough, he or she would be struck with the butt of a rifle or a cudgel, similar to a nightstick. It mattered not that the person was old or feeble, sick or crippled.

People disembarking from the train initially sought two things—their loved ones and their luggage. The Nazis immediately separated them from both. Families were told to leave their luggage; they would get it later. Whether they lived or died, their luggage and belongings including valuable and precious heirlooms were gone forever. The new arrivals were then directed to line up in columns of five—men to one side and women and children to the other. Scared and unsuspecting, they did as they were told. Höss and the Nazis were able to manipulate and control the masses with relative ease using their fear as a weapon against them.[5]

On the train platform, old couples who had been married for decades were separated for the last time with no chance to say goodbye. In that moment, husbands would get a last glimpse of their wives and children. Of course, almost none of them knew this. Pretense and deceit were essential to the killing process, and continuous practice made the Nazis masters of deception. The separation from loved ones in an unfamiliar setting was itself disturbing and distressing. Depending upon the time of arrival, deportees might also sense the terror of impending death. Arriving prisoners would often catch sight of flames spewing from the crematoria or pits. The foul stench of burning bodies would be difficult to miss. Human ashes often floated down upon them. To calm the families, Höss employed an orchestra composed of internees. At Nuremberg, Madame Marie Claude Vaillant-Couturier described the train disembarkation:

Cattle car at Auschwitz II–Birkenau (author photograph).

> The stopping place about 100 meters from the gas chamber, was right opposite our block though, of course, separated from us by two rows of barbed wire. Consequently, we saw the unsealing of the cars and the soldiers letting men, women, and children out of them. We then witnessed heartrending scenes; old couples forced to part from each other, mothers made to abandon their young daughters, since the latter were sent to the camp, whereas mothers and children were sent to the gas chambers. All these people were unaware of the fate awaiting them. They were merely upset at being separated, but they did not know that they were going to their death. To render their welcome more pleasant at this time—June–July 1944—an orchestra composed of internees, all young and pretty girls dressed in little white blouses and navy blue skirts, played during the selection, at the arrival of the trains, gay tunes such as "The Merry Widow," the "Barcarolle" from *The Tales of Hoffman*, and so forth. They were then informed that this was a labor camp and since they were not brought into the camp they saw only the small platform surrounded by flowering plants. Naturally, they could not realize what was in store for them.[6]

VI. Entrance Into Hell

The groups of men and women were placed in formations of five for "selection." Life or death hung in the balance. At first, selections of mass Jewish transports took place sporadically. Systematic selection began July 4, 1942. Selection served the sole purpose of determining who was fit to work. The decision was usually made by one of the camp physicians, often the notorious Josef Mengele, although sometimes officers of the protective custody camp or the labor department performed the task. If in the moment of decision it was determined that a person could not benefit the Reich labor force, he or she was immediately sent to the gas chamber. No physical examination was conducted, and no records were reviewed. The determination was based upon age, past work experience and present physical condition. If Mengele pointed to the right, you lived; if he pointed to the left, you died.[7]

Although Höss did not regularly participate in the selections, he clearly knew, as the Auschwitz commandant, how the process worked. At Nuremberg, he testified:

> They were there examined by two SS medical officers as to their fitness for work. The internees capable of work at once marched to Auschwitz or to the camp at Birkenau and those incapable of work were at first taken to the provisional installations, then later to the newly constructed crematoria.

By "provisional installations," Höss was referring to Polish cottages near Birkenau which had been converted into gas chambers before four large

Division of men and women on ramp at Auschwitz II–Birkenau prior to selection (courtesy Yad Vashem—the Holocaust Heroes' and Martyrs' Remembrance Authority).

Jews from Subcarpathian Rus undergo selection at Auschwitz II–Birkenau in 1944 (courtesy U.S. Holocaust Memorial Museum, Washington, D.C.).

crematoria were constructed which included gas chambers of their own. In reality, there was no examination; only a cursory inspection by one doctor determined a person's fate. He might ask a new arrival what type of work he or she performed and his or her age.[8]

Höss spoke to Dr. Leon Goldensohn, the prison psychiatrist at Nuremberg, about the trains and selection. Whenever Höss described the workings of Auschwitz, he spoke with a sense of pride. Though the discussion inevitably involved suffering and death, his tone was apathetic and Höss expressed no emotion:

> Höss: Well, it was like this. These transports didn't come daily; sometimes two or three trains arrived on a single day, every train containing two thousand people, but there were periods when no transports arrived for three to six weeks.
> GOLDENSOHN: How long were these people kept at Auschwitz?
> Höss: No time at all. A side track went to Birkenau and unloaded, and there the selection was made. Those who were able to work were sifted from those unable to work.
> GOLDENSOHN: What criteria for selection were used?
> Höss: Well, we had two SS doctors and they sat at tables, and the people from the transports got off the train and walked by these doctors. These people were fully clothed; they just walked by and the doctors judged by their looks, age, and strength.

VI. Entrance Into Hell

GOLDENSOHN: Out of the transport of two thousand, approximately how many were saved for work?

Höss: In all of those years, I figured an average of twenty to thirty percent of the people were able to work.[9]

    The elderly and the infirm were always sent directly to the gas chamber. Women with children, pregnant women and children were selected for the gas chamber. In the selection process, telling the truth about age or occupation might mean certain death. Sometimes, a sympathetic kapo, who knew the answers an SS doctor expected from those fit to work, saved the life of an arriving prisoner. Elie Wiesel arrived at Auschwitz with his mother, father and three sisters. He and his father were immediately separated from his mother and sisters. He would never see his mother and younger sisters again. At 15, Elie, too young to work by generally accepted standards, was destined for the gas chamber. A prisoner functionary told Elie to tell the SS doctor he was 18. He did so. Elie also lied about his profession. The Nazis did not want students, so he said he was a farmer. Elie's father was 50 years old. The kapo directed him to say he was forty. Elie and his father made it through. Passing the selection was all that mattered.[10]

    Following his successful selection on February 21, 1944, Primo Levi from Italy was driven by truck for 20 minutes from the railway ramp to the prison. He and the other men with him were crowded into a large room. With nothing to drink for four days, Levi was extremely thirsty. There was a tap in the room, but also a sign indicating the water was too dirty to drink. After a long wait, an SS man entered the room and asked, "Wer kann Deutsch?" ("Who knows German?"). A man stepped forward to interpret. The men were directed to form rows of five, with intervals of two yards between each man. They were then told to undress and make a bundle of their clothes in a special manner, the woolen garments on one side, all the rest on the other. They were told to take off their shoes, but pay great attention that they were not stolen. Nakedness served two purposes at Auschwitz: one was to weaken the prisoners psychologically and make them less likely to resist. The other purpose was to plunder their personal belongings.[11]

    Another German came in and told the men to put their shoes in a certain corner. They did as they were told. An inmate followed with a broom and swept away all the shoes, outside the door into a heap. Levi thought, "He is crazy, he is mixing them all together, ninety-six pairs, they will be all unmatched." In truth, Levi and the new arrivals would not get their shoes back. They had become Reich property. When the outside door opened, a freezing wind entered; the naked men covered themselves with their arms. The wind blew the door shut. The German reopened it and stood watching as the men writhed to hide from the wind, one behind the other. Then he left and closed it.[12]

Four men with razors, soap, brushes and clippers burst into the room. They also carried trousers and jackets with stripes, with a number sewn on the front. The prisoners were shorn from head to toe. Another door opened and the men, naked and sheared, were ushered into a shower room, alone. Levi recalled:

> Slowly the astonishment dissolves, and we speak, and everyone asks questions and no one answers. If we are naked in a shower-room, it means that we will have a shower. If we have a shower it is because they are not going to kill us yet. But why then do they keep us standing, and give us nothing to drink, while nobody explains anything, and we have no shoes or clothes, but we are all naked with our feet in the water, and we have been travelling five days and cannot even sit down.[13]

The commotion made by the men caused the German officer to re-enter the room. He told them they must be quiet. The men wanted answers to their questions—what were they waiting for, how long will they stay there, what about their women—but he refused to answer. The German left and a prisoner in stripes returned. He spoke to them in Italian. He made a long speech, was very polite and tried to reply to all their questions. They were told they were at Monowitz, near Auschwitz, a work camp; all the prisoners work in a factory which produces a type of rubber called Buna, so the camp itself was called Buna.[14]

Jews from Subcarpathian Rus undergo selection at Auschwitz II–Birkenau in 1944 while others walk to the gas chambers (courtesy U.S. Holocaust Memorial Museum, Washington, D.C.).

VI. Entrance Into Hell

The man told them they would be given shoes and clothes like his. They must remain naked while they waited for the shower and the disinfection, which would take place immediately after reveille; no one could enter the camp without being disinfected. He told the men their women were well and they will see them again soon—a lie. At the sound of the bell, the still dark camp awoke. Unexpectedly, boiling water gushed out from the showers. After five minutes, four men burst in yelling and shoving and driving them, wet and steaming, into the adjoining room, which was freezing. In that room, other shouting people threw unrecognizable rags at Levi and the other men and thrust into their hands a pair of broken-down boots with wooden soles. Often the clothes new arrivals received were taken from murdered prisoners. They had no time to understand. Suddenly, they were in the open, in the blue and icy snow of dawn, barefoot and naked, with their clothing in their hands and a hundred yards to run to the next hut. Only there would they be allowed to get dressed. Finally, Levi received the tattoo 174517 on his left arm, by which he would thereafter be known at Auschwitz and which he carried until he died.[15]

Höss and the Nazis had completed their first task, transforming proud men into what Levi called "miserable and sordid puppets." As they stood together, naked, unable to lift their eyes and look upon one another, it was then, Levi recalled:

> we became aware that our language lacks words to express this offence, the demolition of a man. In a moment, with almost prophetic intuition, the reality was revealed to us: we had reached the bottom. It is not possible to sink lower than this; no human condition is more miserable than this, nor could it conceivably be so. Nothing belongs to us anymore; they have taken away our clothes, our shoes, even our hair; if we speak, they will not listen to us, and if they listen, they will not understand. They will even take away our name: and if we want to keep it, we will have to find in ourselves the strength to do so, to manage somehow so that behind the name something of us, of us as we were, still remains.[16]

As humiliating as the entrance process was for the men, it was more dehumanizing for the women. Priska Löwenbein from Slovakia, who had recently discovered she was pregnant, arrived at Auschwitz with her husband Tibor. Immediately, they were separated. Tibor would not survive. After Mengele selected Priska for work, kapos and SS guards marched her and other women in columns of five past high barbed-wire fences to a remote brick building on the periphery of the camp, known as the Sauna. They were squeezed into a long room with windows and immediately ordered to strip naked to be "disinfected." Many of the women balked at the command, having never been seen undressed even by their husbands. Their hesitation was met with blows from the kapos and SS until they complied. Their discarded clothes, watches, money and jewelry, now property of the Reich, were quickly piled into mounds to be taken to the commercial warehouses of Auschwitz.[17]

Once the women were completely naked, they were hurried down a hallway to another room where their mouths and other body orifices were closely inspected for hidden valuables such as gold or gems. The Germans knew that deportees often hid jewelry on their person in hopes it would not be discovered. Then, as were the men, the women were subjected to the shearers who shaved all the hair off their bodies. Inmate Anka Nathan recalled how she felt:

> You feel more than naked; you feel degraded … like a cockroach you can step on. It didn't hurt but … the humiliation … if you don't do it of your own free will … you can't imagine what you look and feel like without hair.

The hair was collected to serve the Reich. The women were then forced outside, completely naked, for another inspection by Dr. Mengele. Priska watched Mengele question other women as he approached. Outwardly, she tried to appear dignified, but inwardly she had never felt more humiliated or afraid.[18]

Mengele looked carefully at Priska and asked her in German if she was pregnant. She had only a moment to decide whether to tell him the truth. She did not trust him, so she looked back at him directly and lied, "Nein." Mengele then passed nonchalantly to the woman next in line. Priska had just saved her life and the life of her child. Mengele would not always trust a woman's answer to that question. Sometimes, he would just grab her breast. If she was lactating, she and her baby were taken to the gas chamber. After the roll call, Priska and the other women were hurried to a concrete shower room where the kapos forced them to stand under water pipes and large showerheads. They were real. Hot water poured onto the women. There was no soap or towels. Instead, the kapos sprayed their heads and underarms with a stinging disinfectant that burned their sores and razor nicks.[19]

The women's ordeal was not yet over. Still wet, they were rushed by the yelling guards into another room and given only a few moments to dry off. Next, they were forced into a small latrine and commanded to squat over holes in the floor five at a time. Prodded with batons and without any paper, few were able to perform. The women were then taken to a room in which there was a huge pile of discarded clothes. As each woman entered, inmates threw her an item or two of leftover clothing. The clothes often did not fit. The women, as the men, were registered with tattoo numbers on their left forearms.[20]

Personal data of prisoners were taken down when they were given their identification numbers. Once an inmate received a tattoo, he or she became nameless; the number was the sole means of identification. The prisoner's camp number, stamped on a special piece of cloth, had to be sewn on the trousers and coat. A triangle pointing downwards, known as a Winkel, was added above the number, showing the prisoner's category. The Winkel was also applied to the hem of the right trouser leg. A red triangle indicated that the person was a political prisoner. Green Winkels were worn by "criminals" and prisoners in "preventive custody," known in the jargon of the camp as "professional criminals." The color black indicated an "anti-social" inmate, such as a prostitute or Gypsy. The triangles of the Jehovah's Witnesses, known as "Bible-researchers," were purple. Homosexuals wore a pink Winkel, emigrants blue and Jews, who formed a category of their own regardless of nationality, yellow. A letter on the triangle gave the nationality of non–Jews: "P," for example, meant Pole; "F" for French; Reich Germans—most of them falling under the category of "criminals"—were not obliged to wear a letter. Jews had to wear a different-colored Winkel over the yellow one according to the reason for their imprisonment, so that their clothes were adorned with a Star of David; from mid–1944 a yellow strip over the Winkel replaced the second triangle.[21]

After prisoners were subjected to the registration process, they were sent to the quarantine section for 6–8 weeks. While ostensibly intended to protect existing inmates from any new disease or contagion, quarantine also served as Auschwitz boot camp. Prisoners were drilled and taught German marching songs, and, as if to prepare them for what was to come, they were constantly beaten and mistreated. Quarantine served the objective of terrorizing prisoners and breaking down their will to resist. As they did not yet work, their food rations were smaller than inmates within the camp. One prisoner described quarantine as "…a menagerie with defenseless animals that were subjected to drills by tamers without compassion."[22]

Auschwitz survivor Ludwik Rajewski recalled:

> As a rule everything we did was wrong and the punishment was—jump, roll, run, turn round, etc. After having been so harassed, it was a relief to go marching and singing, even if our bare feet, unused to such marching, were treading on broken bricks, glass, etc. which caused cuts and in consequence festering, infected wounds.… The persecutors pounced upon us, their ready prey. We were beaten in a horrible manner. For hours we had to run, jump, crawl, turn round while kneeling on the gravel and sharp pebbles. Weaker prisoners collapsed, older and stouter men fainted.…

Quarantine was also used for prisoners fortunate enough to be transferred out of Auschwitz to assure diseases in the camp did not spread elsewhere. Despite periodic fumigation, lice infested the camp and everyone in it. As a result, typhus, among other diseases, was widespread.[23]

Höss stated that he was never cruel, never mistreated a prisoner and never sanctioned mistreatment. As commandant, he was well aware of the emotional and physical trauma inflicted by the selection process. He knew that the deportees who were not immediately sent to the gas chambers were deprived of their personal property, stripped naked and shorn of their hair. Höss made no effort to render this process more humane or respectful. By degrading and humiliating the new prisoners, Höss maintained discipline and control. He claimed to be "powerless" when it came to stopping the mistreatment of prisoners meted out by the SS. Yet, SS-Obersturmbannführer Arthur Liebehenschel, who replaced Höss as commandant of Auschwitz in November 1943, apparently had little difficulty in restraining abusive SS men and prisoner functionaries. According to statistics relating to the quarantine section in Birkenau, there was a marked decrease in random killings after the change in leadership.[24]

VII

Life Within the Wire

The day of a prisoner at Auschwitz began and ended with roll call—the time for the SS to assure all inmates were accounted for. The camp was awakened at 3:30–4:00 a.m. by a shrill bell or the banging of a gong. Inmates were driven from their bunks by the shouting of the guards and kapos delivering bruising and painful blows with clubs. Prisoners were given a brief time to wash, then forced to line up. No excuse could release an inmate from roll call; even those who were dying were dragged outside the barracks to be counted. Madame Vaillant-Couturier testified at Nuremberg:

> We had to stand there in rows of five until dawn, that is, 7 or 8 o'clock in the morning in winter; and when there was a fog, sometimes until noon. Then the kommandos (work groups) would start on their way to work.
>
> ...we waited until daybreak, until the Aufseherinnen, the German women guards in uniform, came to count us. They had cudgels and they beat us more or less at random.

Roll call could be extended for many reasons, usually because the count did not match the number of inmates who should be present or sometimes roll call was protracted as punishment. During the entire process, prisoners stood at attention with their caps in hand and heads uncovered. The evening roll call of July 6, 1940, lasted from 7 p.m. until 2 p.m. the following day. Many inmates, due to weakness or illness, could not withstand extended roll calls. Survivor Kitty Hart remembered a roll call that lasted two hours in the sleeting rain; the women were naked, and some died.[1]

Madame Vaillant-Couturier recounted an incident she witnessed during one roll call, when a fellow prisoner from France, Germaine Renaud, was struck in the head with a club that fractured her skull. She testified that on February 5, 1943, at 3:30 a.m., the whole camp was awakened and sent outside, where they remained until five in the afternoon in the snow with no food. When the signal was given, the women were forced through the door of the barracks one by one and were struck in the back with a club to make them run. Those who could not run, either because they were too old or too ill, were taken to Block 25, the "waiting block," for the gas chamber. On that day, 10 of the French women from her convoy were taken to Block 25. When all the internees were back in the camp, she was sent out with other women to pick up the bodies of the dead. Approximately 1,000 women died that day.[2]

Prisoners feared SS guards at Auschwitz, and with good reason. The number of SS personnel at the camp varied over time from 500 in 1,940 to more than 4,400 in January 1945. Overall, about 6,800 SS men and 200 SS women served at Auschwitz. When the time for reckoning came after the war, only about 750 were punished for their misdeeds. SS personnel at Auschwitz came from various social groups with different job and education experiences. Those factors, as well as the motivation to excel at a personal level, precluded group cohesiveness. Camp authorities used rewards to motivate the behavior sought in the SS, usually at the expense of prisoners. Commendations, promotions, bonuses for shooting prisoners attempting to escape and extra food or alcohol rations for participating in mass extermination operations were sometimes given out. Many SS guards sought a reward for stopping an attempted escape by forcing the inmate to initiate the attempt. They would throw a prisoner's cap beyond the sentry line and order him to retrieve it, where he would, inevitably, be shot.[3]

SS men often welcomed their tour of duty in the camp as a means to avoid the front. The life of a guard was perfectly suited for bullies and power-hungry individuals needing to compensate for feelings of inferiority. Despite regulations to the contrary, the SS were given the freedom to beat, brutalize and even murder prisoners. Not all the guards acted maliciously; instead, witness testimony indicates some SS treated the prisoners humanely, though they were few in number. SS guards could benefit significantly from the deaths of persons killed in the Auschwitz gas chambers. The property of the victims, which had been confiscated on behalf of the Reich, was often pocketed by the SS. At Auschwitz, this plundering occurred to an exceptionally high degree until, in 1944, Himmler was forced to appoint a special commission to investigate the matter. The commission's findings resulted in the downfall of SS-Untersturmführer Maximilian Grabner, the head of the Political Department. Höss was also implicated. Only through the protection of higher authority in Berlin did Höss escape being arrested and tried.[4]

Kapos and Mistreatment of Prisoners

A camp the size of Auschwitz could not be controlled by the SS alone. A system of prisoner functionaries, many of whom were as brutal, and sometimes more so, than the SS, imposed order and discipline on the inmates. The SS chose kapos who would carry out SS orders. The kapos were given almost unlimited power over the inmates. They could beat and abuse prisoners over the most minor of infractions. If an inmate died, the kapo would not be held responsible; it was only necessary that the death be reported so the SS could keep track of the number of inmates. Inmates in the barracks had no means of redress. Höss was well aware of the mistreatment imposed by the prisoner functionaries.[5]

Reichsführer-SS Heinrich Himmler described how the kapo system worked:

> His job is to see that the work gets done … thus he has to push his men. As soon as we are no longer satisfied with him, he is no longer a kapo, and returns to the other inmates. He knows that they will beat him to death his first night back.… Since we don't have enough Germans here, we use others—of course a French kapo for Poles, a Polish kapo for Russians; we play one nation against another.

Above the kapos were block elders who were responsible for maintaining order and assuring that all commands were followed satisfactorily. Next in the inmate hierarchy was the "camp eldest," chosen by the camp commandant. The block elders reported to the "camp eldest," who in turn reported to the SS-Rapportführer. Inmate functionaries were identified with armbands and enjoyed a number of privileges that fostered rivalry among the prisoners. In fact, as soon as an inmate became a kapo, he or she no longer slept in the same area as the other inmates. The impact of prisoner functionaries was magnified in Auschwitz because of its size. There simply were not enough SS.[6]

The camp administration preferred to use prisoners with criminal records as functionaries—the ones that wore a green triangle. The "greens," as they were known in camp, tended to have unstable personalities and were accustomed to being objects of scorn. Many of them were chosen specifically because of their sadistic temperaments. The SS gave them a great deal of power, and inmates flattered them to get on their good side. Höss, who had trained at Dachau and Sachsenhausen, knew well the value of the greens. Hermann Langbein, an Auschwitz survivor, wrote that Höss once stated that from the standpoint of running a camp, 10 green functionaries were better than 100 SS men. One of the most notorious kapos, Ernst Krankeman, was brought from Sachsenhausen shortly after Auschwitz opened. Krankeman, like Vacek, who inmate Filip Müller encountered in the courtyard of Block 11 at Auschwitz I in May 1942, was a Funktionschäftling, a prisoner trained in brutal methods to be used against inmates. Krankeman, Vacek and SS-Hauptscharführer Gerhard Palitzsch, notorious for murdering thousands at the Death Wall in the courtyard of Block 11, all came from Sachsenhausen with Höss. Under the prisoner functionary system, nationality mattered; Germans were at the top. Inmates from other nations were also ranked—Slavs toward the bottom, Russians below the Slavs. Jews, no matter their nationality, were at the bottom.[7]

In his memoirs, Höss, thinking back to his own time in prison, alluded to the comradeship created by sharing a common fate and misery and wondered how the prisoner functionaries could be so cruel to fellow prisoners. Höss knew very well the reason. Confinement in Auschwitz was unlike his imprisonment. At Auschwitz, survival was extremely tenuous; any day could be an inmate's last. Acting as a prisoner functionary, with its accompanying privileges, was one way of increasing the chances of survival. Brutal treatment of other prisoners by the prisoner functionaries was part of the job and served to extend the hand of Höss and the SS in maintaining strict order.[8]

Having observed the abuse heaped on prisoners by kapos and block elders, Höss noted the effect of such behavior, particularly on the newer inmates, "Quite apart from the physical effects of such mean and vile treatment, its psychological results were unspeakably worse for those of their fellow-prisoners whose sensibilities had not yet been blunted by the harshness of camp life." Höss stated that "…for reasons of self-preservation the harder the life, the crasser that egotism. … Even people, who in ordinary life outside the camp were at all times considerate and good-natured, became capable, in the hard conditions of imprisonment, of bullying their fellow prisoners mercilessly, if by so doing they could make their own lives a little bit easier." Höss and the Nazis took full advantage of this survival instinct.[9]

As an inmate himself, Hermann Langbein attested that the punishment inflicted by his fellow prisoner could be more damaging than the beatings and whippings they received from the SS. Höss also knew this:

> The treatment they received from the guards, however brutal, arbitrary and cruel, never affected them psychologically to the same extent as did this attitude on the part of their fellow inmates.
>
> The very fact of having to watch helplessly and without any power to intervene, while Capos of this sort tormented their fellows, had a thoroughly crushing effect on the prisoners' psyche. Woe betide the prisoner who tried to interfere, to stand up for the oppressed! The system of terrorization that prevailed within the prison camp was far too great for any man to take such a risk.[10]

In his memoirs, Höss indicates that his SS subordinates not only mistreated the prisoners, but instructed the prisoner functionaries to do the same. He claims that they disregarded his instructions to treat the inmates humanely, and he was powerless to stop it. Höss' actions and words belie his self-exoneration. The entire prisoner functionary system was premised upon maintaining control and order in the absence of a sufficient number of SS. Höss knew very well that the kapos would impose harsh, even lethal, discipline for minor offenses. The use of barbaric prisoners such as Krankeman and Vacek, who came with him from Sachsenhausen, to demean and punish inmates is clear evidence of his mindset. Höss' statement regarding his preference for the use of "green" prisoners further reflects his intent to brutalize and dehumanize Auschwitz prisoners to maintain order.[11]

No rational person can believe Höss' statement that the order of a camp commandant in the Third Reich would be ignored by his SS subordinates. Höss indicated that, when Himmler gave him the order for the Final Solution, he did not reflect on it: "I had been given an order, and I had to carry it out." If, in the SS universe, according to Höss, every order must be obeyed, then certainly any order from Höss that prisoners not be mistreated would be followed. In fact, SS rules and regulations required that SS give decent treatment to inmates and prohibited arbitrary treatment by subordinate SS men. "The camp leader is responsible for the entire domain of the inmates of the camp.... In particular, he has to make sure that the inmates are treated with strictness, but justly. Mistreatments must be reported immediately to the commander of the camp." Höss was well aware of these requirements from his training. If Höss had, in fact, forbidden prisoner abuse, brutality by the SS would have been far less frequent.[12]

Even less credible is Höss' suggestion that he could not control the mistreatment of the inmates by their fellow prisoners. In August 1942, the SS Main Economic and Administrative Office (WVHA) advised the camp commandants that concentration camp prisoners could be punished by German courts for severe abuse of their fellow prisoners. The commandants were ordered to stop this practice. Nothing changed at Auschwitz. The cruelty and brutality of the kapos and block elders were essential to the Auschwitz system. Höss knew this and used them as Himmler envisioned. Höss allowed the SS to be cruel and knew they would teach kapos to brutalize their fellow prisoners to maintain order. According to Höss, the influence of Kapos "was a factor of decisive importance in Auschwitz-Birkenau where the masses of prisoners could not be supervised."[13]

Höss claims he received conflicting guidance from Himmler regarding the treatment of prisoners. Himmler once decreed, "Strictest, merciless treatment of prisoners without consideration," then next he decreed, "Gentle treatment, watching carefully over the prisoners' health conditions and trying to educate them with rehabilitation and discharge in mind." Another time, "Increase the work day to twelve hours and the harshest punishment for laziness," the next, "Increase in prisoner privileges and construction of brothels to voluntarily get higher work quotas performed; supplementary food for prisoners has to be curtailed in order not to deprive the surrounding, hard-working civilian population of their necessary food supply," then next, "The camp Kommandant has to do everything in his power to see to it that the rations allocated by the Ministry of Food will be increased for the prisoners and to add to that supply by gathering edible things growing in the wild." Then, "In view of the importance of defense contract plans there can be no consideration given to the health of the prisoners; they must be used to the utmost to get as much work out of them as possible." Then again, "So that prisoners can be deployed as long as possible in the arms factories, any unreasonable demands by the foreman to work harder must be vigorously opposed." Himmler's orders regarding penalties also changed according to Höss. One time he complained there was too much corporal punishment. Another time, "Discipline in the camps has become very lax, drastic steps must be taken, and there must be harsher punishments." As a consequence of Himmler's conflicting directives, Höss, who was on site and in the best position to judge the situation, felt free to impose discipline and manage prisoner conditions that would be most effective in accomplishing his goals.[14]

In his Nuremberg testimony and in his memoirs, Höss made a concerted effort to distance himself from the barbaric treatment imposed on the inmates of Auschwitz. Paradoxically, he was far more willing to admit to his participation in the extermination of one million Jews in the gas chambers. Most of the victims who were gassed arrived on a train, were deceived about their fate and within one to two hours in Auschwitz were dead. After several minutes of terror, their lives were over. He could watch them die, knowing the suffering was momentary. Under Höss' twisted thinking, it made more sense to be associated with the quick murder of innocent men, women and children, especially because they were Jews, than with the daily inhumane conditions which slowly destroyed the lives of human beings, both physically and mentally, in Auschwitz day after day, week after week, month after month.

Food and Barracks

According to Höss' affidavit introduced into evidence at Nuremberg, starvation and disease accounted for half a million deaths at Auschwitz. Primo Levi, an Auschwitz survivor, recalled that prisoners received three meals. In the morning, after reveille, they were provided 350 grams of bread on four days of the week and 700 grams on the other three, averaging 500 grams per day—an amount he says would have been fairly reasonable if the bread itself had not indisputably contained a very large quantity of dross, including sawdust. With the bread in the mornings, inmates received 25 grams of margarine with about 20 grams of sausage or a spoonful of jam or soft cheese. The margarine was distributed on six days of the week only, and later this was reduced to three. At noon, a liter of turnip or cabbage soup was provided, though it was completely tasteless, and every evening after work another liter of a slightly thicker soup with a few potatoes, or now and then some peas and chickpeas. This soup also lacked any flavor. A few shreds of meat, a slice of poor quality sausage, or a little bit of cheese might also be supplied. To drink, half a liter of coffee was distributed morning and evening. Medical examination of the Auschwitz prisoners who were liberated by the Soviet Army in January 1945 showed them to be 50–70 percent below their normal weight.[15]

To avoid starvation, prisoners needed more food. Inmates often traded or bartered to obtain something extra to eat. In Auschwitz, the term used to describe the process of securing enough food to survive was "organize." It was distinct from stealing. If someone took property from a fellow inmate, he was treated as a thief and severely punished by others. "Organizing," however, was regarded as honorable and commendable. An inmate who wanted to stay alive had to "organize" by appropriating goods from stockrooms, larders or kitchens.[16]

Hunger was constant, gnawing and unabating. First in line did not necessarily mean the first to be satisfied. Primo Levi stated, as noon of a work day finally arrived, "…we have an animal hurry to swell our bellies with the warm stew, but no one wants to be first, as the first person receives the most liquid ration. As usual, the kapo mocks and insults us for our voracity and takes care not to stir the pot, as the bottom belongs notoriously to him." He also explained how prisoners would "organize" for food:

> Here scores of prisoners driven desperate by hunger prowl around, with lips half-open and eyes gleaming, lured by a deceptive instinct to where the merchandise shown makes the gnawing of their stomachs more acute and their salvation more assiduous. In the best cases they possess a miserable half-ration of bread which, with painful effort, they have saved since the morning, in the senseless hope of a chance to make an advantageous bargain with some ingenuous person, unaware of the prices of the moment. Some of these, with savage patience acquire with their half-ration two pints of soup which, once in their possession, they subject to a methodical examination with a view to extracting the few pieces of potato lying at the bottom; this done, they exchange it for bread, and the bread for another two pints to denaturalize, and so on until their nerves are exhausted, or until some victim, catching them in the act, inflicts on them a severe lesson, exposing them to public derision. Of the same kind are those who come to the market to sell their only shirt; they well know what will happen on the next occasion that the Kapo finds out that they are bare underneath their jackets. The Kapo will ask them what they have done with their shirt; it is a purely rhetorical question, a formality useful only to begin the game. They will reply that their shirt was stolen in the washroom; this reply is equally customary, and is not expected to be believed; in fact, even the stones of the Lager (i.e., the camp) know that ninety-nine times out of a hundred whoever has no shirt has sold it because of hunger, and that in any case one is responsible for one's shirt because it belongs to the Lager. Then the Kapo will beat them, they will be issued another shirt, and sooner or later they will begin again.[17]

A major cause of the spread of epidemics was the unsanitary mess tins which inmates were required to eat from. At best, they were rinsed in cold water after each meal. Many inmates were ill and lacked the strength to go to the lavatory during the night, so they used these containers as bedpans. The next day, the mess tins were collected and taken to a refuse heap. Then, they would be washed in cold water, and reused for the next meal.[18]

Prisoners slept on wooden planks and straw. Because of Karl Bischoff's decision to crowd more inmates into the same space, people were forced to sleep body-to-body on three tiers. Those on the lower tier faced the prospect of scurrying rats, as well as the uncontrollable bowels of sick prisoners above. With one wash barrack for each 7,800 inmates and one latrine for each 7,000 inmates, 744 prisoners in each barracks competed with the inmates from nine other blocks for use of the washing room. They also had to share the latrine with eight other blocks. It requires little imagination to see how typhus, malaria, dysentery and other communicable ailments spread so rapidly through the population. When a case of typhus was diagnosed at Birkenau, prisoner disinfection was ordered. The disinfection process consisted of submersion, naked, into a vat of Lysol solution. The procedure did not kill the lice or stop the typhus. It did lead to the death of some prisoners.[19]

Something as simple as shoes could be the difference between life and death. In the snow and mud, leather shoes were destroyed within a short time. An inmate's feet were often frozen and became covered with sores. Prisoners slept with their muddy shoes on, lest they be stolen. If shoes were lost, the victim was forced to desperately seek replacements, even if it meant two left shoes or two right shoes. Inmates appearing at roll call without shoes were taken to the gas chamber. Working with unfitting shoes could easily result in sores and infected feet and a trip to the infirmary from where many prisoners never returned.[20]

Medical Care and Experimentation

Before an inmate could go to the infirmary, permission had to be obtained from the block elder, who often refused. If authorization was given, prisoners were marched in columns and, no matter what the weather or the prisoner's condition, forced to wait for several hours in a line standing outside the infirmary. Frequently, patients died before they were admitted. Madame Vaillant-Couturier related that lining up in front of the infirmary could be dangerous because, at any time, if the SS felt the line was too long, they could take the women who were waiting to Block 25 to await a trip to the gas chamber.[21]

A prisoner accepted into the infirmary had two advantages: there was no roll call and no work. However, medical care for prisoners was atrocious. The SS doctors cared nothing for the welfare of the Auschwitz inmates as patients and did not examine them personally. Any medical care came from prisoner doctors and nurses. Very little medicine was available. Conditions in the hospital were themselves sickening. For a long time, no sewer facilities existed. Human waste covered the floor. The hospital was overcrowded and filthy. Madame Vaillant-Couturier stated:

> [O]ne lay in appalling conditions, four in a bed of less than 1 meter in width, each suffering from a different disease, so that anyone who came for leg sores would catch typhus or dysentery from neighbors. The straw mattresses were dirty, and they were changed only when absolutely rotten. The bedding was so full of lice that one could see them swarming like ants.... the patients were left in their beds without any attention, without hygiene, and unwashed. The dead lay in bed with the sick for several hours; and finally, when they were noticed, they were simply tipped out of the bed and taken outside the block.

From morning until night, the carriers of the dead went from the infirmary to the mortuary. Fleas and lice infested the patients, and rats chewed the dead bodies. While the infirmary served as a temporary respite from the tribulations of everyday life in the camp, extended stays could be fatal. As is evident from Auschwitz records, prisoners in the infirmary not expected to recover quickly were selected and killed, often by a phenol injection to the heart.[22]

Not only did the SS doctors make little or no effort to heal the sick and dying, they engaged in some of the most despicable and repugnant practices ever performed by medical professionals. The classic Hippocratic Oath required that the Nazi doctors "abstain from whatever is deleterious and mischievous," "give no deadly medicine to anyone" and "go into [houses] for the benefit of the sick, and ... abstain from every voluntary act of mischief and corruption." The Nazi doctors violated this oath repeatedly by using inmates at Auschwitz as their personal lab rats and subjecting them to painful and often lethal clinical procedures with no potentially valid medical purpose. Some of the testing and experimentation was undergone for the specific purpose of racial demolition—to destroy the ability of young Jewish men and women to reproduce. In addition to deciding life and death on the platform as trains arrived, the Nazi doctors tortured and murdered the prisoners within Auschwitz without compunction.[23]

All of this occurred under the watchful eye of, and with no interference from, Commandant Höss. In his Nuremberg affidavit of April 5, 1946, Höss said that "[f]rom time to time we conducted medical experiments on women inmates, including sterilization and experiments relating to cancer. Most of the people who died under these experiments had been already condemned to death by the Gestapo." That was a lie. At his trial in Poland, Höss would be held accountable for the medical atrocities. The Indictment alleged that Höss deprived millions of people of their lives by "gas-chambers, shooting, hanging, lethal injections of phenol or by medical experiments causing death, systematic starvation, by creating special conditions in the camp which were causing a high rate of mortality, by excessive work of the inmates, and by other methods." While disputing the number of persons killed, Höss did not otherwise deny the claims against him.[24]

The center for experimentation at the Stammlager was Block 10. All the subjects were Jews. Drs. Carl Clauberg and Horst Schumann were best known for their sterilization and castration experiments. Clauberg's method of sterilization was the injection of a caustic substance into a woman's cervix to obstruct the fallopian tubes. On April 30, 1943, according to Auschwitz records, Höss' office notified the WVHA that 242 female prisoners had been earmarked for experimental purposes performed by Dr. Clauberg. On June 7, 1943, Clauberg wrote Himmler that it would be possible to sterilize up to 1,000 women a day by injection. Schumann, on the other hand, used x-rays to sterilize healthy men and women. X-ray treatment often caused burns and was followed by castration. Chief camp physician Eduard Wirths sought a treatment for contagious diseases that might threaten the health of German troops, normally a laudable medical goal. However, he did so by injecting Jewish inmates with the diseases against their will, which often led to their deaths. Dr. Johann Paul Kremer, who was brought to Auschwitz to help address the typhus epidemic, kept a diary. He often spoke excitedly of receiving fresh organs for his experiments.[25]

The Tribunal at Höss' trial also heard evidence of premature termination of pregnancy and other experiments on pregnant or childbearing women. Nazi doctors engaged in experiments of artificial insemination without the voluntary consent of the subjects. These experiments were performed as a means to check the results of x-ray castrations and the effects of fluid injections into the uterus and fallopian tubes. Excisions were made on completely healthy women with no suspicion of cancer of the genital organs. Experiments of transplanting cancerous bodies to the uterus and cervical channel were also carried out. After a certain time, the uterus was removed, and results of the transplanting observed. As in most cases these experiments were successful, however, and victims usually died within one-and-a-half years, or at least temporary illness followed.[26]

The most notorious of Nazi doctors was Josef Mengele. Besides regularly appearing at the train platform to select new arrivals for the gas chambers, Mengele took a particular interest in noma, a facial infection prominent among the Gypsy population at Auschwitz. He also sought out twins and dwarves for study and experimentation. Twins, usually children, would be forced to stand naked for hours as measurements were taken of every part of their bodies and recorded. Often body fluid samples were taken, sometimes in quantities so large as to be fatal. On one occasion, he sewed the veins of

(Left to right) SS officers Richard Baer, Josef Mengele, and Rudolf Höss (courtesy U.S. Holocaust Memorial Museum, Washington, D.C.).

two twins together for no apparent reason. Their misery and suffering ended only when their own mother terminated the lives of her children. Mengele attempted to change eye color by injecting unknown chemical substances into the eyes of children. He never examined or touched actual sick patients. In September 1942, SS Chief Doctor and Head of the Sanitation Central Office SS-Obergruppenführer Dr. Ernst-Robert Grawitz, who was also president of the German Red Cross, inspected the camp and found medical supervision by the doctors unsatisfactory and that patients did not receive adequate care. He noted the general bad health of prisoners and witnessed the gassing of Jews. Conditions did not improve.[27]

Slave Labor

Everyone "fortunate" enough to have escaped the gas chambers upon entry into Auschwitz was required to work. In this way, Auschwitz satisfied the dual purposes of serving the German war effort and exterminating more Jews. The primary benefactor of the slave labor provided by the Nazis was I. G. Farben, which operated facilities intended to manufacture Buna—synthetic rubber. The plant was seven kilometers from the camp. In 1943, there were 7,000 Auschwitz prisoners at I .G. Farben, and in 1944, 11,000. Prisoners were grouped into work groups or kommandos; an inmate kapo was placed in charge of the kommando. Primo Levi recalled:

> Every morning we leave the camp in squads for the Buna; every evening, in squads, we return. As regards the work, we are divided into about two hundred Kommandos, each of which consists of between fifteen and one hundred and fifty men and is commanded by a Kapo. There are good and bad Kommandos; for the most part they are used as transport and the work is quite hard, especially in the winter, if for no other reason merely because it always takes place in the open. There are also skilled Kommandos (electricians, smiths, bricklayers, welders, mechanics, concrete-layers, etc.), each attached to a certain workshop or department of the Buna, and depending more directly on civilian foremen, mostly German and Polish. This naturally only applies to the hours of work; for the rest of the day the skilled workers (there are no more than three or four hundred in all) receive no different treatment from the ordinary workers.[28]

After a time, due to the distance from the concentration camp, a special camp for the slave laborers employed at I. G. Farben was set up and called Monowitz after the nearby town. Conditions were no better there than in Auschwitz. At any time, a prisoner who was not working quickly or efficiently enough would be beaten or kicked by the SS, a kapo or a German I. G. foreman. Often, a worker unable to keep pace would be struck multiple times and left on the floor bleeding. Laborers who were no longer fit to work and did not die on their own were selected for the gas chamber or shot by the SS. Other private German companies soon followed I. G. Farben and established themselves near Auschwitz. More than thirty sub-camps arose, though Monowitz was the largest.[29]

As the war progressed, more and more prisoners were used in the German munitions industry. Höss sought to further this effort by repeatedly issuing orders to employ as many inmates as possible in arms factories. Most prisoners in satellite camps were Jews. They received half of the rations of food of German prisoners and were provided inadequate clothing and equipment. Forced labor was simply a slower death. Prisoners worked 12 hours a day, with one hour for lunch, six days per week. After an average of three to four months, most of the prisoners forced to work were dead, having succumbed to beatings, hunger, weakness and inhuman living conditions. Of approximately 35,000 Auschwitz inmates that worked for I. G. Farben alone during the war, more than 25,000 died.[30]

Women at Auschwitz

Women resided in Auschwitz I until August 16, 1942, when they were moved to section BI of Birkenau. Until July 1942, the women's camp on the grounds of the main camp was technically within the jurisdiction of the headquarters of the Ravensbruck concentration camp; thereafter it was placed under the Auschwitz commandant, Höss, where it remained until November 1943. The women occupied sections BIa and BIb, closest to crematorium II. Höss found the chief female supervisor, Frau Langefeldt, to be incompetent, so he established a parallel chain of authority for the women's camp.[31]

SS supervisors distinguished themselves in their savage treatment of women prisoners. Their brutality was shocking even by Auschwitz standards. As bad as conditions were at the Stammlager, they were worse at Birkenau due to the boggy ground, overcrowded barracks, lack of sanitation, spread of disease and lack of water. Höss acknowledged that "the most wretched conditions prevailed in the women's camp." He knew that "[w]ash houses and latrines were sufficient, at the most, for a third of the number of inmates that the camp contained." Madame Vaillant-Couturier testified at Nuremberg:

> There was the complete lack of washing facilities. When we arrived at Auschwitz, for 12,000 internees there was only one tap of water, unfit for drinking, and it was not always flowing. As this tap was in the German wash house we could reach it only by passing through the guards, who were German common-law women prisoners, and they beat us horribly as we went by. It was therefore almost impossible to wash ourselves or our clothes. For more than 3 months we remained without changing our clothes.[32]

If a Jewish woman came into Auschwitz in the first months of pregnancy, the pregnancy was aborted. If her pregnancy was near the end, then after delivery, her baby was drowned in a bucket of water. Non-Jewish women were allowed to keep their babies, but they usually lived only a short time. Most newborns died of malnutrition or from the unsanitary and primitive hygienic conditions.[33]

Family Camp and Gypsies

For one group of Jewish families, entrance into Auschwitz did not mean separation and immediate death. In September 1943, 5,000 Jewish prisoners from the Theresienstadt concentration camp in Czechoslovakia were placed in a family camp, section BIIb, located not far from the main gate. The Theresienstadt families were not subject to the selection process. They were allowed to keep their civilian clothes and their hair, while living together in their own area. In December 1943, another 5,000 from Theresienstadt arrived and were treated the same way. Living conditions for these families were as bad as they were for everyone else.

The Nazis did not have any particular compassion for Czech Jews. The Theresienstadt families were held up to the outside world as examples of what camp life was like for prisoners at Auschwitz. Once this false impression was made, they were of no more use. On March 7, 1944, after six months of suspended death, the Theresienstadt families were taken to the gas chambers. Before they were killed, they were told to write postcards to their relatives telling them of how well they were being treated. The Nazis offered the postcards to refute allegations of mass exterminations of the Jews. Other transports came from Theresienstadt with the same life expectancy—six months.[34]

Another group of families was also allowed to stay together, but they were not Jewish. They were Sinti and Roma Gypsies. Similar to the Jews, anti–Gypsy prejudice existed in Europe for centuries. Although they were Aryan, they were deemed antisocial, so they were rounded up and deported to concentration camps. On February 26, 1943, the first transport of Gypsies arrived at Auschwitz. The Gypsy family camp was established in section BIIe. The conditions to which they were subjected were as bad as other inmates. In March and May 1943 and again in August 1944, those Gypsies who had not perished from hunger and disease were taken to the gas chamber.[35]

Musselman and Subsequent Selections

When starvation and malnutrition had reduced an Auschwitz prisoner to the point he or she could no longer work and lacked the strength or energy to even stand and walk, the person was accorded a special designation—"musselman" or "Moslem." Musselmänner were prisoners who looked miserable, sick and emaciated. Inmates who had become weak and inept and who were no longer able to perform hard physical labor were Musselmänner. The term derived from the body posture of the prisoner, which appeared as a Muslim praying. Inmates with camp experience could quickly tell whether a newcomer could survive or would perish. One prisoner said the trick to avoid looking like a Musselman was to avoid shuffling one's feet. If the willpower of a person was crushed by the burden of Auschwitz, it would not be long before the marks of impending death appeared on his face. One prisoner observed:

> We knew that such a man would soon not react any more, that he would lose interest in his surroundings and stop obeying commands. His movements were going to become slow and his face masklike; his reflexes would stop functioning, and he would become incontinent without noticing it. He was not going to rise from his pallet but would remain lying on it motionlessly—in short, he would turn into a Musselmann, a corpse standing on swollen legs. When we had to come out for roll call, we would place such men against the wall with their arms raised. It was only a skeleton with a gray face that now leaned against the wall without moving, for it had lost its sense of balance.

Another prisoner presented this picture:

VII. Life Within the Wire

This person of skin and bones, barely capable of moving, lacking will and strength, with a discharge running from his nose onto his mouth and chin, this dirty being dressed in rags, often with lice, usually with severe diarrhea and an accordingly dirty uniform, with fallen in or bulging eyes, was a true picture of misery, of weakness, hopelessness, and horror.

Musselmänner were doomed to die either naturally or by selection.[36]

Survivor Hermann Langbein describes the selection of a group of Musselmänner:

> On such days the SS roll call leader picks out from the details marching off to work in the morning all those who attract his attention and do not appear to be fully fit for work. A black day for the camp.
>
> "Strip completely!"
>
> Now they have to undress in the cold, helped along by screams and beatings.
>
> Most of them surely know what is going to happen to them. I can read it in their faces. Thinking that he is not being observed, one man stealthily and quickly puts on his clothes again, but a capo catches him. I can hear the blows and his screams through my window. Everyone wants to be the last to take off his clothes. Perhaps the terrified inmates hope that this will enable them to cheat their way out of their fate.
>
> "Faster, faster! On with it!" In the background stands an SS man with his legs apart.
>
> Now everyone has undressed. Pitiful skeletons. Their numbers are taken down, and they are chased into the block. The sun is shining, and the snow is glistening and merrily dripping from the roof. No one is in front of my window; all I can see are big piles of dirty prison clothes along the wall. Then I hear footsteps and muted voices from the corridor. I look outside. Now there are long lines of naked inmates. The clerk of our block walks up to each one with file cards in his hand, compares names and numbers, and writes each inmate's number on his chest with indelible ink. The corpses in Auschwitz bear that number on their chests; these inmates are already counted among the dead, and there has to be order. (In late 1942 not all inmates had had their numbers tattooed.)
>
> How they look at me, these freezing skeletons, as if I could help them, as if I were to blame for what is to come. I quickly close the door again.
>
> How must such a human being feel, standing naked in a corridor and waiting to be loaded on a truck that will take him to the gas chamber?
>
> But I don't hear any motor vehicle drive up. Those men are still there each time I have to cross the corridor on my way to the toilet. Some are apathetic and in a squatting position, others have flickering eyes. Do they still have hope—are they still seeking a way out? Those who sit are repeatedly roused; the corridor has to be clear. It was in the morning, after the early roll call, that I saw them being herded together in front of my window. Now it is evening, and they haven't had anything to eat all day. And why should they still be fed? If they want to drink, their only resource is water from the toilets.
>
> Now many are lying down. They are too weak to fear the blows that are intended to shake them awake. Three of them are lying in front of my door, and I have to step over them if I want to leave the room. One is dead, but the two next to him are still alive. There is little difference among these three.[37]

Selection for the gas chamber was not a onetime occurrence. From time to time, without warning, a block or the infirmary would be subject to another selection to reduce the population. Malnutrition and work had usually worn the prisoners down, increasing the likelihood of selection as time passed. Priska Löwenbein remembered Dr. Fritz Klein, a Jew hater, who conducted some of the selections. He inspected the bodies of the women for eczema, blemishes or deformities, anything that would warrant a trip to the gas chamber. At his war crimes trial, Klein said that Jews were the "inflamed appendix" of Europe that needed to be removed. Most prisoners, once selected, knew they were going to the gas chamber and went with relative calm, though isolated incidents of resistance did occur. One Jewish woman snuck out of the infirmary during a selection and, prohibited from entering a nearby barracks by the block elder, hid under a pile of corpses for several hours until the selection concluded. Inmates in the infirmary who had been selected to be killed were given a phenol injection to the heart. SS-Untersturmführer Maximilian Grabner, who led the Political Department, gave orders to chief camp physician Eduard Wirths to execute prisoners by lethal injection of phenol. Wirths always went to Höss to confirm the order.[38]

In *Return to Auschwitz* Kitty Hart wrote about a selection in her block:

> Two S.S. women came in, with the Blockälteste [block elder] fawning beside them and began to write down the tattoo numbers of a random selection of girls. The choice seemed quite arbitrary; you got the impression the S.S. needed a certain quantity, just as for work Kommandos, and when they had reached it they would be satisfied. When they had left, girls whose numbers had been noted down began to cry. "They're going to kill me," one screamed over and over again. We tried to reassure them. It couldn't happen just like that, it was all to do with something else. It had to be.

It was just that simple. At roll call, the tattoo numbers were read out. The girls were taken to Block 25, and after a couple of days the trucks came to take them to the gas chamber.[39]

Dr. Johann Paul Kremer was present on September 5, 1942, during one of the in-camp selections. In his diary, he described it as "the most horrible of all horrors." It resulted in the killing in the gas chambers of about 800 women prisoners. In the formal record at his trial on July 18, 1947, at Krakow, Kremer explained that diary entry as follows:

> Particularly unpleasant had been the action of gassing emaciated women from the women's camp. Such individuals were generally called "Muselmänner" ("Moslems"). I remember taking part in the gassing of such women in daylight. I am unable to state how numerous that group had been. When I came to the bunker they sat clothed on the ground. As the clothes were in fact worn out camp clothes they were not let into the undressing barracks but undressed in the open. I could deduce from the behavior of these women that they realized what was awaiting them. They begged the SS men to be allowed to live, they wept, but all of them were driven to the gas chamber and

gassed. Being an anatomist I had seen many horrors, had to do with corpses, but what I then saw was not to be compared with anything seen ever before.[40]

Höss himself participated in these supplemental selections. Survivor Ester Sendrowicz recalled that she was one of approximately 1,000 women taken out of the barracks one day. Room had to be made for more transports, so these women were subjected to a selection supervised by Höss and SS-Obersturmführer Franz Hössler, head of the women's camp. Being small, Sendrowicz expected to go to the gas chamber. That day she was lucky. Höss saw her and with his finger motioned for her to move to the group of women who would go back to the barracks. She was one of only a little more than one hundred women out of a thousand who were saved that day.[41]

Orchestras

In the category of unexpected and bizarre were the Auschwitz orchestras. An orchestra was authorized by Höss in the main Auschwitz camp in 1941. At that time, most of the inmates were Poles, and enough qualified musicians could be found to form a fine musical company. Once Birkenau was built, an orchestra was established in that camp as well. The orchestras played when the trains arrived to calm and deceive the deportees as to their fate. An orchestra also played in the morning after roll call to send the inmates off to work and in the evening to welcome them back to camp. The music improved the march of the prisoners in the kommandos. The orchestras also performed concerts, which usually took place on Sundays in front of Höss' villa.[42]

Acceptance as a musician in the orchestra served as a reprieve from some of the hardships experienced by ordinary prisoners at Auschwitz. The musicians worked during the day in the camp kitchen, so they could be quickly summoned, if necessary, to perform for SS visitors. The orchestra members wore clean white suits and were better nourished because they worked in the kitchen. The orchestra at the Stammlager rehearsed in a large room adjacent to the central office in Block 24, next to the camp gates. For prisoners close enough to hear, the music served to take them away, if only briefly, from the misery and degradation that was otherwise their day-to-day existence.[43]

The women's orchestra at Birkenau was the most famous. The head of the women's camp, Maria Mandl, who would later be executed as a war criminal, was a music lover and created the orchestra. Alma Rose, a famous musician and the daughter of a first violinist of the Vienna Philharmonic, was made conductor, despite the fact she was Jewish. The orchestra's performances were not limited to roll calls and work kommandos. According to one observer, "It had to play at all official occasions—for the camp commander's speeches, for transports, and for hangings. It also served as the entertainment for the SS and the inmates in the medical barracks."[44]

Random Violence and Discipline

As an officer at Dachau, Höss learned that the worst aspect of concentration camp life was the uncertainty of the term of imprisonment, which had a significant psychological effect on the prisoners. Viktor Frankl, a survivor of several camps, including Auschwitz, voiced the same observation: "Former prisoners, when writing or relating their experiences, agree that the most depressing influence of all was that a prisoner could not know how long his term of imprisonment would be." Auschwitz added a new and terrifying dimension to the uncertainty of life. Beating, whipping, punishment and death could come at almost any time for the most arbitrary and random reasons.[45]

For their own amusement when they were bored, SS guards would set their dogs on the prisoners, lacerating their skin and tearing their already worn clothes to shreds. Höss was aware of this practice and did nothing to stop it. "Because of the time and trouble it took to train fresh dog-handlers, they could only be relieved of their posts if they had been guilty of some grave offense, such as one that entailed punishment by SS court-martial, or alternatively if they had badly ill-treated or neglected their dogs," said Höss.[46]

Pity by the SS was rare. Even mercy shown by prisoners to one another was punished. Madame Vaillant-Couturier testified at Nuremberg that prisoners in Block 25 received little food and water because they were condemned to death. She recalled a young woman who, passing Block 25 one day, was overcome with pity for the women who moaned from morning until night in all languages, "Drink. Drink. Water!" She came back to get a little herbal tea, but as she was passing it through the bars of the window she was seen by the female guard, who took her by the neck and threw her into Block 25. Two days later, she was taken to the gas chamber.[47]

Offenses such as a missing button or an unsuitable facial expression could subject a prisoner to many different penalties, including beating or detention, solitary confinement, the standing cell or being hung from a post with his arms behind his back. Inmates who failed to march in step, an activity made difficult by the wooden shoes and blisters, could be mercilessly kicked or smacked in the face. In addition to hunger, hard labor and illness, prisoners regularly died of abuse. Auschwitz records reveal that on March 15, 1942, 131 prisoners were killed by drunken SS men. Later that same day, 147 prisoners and 103 Soviet POWs were tortured to death. On December 5, 1942, 2,000 young and healthy women were selected to be gassed. One prisoner was hanged because he bound the sole of his torn shoe with a piece of wire.

Then there was the 15-year-old Jew from Warsaw who drank coffee from a canteen while at work without knowing that it belonged to an SS man. He, too, was selected to be killed.[48]

Prior to Reichsführer-SS Himmler's second visit to Auschwitz in July 1942, a group of prisoners were lined up outside the barracks while the orchestra stood ready at the gate. The SS and prisoner functionaries were already under great stress when "catastrophe" happened, as related by survivor and Auschwitz escapee Rudolf Vrba:

> In the tenth row outside our Block, the Block Senior found Yankel Meisel without his full quota of tunic buttons.
> It took some seconds for the enormity of the crime to sink in. Then he felled him with a blow. An uneasy shuffling whispered through the ranks. I could see the SS men exchange taut glances and then I saw the Block Senior, with two of his helpers, hauling Yankel inside the barrack block.
> Out of sight, they acted like men who have been shamed and betrayed will act. They beat and kicked the life out of him. They pummeled him swiftly, frantically, trying to blot him out, to sponge him from the scene and from their minds; and Yankel, who had forgotten to sew his buttons on, had not even the good grace to die quickly and quietly.
> He screamed. It was a strong, querulous scream, ragged in the hot, still air. Then it turned suddenly to the thin, plaintive wail of abandoned bagpipes, but it did not fade so fast. It went on and on and on, flooding the vacuum of silence, snatching at tightly-reined minds and twisting them with panic, rising even above the ugly thump of erratic blows. At that moment, I think, we all hated Yankel Meisel, the little old Jew who was spoiling everything, who was causing trouble for all of us with his long, lone, futile protest.[49]

Yankel Meisel died, and the orchestra played for Himmler, who was unaware of the man whose life had just ended on his account.

Punishment by assignment to a penal company could also result in death. Höss stated, "…penal companies were assigned the hardest tasks, such as digging drainage ditches at Birkenau…. Prisoners in penal companies had to work all day long, also at hours when other prisoners were resting." Höss acknowledged that "particularly energetic Kapos were chosen to supervise such companies; I remember, among others, prisoner Krankeman [who came with Höss from Sachsenhausen] as one of the penal company Kapos."[50]

One of the worst prisoner-on-prisoner acts of violence occurred on October 5, 1942, at Budy, a village near Auschwitz where a penal company of prisoners was performing drainage work. The Budy unit was separate from Auschwitz, and the kapos of both genders, who were recruited criminals, treated the other inmates without mercy. According to SS-Unterscharführer Pery Broad, the SS guards provoked the German women prisoners to mistreat the Jewish women. The SS took pleasure in seeing the Jews suffer. As a result of this abuse, the Germans feared revenge by the Jews. One day, as a female Jewish prisoner was returning from the lavatory, a female German prisoner told her SS lover that the Jewish woman had struck her with a stone, which was untrue.[51]

The SS guards ran upstairs and, with the German women inmates, began beating the Jewish prisoners. Some of the Jewish women were thrown from the window, others were driven into the yard where they were shot or bludgeoned. A few managed to hide and avoid the joint attack by the SS guards and German inmates. About 90 women were beaten to death with clubs, rifle butts and axes. Notified of the incident, Höss drove to the site and conducted a brief inspection. He assigned SS-Untersturmführer Maximilian Grabner of the Political Department to perform an investigation. As soon as Höss left, most of the wounded Jewish women were shot.[52]

Some of the wounded Jewish women who had hidden were interrogated by the SS then injected in the heart with phenol. Photographs were taken during the investigation. However, the SS investigators developed only one copy of each photograph. Broad states, "The plates had to be destroyed in the presence of the commandant (Höss) and the photos were put at his disposal." Six German female prisoner functionaries were interviewed about the incident. On October 24, the six German female prisoners were killed by injection for the murder of the female Jewish inmates on October 5. The families of the Germans were sent a note of condolence by Höss for the tragic death of their daughter due to disease despite "the best medical care." As Germans, these families could receive an urn with ashes, though the families would not know it was just a mixture of ashes of several bodies from the crematorium.[53]

Höss transferred the sentry commander and the SS Head Supervisor, but otherwise did nothing to the SS who participated in the Budy massacre. At Nuremberg, Höss was asked:

> Did you make any observations as to whether there was any ill-treatment of prisoners to a greater or lesser degree on the part of those guards, or whether the ill-treatment was mainly to be traced back to the so-called Kapos?

Höss responded, "If any ill-treatment of prisoners by guards occurred—I myself have never observed any." Höss chose to be very literal, as he was when relating whether *he* had ever been cruel to or mistreated prisoners. At Budy, he did not observe the SS beat and shoot the Jewish female prisoners, but he knew it happened and covered it up.[54]

Kitty Hart reflected upon an incident which almost cost her her life. It was nighttime, and the weather was cold. She attempted to sneak some wood into the barracks for the stove, but was caught by the SS. The next day, Hart was taken to the punishment compound. While two kapos held her down, she was flogged and forced to count each of the lashings. She remembered counting to six. When she awoke, her body was soaked with blood, and every

VII. Life Within the Wire

part of her body hurt. She staggered back to her block with a gaping wound in her thigh and one eye completely closed. She was lucky. Those, like Anka Nathan, who would not be defeated by Auschwitz related a valuable lesson for survival. A prisoner needed to blend in and not attract unwanted attention—become invisible.[55]

Sometimes, a prisoner could not bear anymore suffering. Loved ones had been taken from them when they arrived. Starvation had taken its toll. Day after day, they struggled for food. Only the strongest could bear the work. Beatings, selections and random killings meant inmates never knew how long they would live. People who lost hope and could no longer stand the barbaric conditions committed suicide by running into the electrified wire to be electrocuted or by entering the restricted zone near the fence to be shot by the guards. Höss rewarded guards for killing prisoners near the wire for attempted escape. Himmler and Höss' superior SS-Oberführer Richard Glücks appreciated the effort to reduce the number of escapes and attempted escapes from Auschwitz. The killings of registered inmates, whether they died by injection, gassing, beating or shooting, had to be recorded in the Totenbuch—the Death Book. Of course, the actual cause of death was not listed. If a group of prisoners was shot at the Death Wall of Block 11, their names and the time of their deaths would be entered in 5- to 10-minute intervals. No one questioned why 50–60 young and healthy men died of heart failure five minutes apart.[56]

The Nazi effort near the end of the war to destroy evidence of their atrocities was only partially successful. The following is just a sample of Auschwitz records from the latter half of January 1941, providing a brief glimpse of the effects of the inhumane conditions and abusive treatment:

> January 21—As a result of hunger, hard labor, illness, and torture, 25 prisoners die in Auschwitz, among them 18 Poles, four Jews, two Czechs, and a German political prisoner. 22 Russian POWs die in the prisoner-of-war camp.
> January 22—As a result of hunger, hard labor, illness, and abuse, 26 prisoners and 27 Russian prisoners of war die in Auschwitz.
> January 23—As a result of hunger, hard labor, illness, and abuse, 21 prisoners and 24 Russian prisoners of war die in Auschwitz.
> January 24—As a result of hunger, hard labor, illness, and abuse, 18 prisoners and 15 Russian POWs die in Auschwitz.
> January 25—As a result of hard labor, illness, and abuse, 26 prisoners and 27 Russian POWs die in Auschwitz.
> January 26—As a result of hunger, hard labor, illness, and abuse, 31 prisoners and 10 POWs die in Auschwitz.
> January 27—As a result of hunger, hard labor, illness, and abuse, 31

prisoners and 13 Russian POWs die in Auschwitz. The deceased include 24 Poles, five Czechs, one Jew, and one German criminal prisoner.

January 28—As a result of hunger, hard labor, illness, and abuse, 46 prisoners and 14 Russian POWs die in Auschwitz.

January 29—As a result of hunger, hard labor, illness, and abuse, 34 prisoners and 8 Russian POWs die in Auschwitz.

January 30—As a result of hunger, hard labor, illness, and abuse, 29 prisoners and 13 Russian POWs die in Auschwitz.

January 31—As a result of hunger, hard labor, illness, and abuse, 27 prisoners and 10 Russian POWs die in Auschwitz.[57]

While prisoners starved, were beaten to death or shot, died of disease or were subjected to medical experimentation, Höss and his family lived in a two-story villa a short distance from Auschwitz I and within easy sight of the crematorium. When Höss became the commandant at Auschwitz, he and Hedwig had four children: Klaus, 10, Heidetraut, 8, Inge-Brigitt, 6, and Hans-Jurgen, 3. Their fifth child, Annegret Höss, was born November 7, 1943. Their home was decorated with furniture and artwork stolen from prisoners. The Höss family enjoyed the services of cooks, nannies, gardeners, chauffeurs, seamstresses, haircutters and cleaners, some of whom were prisoners. From time to time, Höss and Hedwig entertained Himmler and other SS dignitaries at the villa.[58]

Despite the grotesque appearance of contented family life in the shadow of abject depravity, Höss wrote that he was "no longer happy in Auschwitz once the mass exterminations had begun." Despite this claim, by all appearances, as Höss acknowledged, "…everyone in Auschwitz believed that the commandant lived a wonderful life." Höss conceded:

> My family, to be sure, were well provided for in Auschwitz. Every wish that my wife and children expressed was granted them. The children could live free and untrammeled life. My wife's garden was a paradise of flowers. The prisoners never missed an opportunity for doing some little act of kindness to my wife or children, and thus attracting their attention.
>
> …
>
> The children always kept animals in the garden, creatures the prisoners were forever bringing them. Tortoises, martens, cats, lizards: there was always something new and interesting to be seen there. In summer they splashed in the paddling pool in the garden or in the Sola [River]. But their greatest joy was when Daddy bathed with them.[59]

Photographs of Höss at Auschwitz after the gassing began do not show him to be an unhappy man. Aside from the mass exterminations in the gas chambers, it did not appear incongruous to Höss as he lived with his family in ease and comfort that tens of thousands of human beings over whom he

VII. Life Within the Wire

(Left to right) SS officers Richard Baer, Rudolf Höss and Karl Hoecker (courtesy U.S. Holocaust Memorial Museum, Washington, D.C.).

exercised complete control had insufficient potable water, were dying of starvation, slept on straw and boards covered with lice and suffered excruciating physical pain at the hands of unscrupulous Nazi doctors. Not one shred of evidence exists demonstrating that Höss attempted to alleviate any of the demonic conditions perpetrated at Auschwitz. Despite his own inherent love for and need to protect his family, he never empathized with the separation of loved ones at the train platform and the helplessness and terror imposed on men, women and children by the Nazis. If such humanity, buried deep down in his religious childhood, ever did pry its way into Höss' life, he ignored it in the name of Adolf Hitler and the Third Reich. Each day as hundreds of bodies were taken to the crematorium to be burned, Höss whispered to himself what he said aloud at Sachsenhausen: "Those are not people, they are inmates."

It is difficult, if not impossible, for those who did not endure Auschwitz to imagine the depth of hunger, deprivation, filth and desperation of its prisoners. As Höss happily played with his children, ate with his family and entertained Himmler, Auschwitz was eating away at human beings physically and mentally. Each day, people were suffering horrifically and needlessly. Lives with promise of love and joy were slowly being extinguished. Selfless, giving spirits were being transformed into cold, hardened souls.

Höss was aware of the appalling barbarity and deprivations and did nothing. Even more condemning is that he perceived what was devouring

(Left to right) SS officers Richard Baer, Josef Mengele, Josef Kramer, Rudolf Höss and Anton Thumann (courtesy U.S. Holocaust Memorial Museum, Washington, D.C.).

Auschwitz prisoners from the inside. Whether it was his own incarceration or his extensive experience in the Nazi concentration camp system, Höss knew full well that the tormented life imposed on Auschwitz inmates was destroying their souls. Höss said, "[Oh it] is not the physical hardships which make the prisoner's life so unbearable, but the indelible mental suffering caused by the tyranny and wickedness and meanness of indifference or malicious individuals among the guards and supervisors. The prisoner can cope with stern but impartial severity, however harsh it may be, but tyranny and manifestly unjust treatment affect his soul like a blow with a club." Eicke was right when he said no one was better qualified than Höss for work in a concentration camp.[60]

Primo Levi confessed, from the standpoint of one who withstood the many abominations of Auschwitz, how difficult it became to hang on to one's humanity:

> Survival without renunciation of any part of one's own moral world—apart from powerful and direct intervention by fortune—was conceded only to very few superior individuals, made of stuff of martyrs and saints.

Levi learned a valuable lesson about survival from a friend, Steinlauf:

> I suddenly see Steinlauf, my friend aged almost fifty, with nude torso, scrub his neck and shoulders with little success (he has no soap) but great energy. Steinlauf sees

me and greets me, and without preamble asks me severely why I do not wash. Why should I wash? Would I be better off than I am? Would I please someone more? Would I live a day, an hour longer?

Levi could not recall precisely how Steinlauf answered, but the meaning of his words remained with him. It was precisely because Auschwitz was a great machine intended to reduce them to beasts that they must not become beasts; that even in that place, one can survive, and, therefore, one must want to survive, to tell the story, to bear witness; and that to survive they must force themselves to save at least the skeleton, the scaffolding, the form of civilization. Although they are slaves, deprived of every right, exposed to every insult, condemned to certain death, they still possess one power, and they must defend it with all their strength, for it is the last: the power to refuse their consent. So, they must certainly wash their faces without soap in dirty water and dry themselves on their jackets. They must polish their shoes, not because the regulation demands it, but for dignity and propriety. They must walk erect, without dragging their feet, not in homage to Prussian discipline, but to remain alive, and to not begin to die.[61]

VIII

Crystal Death

Violence came naturally to the Nazis. They used brutal force to gain strength by suppressing opposition and to maintain power by eliminating any person or group who posed a threat. It was a small step for Hitler and the Nazis from the street violence of the SA to state-sponsored murder. As time passed, being an "enemy of the State" was not the only brand that caused an individual to be captured on Nazi radar and subjected to "special treatment." Hitler wanted Germany to be populated by Aryans with pure blood, blond hair and blue eyes. Being "undesirable" could take many forms. For those souls "unfortunate" enough to be born racially impure or with a physical deformity or mental illness, Hitler exercised his dictatorial power of execution.

In July 1939, approximately 5,000 German children, who displayed severe hereditary diseases or handicaps, were killed by tablets, injections and starvation. Beginning in October 1939, under what was known as the T4 program, about 65–70,000 psychiatric patients were put to death, many based upon the fact that they were Jews, Gypsies or non–European. The T4 program was used not only to kill the mentally ill but also the blind, deaf, epileptic and people with learning disabilities. The first use of poisonous gas to murder the mentally ill occurred in Poland in November 1939, little more than two months after Germany invaded that country. As early as June 1938, Jewish patients in psychiatric institutions were separated from other patients. Beginning in 1940, they were transported to killing centers regardless of their medical diagnosis or ability to work.[1]

The Nazis transferred the gas killing technology developed in the context of the euthanasia programs to the concentration camps. In the spring of 1941, at the prompting of Reichsführer-SS Heinrich Himmler, the T4 organization began to deploy medical commissions to four concentration camps. These medical commissions initiated a systematic selection and extermination of concentration camp prisoners.[2]

The killing of Jews by the Nazis began in earnest in the summer of 1941. In Operation Barbarossa, Hitler turned against his former ally by invading the Soviet Union in June 1941. Initial German success brought Latvia and Lithuania as well as parts of the Soviet Union within Nazi control. Following the German armies were several *Einsatzgruppen*, SS death squads. SS-Obergruppenführer Reinhard Heydrich, the chief of the Reich Main Security Office (RSHA), ordered the heads of these units to exterminate Communists and Jews. Local police and volunteers aided the *Einsatzgruppen*, as did, on occasion, the German Army—the Wehrmacht. In Kaunas, Lithuania, 3,800 Jews were shot between June 25 and June 28, 1941. On November 29–30 and December 8–9, 1941, almost 28,000 Jews were shot in the Rumbula Forest outside Riga, Latvia. At Babi Yar in Kiev, Ukraine, over 33,000 Jews were shot between September 29 and 30, 1941. By the end of 1941, the total number of Jewish men, women and children killed exceeded 500,000 and may have been as high as 800,000.[3]

Extermination Camps

As the killings continued, the Nazis determined that shooting was not an effective long-term solution for the extermination of large numbers of people. The problem, however, was not finding a more humane means of murder; Himmler was concerned about the strain that mass executions imposed on the perpetrators—SS men and police. Many were reporting sick, some had emotional breakdowns and some even committed suicide. One alternative— an attempt to kill mentally ill people near Minsk with explosives—led to predictable and terrible results. Mobile vans, which rerouted carbon monoxide from the engine exhaust directly into the enclosed vehicle, were used for a while beginning in November 1941.[4]

Auschwitz I was not intended as an extermination camp when it was constructed. In fact, even when Birkenau was built in 1941, there were no gas chambers or crematoria in the plans. At the start of 1942, the only operational extermination facility where poison gas was used for murder was at Chelmno, a camp 50 kilometers north of Lodz, Poland. The decision to build the first extermination camp in Belzec, Poland, where murder was to be carried out with exhaust fumes from a solidly mounted engine, was made in mid–October 1941 and work on the facility began in early November. Belzec began operating in March 1942, the same month work began on the Sobibor extermination camp. Killings started at Sobibor in May 1942 at the same time work began on the Treblinka extermination camp near Warsaw. Treblinka became operational in July 1942. Unlike Auschwitz, which housed prisoners for slave labor, the camps built at Belzec, Sobibor, Treblinka and Chelmno were built strictly for extermination.[5]

By Höss' own estimate, 70–80 percent of persons arriving in Auschwitz would die, most in the gas chamber. The exact number will never be determined, because victims selected upon arrival to go directly to the gas chamber were not registered. Unlike the early inmates of the concentration camps, these poor souls had not said or done anything against Hitler or the Nazis. They had committed no crime. They were Jews and had been labeled "enemies of the State" because of their religion and their race. For Höss, nothing else mattered. Even the children had to die, because, one day, they would grow up and constitute a threat. Hitler and Himmler had repeatedly warned Germans that the Jews would destroy Germany if Germany did not first destroy the Jews. Because Hitler said so, it must be true, according to Höss. Besides, an order of the Reichsführer-SS, in the name of the Führer, was sacred.[6]

Meeting with Himmler

At Nuremberg, Höss testified that, in the summer of 1941, he was summoned to Berlin to receive personal orders from Reichsführer-SS Himmler. Höss was told that Hitler had given the order for the "Final Solution" of the Jewish question and had chosen Auschwitz to implement the policy on account of its easy access by rail and also because the extensive site offered space for measures ensuring isolation. In his affidavits of March 14 and April 5, 1946, Höss specified the meeting with Himmler occurred in June 1941. Auschwitz records suggest the meeting took place in late July in Berlin. Höss' accuracy as to the date of the meeting has been questioned. In his affidavit of April 5, 1946, given at Nuremberg, Höss states that at the time he was summoned to Berlin by Himmler, the extermination camps at Belzec, Treblinka and Wolzek (Sobibor) were "already in the general government (German-occupied Poland)" (see Appendix II). In fact, those camps did not exist until 1942.[7]

Though Höss incorrectly stated that Belzec, Treblinka and Sobibor were in existence at the time of his meeting with Himmler, substantial reasons exist to believe that Höss accurately recollected that his meeting with Himmler occurred in the summer of 1941. By then, it was clear that Hitler intended to destroy, as opposed to merely emigrate, European Jews. In fact, Hitler told the world long before 1941 what he would do to the Jews if given the opportunity. There should be little doubt that, by the summer of 1941, Hitler, Göring, Goebbels, Himmler, Heydrich and the Nazis intended to murder European Jews.

In *Mein Kampf*, Hitler's hatred for the Jews was clearly expressed. He blamed them for the fall of Germany at the end of World War I and the failed German economy thereafter. On January 30, 1939, Hitler spoke at the Reichstag to the German Parliament and the German people and prophesied that if war was to break out, it would mean "the annihilation of the Jewish race throughout Europe." On October 25, 1941, Hitler hearkened back to his "prophecy," adding, "This race of criminals has the two million dead from the World War on its conscience and now hundreds of thousands more. Let nobody say to me: we can't send them into the swamps [in Russia]! Who's worrying about our people? It's good if the fear that we are exterminating the Jews goes before us." Joseph Goebbels, on November 16, 1941, in an article entitled "The Jews are to blame," referenced Hitler's January 1939 prediction: "At present we are experiencing the realization of this prophecy, and in the process, Jewry is suffering a fate, which may be harsh but is more than deserved. Pity or regret is entirely inappropriate in this case."[8]

On September 21, 1939, Chief of the Reich Main Security Office Reinhard Heydrich sent a memo to the Chiefs of the *Einsatzgruppen* regarding the Jewish question in the occupied territory. He indicated that "the planned overall measures (i.e., the final aim) are to be kept strictly secret." He referred to "(1) The final aim (which will require extended periods of time), and (2) The stages leading to the fulfillment of this final aim (which will be carried out in short terms)." Heydrich stated, in typical secretive Nazi fashion, "It is obvious that the tasks that lie ahead cannot be laid down in full detail from here." The *Einsatzgruppen* followed the Wehrmacht east in June 1941 into the Soviet Union, killing Jews from Latvia to the Ukraine. On July 17, 1941, Heydrich issued an order, *in accordance with Hitler's guidelines of March 30, 1941*, to shoot all Soviet prisoners of war who might be a threat to National Socialism, as well as Russian intelligentsia, agitators or fanatical Communists and Jews.[9]

On July 31, 1941, Reich Marshal Herman Göring sent a memorandum to Heydrich "to solve the Jewish question by *emigration* and *evacuation* in the most favorable way possible." Heydrich was authorized to make all necessary preparations "for a total solution of the Jewish question in the German sphere of influence in Europe."[10] As became clear at the Wannsee Conference in January 1942, a meeting convened to bring other Nazi officials "on board" with Jewish genocide, "evacuation" meant murder. There could be no question what Göring intended. Certainly, Himmler would have known in June 1941 that Nazi policy going forward was extermination of the Jews. The "benefit of the doubt" does not weigh in favor of Hitler and the Nazis. The existence of a written document that can be heralded as "smoking gun" proof of Hitler's intention to begin the Final Solution is hardly necessary. Abundant evidence suggests that by the time Germany launched Operation Barbarossa, Himmler, Göring, Goebbels and Heydrich were aware of Hitler's mandate to eliminate all European Jews, a plan in which they fully concurred and wholeheartedly participated.

Clearly, Höss was wrong when, looking back in 1945, he said that Belzec, Treblinka and Sobibor were already in existence in 1941. That misstatement does not mean he was wrong about the date of the meeting with Himmler. No one disputes that Höss did, in fact, meet with Himmler in the summer of 1941 in Berlin. If that meeting had some purpose other than to discuss the use of Auschwitz in exterminating Jews, no one has speculated what that purpose could have been. Meetings in Berlin between camp commandants and the Reichsführer-SS would not have been customary.

The fact that Auschwitz did not yet have the mechanism in place for mass murder also does not undermine Höss' statement that Himmler told him in the summer of 1941 that Auschwitz would become central to Hitler's Holocaust plan. Himmler told Höss that Adolf Eichmann would meet with Höss to give him further details. Auschwitz records establish that, in late summer 1941, Eichmann traveled to Auschwitz to visit with Höss. At that time, Eichmann told Höss he could not give him the starting date for the operation because "everything was still in the preliminary stages and the Reichsführer-SS had not yet issued the necessary orders."[11]

SS-Obersturmbannführer Adolf Eichmann played a pivotal role in the deportation of Jews from their homes and transportation to Auschwitz for extermination. The Gestapo was Office IV of the Reich Security Head Office under the direct command of Heinrich Müller. Section B of the Gestapo dealt with political churches, sects and Jews, and B4 was responsible for Jewish affairs, matters of evacuation, means of suppressing enemies of the people and state and dispossession of rights of German citizenship. The head of B4 of the Gestapo was Eichmann, who had direct operational responsibility for the extermination of European Jewry. His primary function was to round up the Jews and deport them to the great extermination centers established under Himmler's orders.[12]

When Eichmann traveled to Auschwitz several weeks after the Höss-Himmler meeting, he and Höss discussed how the Final Solution should be carried out. Eichmann told Höss where the transports would come from and how many transports to expect. According to Eichmann, the initial victims would arrive from eastern Upper Silesia and neighboring parts of Poland under German rule. In fact, the first train of Jews came from Upper Silesia in February 1942, as did the deportees throughout May and June. Höss and Eichmann agreed the killing should be accomplished by gas since shooting put too much strain on the SS. Eichmann mentioned that mobile vans had been used to kill people. The use of fake showers that would dispense carbon monoxide was discussed but was determined to be unworkable. The matter was left unresolved. Höss and Eichmann also identified a farmhouse which would be used as the initial gas chamber in Birkenau.[13]

Events at Auschwitz during this time were consistent with mass extermination. August 1941 saw the first experiments at Auschwitz of killing prisoners by phenol injections to the heart. More significantly, a use

VIII. Crystal Death

was found for Zyklon B, a pesticide, that would be consistent with the planned use of Auschwitz for implementation of the Final Solution. Zyklon B came in the form of crystals stored in airtight sealed metal tins and was initially deployed starting in July 1941 in the battle against vermin to disinfect housing and clothes. The manufacturer was Deutsche Gesellschaft für Schädlingsbekämpfung (Degesch) (German Pest Control Company) in Frankfurt am Main, a subsidiary of I. G. Farben. At a temperature of about 26 degrees Celsius, the hydrogen cyanide (prussic acid) granules turned into gas upon contact with air and was deadly even in small quantities. In late August 1941, while Höss was away from camp, SS-Obersturmführer Karl Fritzsch, on his own initiative, successfully tested Zyklon B on a small group of prisoners.[14]

Fritzsch repeated the experiment on September 3 in the cellar of Block 11 with 250 ill inmates and 600 Soviet POWs. After the gas was thrown into the cells with the prisoners, the doors were locked and sealed. The next morning, the doors were opened. All but one prisoner was dead. More Zyklon B was thrown in to kill the last prisoner. After the gas cleared, other prisoners transported the bodies to the crematorium. Incineration of the bodies of the victims took several days. On September 16, another 900 Soviet POWs were gassed in the mortuary next to the crematorium. Within a relatively short time after Höss' meetings with Himmler and Eichmann, an established method for killing large numbers of people was discovered at Auschwitz, further substantiating Höss' timeline.[15]

Höss observed the second and third gassings with Zyklon B:

Used Zyklon B canisters (author photograph).

> Protected by a gas mask, I watched the killing myself. In the crowded cells death came instantaneously the moment the Cyclon B was thrown in. A short, almost smothered cry, and it was all over. During this first experience of gassing people, I did not fully realize what was happening, perhaps because I was too impressed by the whole procedure.

He provided more detail of the exterminations at the mortuary:

> The Russians were ordered to undress in an anteroom; they then quietly entered the mortuary, for they had been told they were to be deloused. The whole transport exactly filled the mortuary to capacity. The doors were then sealed, and the gas shaken down through the holes in the roof. I do not know how long this killing took. For a little while a humming sound could be heard. When the powder was thrown in, there were cries of "Gas!," then a great bellowing, and the trapped prisoners hurled themselves against both the doors. But the doors held. They were opened several hours later, so that the place might be aired. It was then that I saw, for the first time, gassed bodies in the mass.[16]

Höss seemed relieved by what he had seen, even though he said it made him shudder and feel uncomfortable:

> I had always thought that the victims would experience a terrible choking sensation. But the bodies, without exception, showed no signs of convulsion. The doctors explained to me that the prussic acid had a paralyzing effect on the lungs, but its action was so quick and strong that death came before the convulsions could set in, and in this its effects differed from those produced by carbon monoxide or by a general oxygen deficiency.

Höss could relax; his extermination problem was solved:

> I must even admit that this gassing set my mind at rest for the mass extermination of the Jews was to start soon and at that time neither Eichmann nor I was certain how these mass killings were to be carried out. It would be by gas but we did not know which gas or how it was to be used. Now we had the gas, and we had established a procedure. I always shuddered at the prospect of carrying out extermination by shooting, when I thought of the vast numbers concerned, and of the women and children.... I was therefore relieved to think that we were to be spared all these blood-baths, and that the victims too would be spared suffering until their last moment came.[17]

First Mass Killings of Jews

The crematorium mortuary, rather than the cellar of Block 11, remained the gas chamber for Auschwitz for the rest of 1941. Höss did not want to move hundreds of bodies down the main street of Auschwitz from Block 11 to the crematorium when the mortuary was in the same building. The Block 11 cellar also lacked proper ventilation. Unlike the carbon monoxide gas chamber, with its system of pipes and perforated vents and its cumbersome gas cylinders, the hydrocyanide gas chamber required only a small porthole through which to drop the Zyklon B crystals. The morgue in the Stammlager had a flat roof; three square portholes were pierced in the earth and concrete ceiling, then covered with tightly fitting wooden lids. Also, only a month or so earlier, the morgue had been equipped with a new and powerful ventilation system which not only removed the foul air but also brought in fresh air from the outside. Such a ventilation system was ideal for extracting the poisonous gas. When the killing was done, Auschwitz I was closed off. Noisy engines ran and horns blared to drown out the screams of the dying prisoners. When the use of Zyklon B started, no one knew how much was needed to kill a human being. Experience taught that four kilograms, about nine pounds, would destroy 1,000 individuals.[18]

In January 1942, at the Wannsee Conference outside Berlin, Reinhard Heydrich formalized the Final Solution to the Jewish problem for senior party officials and other members of the SS. They were obligated to use their resources to facilitate "evacuation" (murder) of the Jews, who would begin arriving in Auschwitz soon after the conference. On February 15, 1942, the first transport of Jews from Beuthen (part of Germany before World War II but given to Poland after the war) arrived. They were told to leave their bags on the train platform and were then led to the crema-

Gas chamber at Auschwitz I (author photograph).

torium and killed with Zyklon B. They received what many called "special treatment." Himmler did not like this term. When he saw the phrase "special treatment" refer to the extermination of the Jews on a report, Himmler changed it to reflect that the Jews who were killed had "passed through" the camps.[19]

SS-Unterscharführer Pery Broad, a member of the Political Department at Auschwitz, described how the Beuthen Jews "passed through" Auschwitz I on February 15, 1942:

> From the first company of the SS-Totenkopfsturmbann, stationed in the Auschwitz concentration camp, the sergeant-major SS-Hauptscharführer Veupel selected six particularly trusty men. Among them were those who had been members of the Black General SS for years. They had to report to SS-Hauptscharführer Hössler. After their arrival, Hössler insistently cautioned them to preserve the utmost secrecy as to what they would see in the next few minutes. Otherwise death would be their lot. The task of the six men was to keep all roads and streets completely closed around an area near the Auschwitz crematorium. Nobody should be allowed to pass there, regardless of rank. The offices in the buildings from which the crematorium was visible were evacuated. No inmate of the SS garrison hospital was allowed to come near the windows of the first floor which looked on the roof of the nearby crematorium and on the yard of that gloomy place. Everything was made ready and Hössler himself made sure that no uncalled-for persons should enter the closed area. Then a sad procession walked along the streets of the camp. It had started at the railway siding, located between the garrison storehouse and the German Armaments Works, and branching out from the main railway line, which led to the camp. There, at the ramp, cattle vans were being unloaded and people who had arrived in them were slowly marching towards their unknown destination. All of them had large, yellow Jewish stars on their miserable clothes. Their worn faces showed that they had suffered many a hardship. The majority were elderly people. From their conversation one could gather that up to their unexpected transportation hither they had been employed in factories, that they were willing to go on working and to be useful as much as they could. A few guards without guns, but with pistols well hidden in their pockets, escorted the procession to the crematorium. The SS men promised the people, who were beginning to feel more hopeful, that they would be employed at suitable work, according to their occupations. Explicit instructions as to their behavior were given the SS men by Hössler. Up till then the guards treated new arrivals very roughly, trying to "keep them at arm's length" with blows, but there were no uncivil words at that moment. The more fiendish the whole plan! Both leaves of the big entrance gate to the crematorium were wide open. Suspecting nothing the column marched in, in lines of five persons, and stood in the yard. Somewhat nervously the SS-guard at the entrance waited for the last man to enter the yard. Quickly he shut the gate and bolted it. Grabner and Hössler were standing on the roof of the crematorium. Grabner spoke to the Jews who unsuspectingly awaited their fate.
>
> "You will now bathe and be disinfected, we don't want any epidemics in the camp. Then you will be brought to your barracks and get some hot soup. You will be employed in accordance with your professional qualifications. Now undress and put your clothes in front of you on the ground."
>
> They willingly followed those instructions, given them in a friendly, warm-hearted

voice. Some looked forward to the soup, others were glad that their nerve-racking uncertainty as to their immediate future was over and that their worst expectations were not realized. All felt relieved after their days full of anxiety. Grabner and Hössler continued from the roof to give friendly advice which had a calming effect upon the people. "Put your shoes close to your clothes bundle, so that you can find them after the bath." "Is the water warm? Of course, warm showers. What is your trade? A shoemaker? We need them urgently, report to me immediately after!" Such words dispelled last doubts or lingering suspicions. The first lines entered the mortuary through the hall. Everything was extremely tidy. But the specific smell made some of them uneasy. They looked in vain for showers or water pipes affixed to the ceiling. The hall meanwhile was getting packed. Several SS men had entered with them, full of jokes and small talk. They inobtrusively kept their eyes on the entrance. As soon as the last person had entered, they disappeared without much ado. Suddenly the door was closed. It had been made tight with rubber and secured with iron fittings. Those inside heard the heavy bolts being secured. They were screwed to with screws, making the door air-tight. A deadly, paralyzing terror spread among the victims. They started to beat upon the door, in helpless rage and despair they hammered with their fists upon it. Derisive laughter was the only reply. Somebody shouted through the door, "Don't get burnt, while you take your bath!" Several victims noticed that covers had been removed from the six holes in the ceiling. They uttered a loud cry of terror when they saw a head in a gas-mask in one opening. The "disinfectors" were at work. One of them was SS-Unterscharführer Teuer, decorated with the Cross of War Merit. With a chisel and a hammer they opened a few innocuously looking tins which bore the inscription "Cyclon, to be used against vermin. Attention, poison! To be opened by trained personnel only!" The tins were filled to the brim with blue granules the size of peas. Immediately after opening the tins, their contents were thrown into the holes which were then quickly covered. Meanwhile Grabner gave a sign to the driver of a lorry, which had stopped close to the crematorium. The driver started the motor and its deafening noise was louder than the death cries of the hundreds of people inside being gassed to death. Grabner looked with the interest of a scientist upon the second hand of his wrist watch. Cyclon acted swiftly. It consists of cyanide hydrogen in solid form. As soon as the tin was emptied, the prussic acid escaped from the granules. One of the men, who participated in the bestial gassing, could not refrain from lifting, for the fraction of a second, the cover of one of the vents and from spitting into the hall. Some two minutes later the screams became less loud and only an indistinct groaning was heard. The majority of the gassed had already lost their consciousness. Two minutes more and Grabner stopped looking at his watch. There was complete silence. The lorry had driven away. The guards were called off, and the cleaning squad started to sort out the clothes, so tidily put down in the yard of the crematorium. Busy SS men and civilians working in the camp were again passing the mound, planted with greenery, on the artificial slopes of which young trees peacefully swayed in the wind. Extremely few knew what terrible event had taken place there, only some minutes ago, and what sight the mortuary below the green sward would present. Sometime later the exhausts had extracted the gas and the prisoners, working in the crematorium, opened the door to the mortuary. The corpses, their mouths wide open, were leaning one upon the other. They were especially close to one another near the door, where in their deadly fright they had crowded to force it. The prisoners of the crematorium squad worked like robots, apathetically and without a trace of emotion. It was difficult to tug the corpses from the mortuary, as their twisted limbs had grown stiff with the gas. Thick smoke clouds poured from the chimney. This was the beginning in 1942![20]

Birkenau

The crematorium at the Stammlager could not accommodate the transports of Jews that were expected. Other arrangements had to be made. In February 1942, Hans Kammler, a deputy to Oswald Pohl in the WVHA, arrived at Auschwitz to discuss an alternative location. Two Birkenau farmhouses which belonged to Polish peasants before they had been evicted were converted into gas chambers—Bunker I and Bunker II. Höss had identified Bunker I as a potential site for gas chambers when Eichmann first visited Auschwitz in August 1941. Bunker I was an unplastered brick building with a tile roof, nicknamed the "little red house," and was the smaller of the two. At first, victims of the little red house were forced to undress in the open behind makeshift walls of straw and tree branches before entering the gas chambers. Later, two barracks were built as undressing rooms. On March 3, 1942, gas chambers were utilized at Birkenau for the first time at Bunker I.[21]

The March 3 transport of Polish Jews was taken from the unloading platform at the freight depot in Auschwitz directly to Bunker I without undergoing a selection. The transport was supervised by Deputy Commandant Hans Aumeier and SS-Hauptscharführer Gerhard Palitzsch, as well as some block leaders. They talked with the Jews about general topics, enquiring as to their qualifications and trades, intending to mislead them and ease their fears. After gassing, the corpses were buried in mass graves in the nearby meadow.[22]

Bunker I was also used to kill sick inmates. In the past, the invalids, chronically ill and handicapped prisoners had been transported several hundred miles to facilities such as the Sonnenstein Euthanasia Center in eastern Germany, where they were gassed by carbon monoxide. Once Bunker I became operational, it was only necessary to drive them the short distance to Birkenau. An "isolation station" was used to hold new arrivals before transport to Bunker I. From there, sick prisoners were loaded onto trucks, brought to Bunker I and killed.[23]

The second, larger farmhouse, Bunker II, was modified into gas chambers several months later due to ever-increasing demand. Bunker II was a brick building that had been plastered and, therefore, nicknamed the "little white house." Bunkers I and II were surrounded by woods. Three barracks that served as dressing rooms were nearby. Once both facilities were operational, 2,000 people could be gassed at once—800 in Bunker I and 1,200 in Bunker II.[24]

Signs were posted on the gas chamber doors to warn and to mislead.

Outside the entrance, a sign read "Hochspannung—Lebensgefahr" (High Tension—Lethal Danger) to prevent anyone from accidentally opening the chamber filled with dead bodies and gas. Inside, visible to the victims as they entered, was the sign "Zur Baden" (To the Baths). The sign on the exit door, "Zur Desinfektion" (To the Disinfection), continued the deceit. Beyond that door lay the pits for burning dead bodies.[25]

Crematoria

At the end of the summer of 1942, construction plans at Auschwitz were modified. The new plans included building four crematoria. Crematoria II and III (crematorium I being the original facility in the Stammlager) were surrounded by their own barbed-wire fences. Two gates led to crematorium II and one gate to crematorium III. Trees and bushes were planted around the crematoria in an effort to screen them from prisoners who lived in adjoining barracks. A common fence enclosed crematoria IV, which was built next to the little white house, and crematorium V, which was built next to the little red house. Crematoria IV and V were also screened from view by a tall hedge which concealed the bodies that were burned outside.[26]

Crematoria II and III were constructed according to nearly identical and symmetrical plans. They consisted of three principal parts: the dressing room, the gas chamber and the crematoria. The dressing room and gas chamber were underground. The two underground rooms were made of reinforced concrete and covered with grass turf. Victims were led down a flight of steps to the dressing room. Along the walls were wooden benches and hooks to hang their clothes. The dressing room was nearly twice as large as the gas chamber to enable the victims to undress in relatively uncramped conditions. Both the gas chamber and the dressing room were mechanically ventilated. The outlet of the ventilation shafts was situated above the roof of the crematorium. A narrow passage connected the dressing room with the gas chamber.[27]

The entrance door to the gas chamber included a circular peephole, made of two glass plates 8 mm thick and airproofed with rubber gaskets. After several incidents in which the victims trapped inside broke the glass, the peephole was covered with a semicircular grille on the gas chamber side. The doors were shut by means of iron bolts, which also served as door handles, and secured with screws. The inside walls of the gas chamber were plastered and whitewashed. Electrical installations and lamps were located on both sides of the bearing beam, and perforated plates mounted on wooden blocks were installed beneath the ceiling to look like showers. Ventilation shafts were situated where the walls met the ceiling and the floor. The gas

Crematorium II and gas chambers at Auschwitz II-Birkenau (courtesy Yad Vashem-the Holocaust Heroes' and Martyrs' Remembrance Authority).

chambers in crematoria II and III could accommodate approximately 2,000 human beings each at one time.[28]

Zyklon B was distributed in the gas chamber through four columns custom-made in the metalwork shops of the camp. They were shaped like pillars and made of two wire grids with a movable core. They were fastened to the floor and passed through openings in the ceiling, appearing outside as small chimneys closed with a concrete cover equipped with two handles. The bottom of the core was flat, and the top was a cone. When Zyklon B pellets were dropped into the cone, they spread uniformly throughout the core. After the gas evaporated, the entire core was removed from the gas chamber and the used pellets were poured out.[29]

An elevator carried bodies up to the furnace room. When Dr. G. M. Gilbert, the Nuremberg psychologist, asked Höss how it was possible to kill so many people. Höss replied, coldly, that killing was not the problem; it was disposing of the bodies that took time. He needed better crematoria. To increase the burning capacity of the ovens, camp authorities recommended that the incineration time be reduced to 20 minutes and the number of bodies incinerated in each oven be increased to three, depending on the size of the body. As a result, the capacity of the crematoria almost doubled, reaching about 8,000 bodies in 24 hours. Crematorium II housed a room where Josef Mengele dissected twins, while a similar room in crematorium III was used to

VIII. Crystal Death

Ovens in new crematorium at Auschwitz II–Birkenau (Photo Archives, Auschwitz-Birkenau State Museum, www.auschwitz.org).

melt gold extracted from the teeth of the dead. In 24 hours, about 2,500 could be cremated in crematorium II and 2,500 in crematorium III. Crematoria IV and V, which were smaller, could incinerate about 1,500 bodies each in 24 hours. Höss recalled:

> During the period when the fires were kept burning continuously, without a break, the ashes fell through the grates and were constantly removed and crushed to powder. The ashes were taken in lorries to the Vistula, where they immediately drifted away and dissolved.[30]

None of the crematoria was completed and operational prior to March 1943. Höss told Dr. Leon Goldensohn, the Nuremberg psychiatrist, that the delay in the construction of the crematoria required that he find other solutions to the ever-increasing number of dead bodies. He stated:

> I believed that crematoriums could be erected fast and so wanted to burn the corpses in the mass graves in the crematory, but when I saw that the crematory could not be erected fast enough to keep up with the ever-increasing numbers exterminated, we started to burn the corpses in open ditches like in Treblinka. A layer of wood, then a layer of corpses, another layer of corpses, et cetera. To start the fire we used a bundle of straw dipped in gasoline. The fire was usually started with about five layers of wood and five layers of corpses. When the fire was going strong, the fresh corpses which came from the gas chambers could merely be thrown on the fire and would burn by themselves.

In March 1943, the old crematorium at Auschwitz I was shut down. Bunkers I and II were used until spring 1943. At that time, Bunker I (the little red house) was demolished. Bunker II would come back into use in May 1944 during the most prolific killing period Auschwitz would ever see.[31]

In early 1943, Höss visited Treblinka, a camp built for extermination only, to determine if it held any advantages over Auschwitz. He noted the chambers were small compared to those at Auschwitz, only about eight feet by eleven feet. Along the side of the extermination chambers, motors from old tanks or trucks were set up, and the gases of the motors, the exhaust, was directed into the cells. Höss estimated that about 200 people were forced into each of the cells. Men were killed separately from the women and children. Höss recalled 10 such chambers with no peek holes, just big doors covered with metal sheeting. The victims were kept in these chambers with the motors running for one hour, and then the doors were opened. By that time, everyone inside was dead. As at Auschwitz, the bodies were buried at first, then later burned in open quarries or ditches.[32]

In his affidavit of April 5, 1946, (see Appendix II) given to the prosecutor at Nuremberg, Höss spoke with pride of the "improvements" he made at Auschwitz as compared to Treblinka. Instead of carbon monoxide gas, he used Zyklon B, which killed in 3 to 15 minutes, depending upon climatic conditions, rather than almost an hour. Once the screaming stopped, they knew the people inside were dead. Also, Auschwitz gas chambers could accommodate 2,000 people at one time, whereas the 10 gas chambers at Treblinka could only hold 200 people each. Finally, at Treblinka, the victims knew they were going to be killed. At Auschwitz, Höss said, "we endeavored to fool the victims into thinking that they were to go through a delousing process." Even without Höss' innovations, it is estimated that between 700,000 and 900,000 Jews were murdered at Treblinka between July 1942 and late 1943 when Treblinka closed. By the end of 1943, the Nazis closed the death camps built for the sole purpose of killing Jews. After that point in time, Auschwitz remained the only camp for exterminating European Jews.[33]

Selection

On May 4, 1942, the first selection took place at Birkenau. Train transports that carried the victims were unloaded at the ramp of the freight railway station situated 2.5 kilometers from the bunkers. When transports arrived at night, the victims were hauled in trucks to the killing site. During the day, trucks were only used to transport victims who were unable to walk the distance on their own. The able-bodied were walked past the barracks of the Birkenau camp then under construction and across the meadows. The

Sonderkommando, prisoners themselves, helped the elderly and infirm undress prior to going into the gas chamber. Those who were too weak or infirm or handicapped to walk to the gas chambers were loaded into trucks and literally dumped out. The Sonderkommando then held the victims while the SS shot them in the back of the neck, one by one. In tragic irony, the marching column was accompanied by a car with the emblem of the International Red Cross. The car carried the Zyklon B and an SS doctor with medicines and an oxygen bottle for use in case SS guards taking part in the gassing were accidentally poisoned.[34]

For Höss and the Nazis, the extermination of European Jews was a mechanical process. Unload a transport of Jews, divide them by gender, select who is fit to work and gas the rest. Deceiving all of them as to the fate of those found unfit to work was necessary to maintain order. Humanity was not a consideration. Upon arrival at Auschwitz, the victims were told they must bathe and undergo delousing before entering the camp. They were directed towards the innocent-looking buildings towards the back of the camp. On the way to the gas chamber some victims were even issued a piece of soap and a towel. Once they arrived at the gas chamber, the victims were told to undress. Höss said, "In the undressing room, prisoners of the special detachment, detailed for this purpose, would tell them in their own language that they were

Jewish women and children from Subcarpathian Rus selected for death walk toward the gas chambers at Auschwitz II–Birkenau (courtesy Yad Vashem–the Holocaust Heroes' and Martyrs' Remembrance Authority).

going to be bathed and deloused, that they must leave their clothes neatly together and above all remember where they had put them, so that they would be able to find them again quickly after delousing."

Reluctant victims could be subjected to beatings or were attacked by dogs. If anyone became too suspicious and caused trouble, he or she could be taken aside and dispatched with a small caliber pistol shot (to minimize the noise) administered to the back of the neck. Even with the normally effective efforts at deception, many of the victims became frightened. Shlomo Venezia, a member of the Sonderkommando, recalled seeing families in front of Bunker II: "People were forced to get undressed where they were, in front of the door. The children were crying. You could feel the fear and dread; people were really helpless and terrified." As a rule, women and children went in first, followed by the men. If the men were to become suspicious or panic, it was unlikely they would resist without their loved ones who were already inside the gas chamber. Each group was led inside behind a cordon of SS men that edged toward the door as the chamber filled. The Sonderkommando went inside to act as interpreters, answer questions (usually vaguely or untruthfully) and help anyone who needed assistance. Seeing them go inside was reassuring to the victims. They would slip out before the door was shut.[35]

Jewish woman walks towards gas chambers with three young children and a baby in her arms at Auschwitz II–Birkenau (courtesy U.S. Holocaust Memorial Museum, Washington, D.C.).

VIII. Crystal Death

When the chamber was full or the entire transport was inside and the personnel had left, the doors were shut, the bolts were slid into place and the screws were tightened. On order of the supervising SS doctor, the SS disinfectors opened the Zyklon B cans and poured their contents into the roof vents down the induction shafts inside the chamber. Johann Paul Kremer, one of the Nazi physicians, kept a diary. Upon observing his first selection on September 2, 1942, Kremer commented, "In comparison with it Dante's Inferno seems to be almost a comedy. Auschwitz is justly called an extermination camp!"[36]

In addition to assisting victims as they met their fate in the gas chambers, the Sonderkommando performed the sad, gruesome task of removing the bodies from the gas chambers to be buried. In the beginning, after covering any trace of the crime, Sonderkommandos, or Special Detachments, as they were also called, were taken to the infirmary and stood in a line in front of the clinic. The SS told them they would receive strengthening injections for the exhausting work. Members of the Sonderkommando were then killed in the prisoners' infirmary with a phenol injection to the heart. The Nazis wanted no witnesses. Later groups of Sonderkommandos would be allowed to live, but in barracks separate from other prisoners to maintain the secrecy

Jewish women and children from Subcarpathian Rus selected for death walk toward gas chambers at Auschwitz II–Birkenau (courtesy U.S. Holocaust Memorial Museum, Washington, D.C.).

of the demonic work they were forced to perform. The life of a Sonderkommando was generally four months. Although the SS men responsible for the operations were sworn to strict secrecy, the killing process became known to many prisoners.[37]

Survivor Kitty Hart said that, as ridiculous as it seemed, no one in the camp was supposed to know about the gas chambers and crematoria. A trusted kapo overheard talking about extermination chambers could herself be shot, beaten to death on the spot or taken away to be gassed. Any other prisoner who even mentioned the subject would be gassed for having dared to suggest that gassing occurred. Yet every day the prisoners witnessed the trains bringing more and more people who left their luggage on the platform and walked to the crematorium, never to be seen again. Each incoming transport was followed by a glow in the sky from the cremations and the stench of burning flesh. No matter what they knew, the Auschwitz prisoners could say nothing about the "special treatment." As Hart observed, "The SS wanted no panic and no stampeding mobs: keep everything tidy, steady and methodical."[38]

Systematic selections began in earnest at Auschwitz on July 4, 1942. Despite the nauseating smell, human ash falling from the sky, pollution of

Jewish women and children from Subcarpathian Rus selected for death walk toward the gas chambers at Auschwitz II–Birkenau (courtesy U.S. Holocaust Memorial Museum, Washington, D.C.).

rivers and death of wildlife caused by the buried remains and occasional word spread by escapees, Höss and the Nazis were amazingly successful in concealing their mass murder operation. At the Auschwitz station, the train filled with deportees was first moved onto a side track. There, locomotives were swapped, and the railway staff took over the carriages. A team of three, sometimes four, officials accompanied the transports to the camp. These men were present when the SS drove the inmates out of the carriages, witnessed the selection process and watched the prisoners walking to the crematoria. They brought the empty carriages back to the station, where the duty foreman of the goods dispatch office was waiting for them. The engineers who brought the train from the ghettoes and took them back again never saw the flames leaping from the crematoria or smelled the burning bodies. At the other end of the process, mass graves, screened from view by hedges, were located near Bunker I and Bunker II. The burial sites were later replaced by incinerating pits. Small trolleys or flatbed trucks that rolled on narrow-gauge tracks transported the corpses from the gas chambers to the pits.[39]

Mass Graves

During the summer of 1942, bodies were still being placed in mass graves. According to Filip Müller, a member of the Sonderkommando, at that time:

> the hot sun began to burn, the corpses started to swell and the earth's crust to burst open. A black, evil-smelling mass oozed out and polluted the ground water in the vicinity. One day we were ordered to take several barrels of chlorinated lime there. Large quantities of this chemical were spread over the decomposing bodies but to no avail.

The bodies would later be removed, and the Sonderkommandos who performed the task were murdered.[40]

On July 17–18, 1942, Himmler made his second visit to Auschwitz. Höss recalled that the Reichsführer-SS "watched every detail of the whole process of destruction from the time when the prisoners were unloaded to the emptying of Bunker II." According to Höss, he constantly drew Himmler's attention to the problems in the camp. Himmler saw the emaciated victims of disease, the crowded hospital block, the overcrowded huts and the primitive and insufficient latrines and washhouses. He was furious at Höss' perpetual complaints of the miserable conditions in the camp and said: "I want to hear no more about difficulties! An SS officer does not recognize difficulties; when they arise, his task is to remove them at once by his own efforts! How this is to be done is your worry and not mine!" Yet for all Höss' whining,

Himmler could see he was doing a good job. Himmler promoted Höss to SS-Obersturmbannführer (Lieutenant Colonel).[41]

One problem that required Höss' immediate attention was the mass graves that proved unsatisfactory for body disposal. Shortly after Himmler's visit, SS-Standartenführer Paul Blobel, who helped organize the Babi Yar massacre in late September 1941 in Kiev, Ukraine, where 33,771 Jews were murdered in two days, arrived from Eichmann's office. He carried an order from the Reichsführer-SS stating that all the mass graves were to be opened and the corpses burned. In addition, the ashes were to be disposed of in such a way that it would be impossible at some future time to calculate the number of corpses that had been burned. Blobel had been placed in charge of what was known as Aktion 1005—to find and destroy all the mass graves in the eastern districts. Blobel had already experimented with different methods of cremation at the Chelmno facility, and Eichmann had authorized him to show Höss the apparatus he used. Höss went to Chelmno in mid–September 1942, accompanied by SS-Obersturmführer Franz Hössler.[42]

Blobel constructed various makeshift ovens fueled by wood and petrol. He even attempted to dispose of the bodies with explosives, but, as Höss stated in his memoirs, "their destruction had been very incomplete." The ashes were distributed over the neighboring countryside after first being ground to a powder in a bone mill. The work itself was carried out by a special detachment of Jews who were shot after each section of the work was completed. Auschwitz was continuously called upon to provide Jews for Aktion 1005. On his visit to Chelmno, Höss was also shown the mobile killing vans—trucks designed to kill by using the exhaust gases from the engines. The officer in charge there, however, described this method as being extremely unreliable, because the density of the gas varied considerably and was often insufficient to be lethal.[43]

By the end of September 1942, bodies at Auschwitz were being burned, first on wood pyres, bearing some 2,000 corpses, and later in pits with bodies previously buried. Oil refuse ignited the fire in the beginning; later, methanol was used. The inmates of the Sonderkommando also doused the corpses with the body fat that flowed from the pyres, so they would burn better. Cremation of bodies in the pits continued day and night. By the end of November, all the mass graves had been emptied. The number of corpses disinterred and burned totaled 107,000. This figure included Jews killed in the gas chambers, as well as Stammlager prisoners who died during the winter of 1941–42 and the Birkenau dead. The ashes of the dead were dumped into the Vistula and Sola rivers.[44]

Approximately 1,400 prisoners were used to unbury the dead and burn the corpses. They worked with their bare hands, knee-deep in decomposing flesh, watched over by drunken SS men with whips and machine guns. Of the

VIII. Crystal Death

Burning of bodies at Auschwitz II–Birkenau (Photo Archives, Auschwitz-Birkenau State Museum, www.auschwitz.org).

1,400 prisoners, 1,100 were murdered on the job; the other 300 were killed when the job was complete. SS-Hauptscharführer Hössler was in charge. His mission was to open the graves and burn the corpses, maintaining the utmost secrecy about his job. He found 20 to 30 particularly reliable SS men to assist him and made them sign a pledge that if they betrayed their trust and spoke of the task they had been given, they would be put to death. These SS men were, of course, only expected to supervise; the prisoners would open the graves and burn the bodies. Even so, these SS guards received extra rations—one liter of milk, sausage, cigarettes and, of course, vodka to compensate them for their unholy task. Any prisoners who refused to participate were immediately shot. According to SS-Unterscharführer Pery Broad, "…one could, for long

Burial site of ashes at Auschwitz II–Birkenau (author photograph).

weeks, see dense, whitish smoke clouds rising towards the sky from several spots. Nobody was allowed to come near those places without a special pass, but the stench betrayed the truth about which people round Birkenau had begun to whisper."⁴⁵

Open air cremation was not a long-term solution. Höss noted, "During bad weather or when a strong wind was blowing, the stench of burning flesh was carried for many miles and caused the whole neighborhood to talk about the burning of Jews, despite official counter-propaganda." Even the SS, who were sworn to secrecy and threatened with the most severe punishment for revealing the truth, disclosed what was happening. German air defense sought to stop the fires, which attracted great attention at night. As long as the transports of Jews kept coming in large numbers, burning at night could not be avoided.⁴⁶

Resistance

Not all exterminations ran as smoothly as Höss wanted. On October 23, 1943, 1,800 Jews—men, women and children—arrived from the Bergen-Belsen concentration camp. They had received passports for departure to South

America through Switzerland. Most of them paid a high price for their visas, which had been approved by the Gestapo. The victims were ordered to prepare for departure and told their luggage would follow. Not until they arrived at the unloading platform did they understand that they had been taken to Auschwitz, a place known to and feared by some of them. As they were being unloaded and assembled to go into the undressing chamber, SS-Obersturmführer Franz Hössler, who commanded the women's camp and was playing the part of a representative of the Foreign Ministry, informed the people that the Swiss government insisted that everyone be disinfected before entry into Switzerland was permitted. He was very polite and with the most reassuring voice even told them that their train was scheduled to leave at 7:00 a.m. He gently urged them into the undressing chamber. The women were taken to crematorium II and the men to crematorium III.[47]

Apparently, not all the prisoners were convinced by Hössler's performance. The SS beat some of those who were reluctant to undress. One particularly attractive woman caught the eye of SS guards Walter Quackernack and Josef Schillinger. She began a seductive strip-tease act, first lifting her skirt and exposing her thigh to them, then removing her blouse. The two SS men stood in awe, with their eyes glued to her body. As she leaned against the pillar to remove her high-heeled shoes, she suddenly struck Quackernack in the forehead with the heel of her shoe, leapt on his falling body and snatched the pistol from its open holster.[48]

Quackernack was holding his bleeding face in both hands as the woman shot Schillinger. A second bullet narrowly missed Quackernack. She then disappeared into the crowd. Other women attacked the SS men with their bare hands; they bit one SS man on the nose and scratched the faces of others, forcing the SS men to call for reinforcements. As an SS guard tried to pull Schillinger out of the dressing room, another shot rang out wounding a third SS guard, Wilhelm Emmerich. The lights went out for some time. Moments later, machine guns and blinding spotlights were being set up in both doorways. The doors were flung open and the Sonderkommando trapped inside were ordered out. Höss pulled up in his car just as the machine guns opened fire inside the undressing chamber. The few who survived the hail of bullets were shot later. SS Sergeant Schillinger died on the way to the hospital.[49]

Höss and the Killing

Every night after the selections, the gassing and the burning of bodies, Höss went home to his family. According to his memoirs, if he was deeply affected by some incident, he would mount his horse and ride until the image was gone. Walking through the stables often provided him the relief he sought.

Höss claimed that "[w]hen at night I stood out there beside the transports, or by the gas-chambers or the fires, I was often compelled to think of my wife and children, without, however, allowing myself to connect them closely with all that was happening." Höss' third child, Inge-Brigitt, when interviewed in 2013, was convinced that her father was a sensitive man; she guessed he was involved with something bad. "I'm sure he was sad inside," she recalls. "It is just a feeling. The way he was at home, the way he was with us, sometimes he looked sad when he came back from work."[50]

Apparently, for a long time, Hedwig was not aware that her husband was overseeing the mass extermination of Jews. When she overheard someone at a party talking about the gassing, she confronted Höss, who admitted that Jews by the trainload were constantly arriving at Auschwitz and being sent to the gas chambers under his supervision. Höss explained to Hedwig as Himmler had told him the need to destroy the Jews before they destroyed Germany. After that conversation, Hedwig no longer had any desire for intimacy with Höss.[51]

Married life was not the only time Höss failed to show any passion. At Nuremberg on the witness stand and in his interviews with Drs. Leon Goldensohn and G. M. Gilbert discussing his role in the Final Solution, Höss spoke apathetically and with no emotion. If he ever placed any emphasis on his words, it was in repeatedly insisting, both at his trial and in his memoirs, that he was never cruel and never mistreated anyone. Knowing that the Nazi moral yardstick did not measure the same as the rest of humanity's, Höss' recollections regarding his personal experiences with people in the gas chamber are particularly interesting and enlightening when considering whether or not the horrors of Auschwitz weighed upon him:

> Many of the women hid their babies among the piles of clothing. The men of the Special Detachment were particularly on the look-out for this and would speak words of encouragement to the woman until they had persuaded her to take the child with her. The women believed that the disinfectant might be bad for their smaller children, hence their efforts to conceal them.
>
> The smaller children usually cried because of the strangeness of being undressed in this fashion, but when their mothers or members of the Special Detachment comforted them, they became calm and entered the gas chambers playing or joking with one another and carrying their toys.
>
> I noticed that women who either guessed or knew what awaited them nevertheless found the courage to joke with the children to encourage them, despite the mortal terror visible in their own eyes.
>
> ...
>
> One young woman caught my attention particularly as she ran busily hither and thither, helping the smallest children and the old women to undress. During the selection she had had two small children with her, and her agitated behavior and appearance had brought her to my notice at once. She did not look in the least like a Jewess. Now her children were no longer with her. She waited until the end,

VIII. Crystal Death

helping the women who were not undressed and who had several children with them, encouraging them and calming the children. She went with the very last ones into the gas-chamber. Standing in the doorway, she said:

"I knew all the time that we were being brought to Auschwitz to be gassed. When the selection took place I avoided being put with the able-bodied ones, as I wished to look after the children. I wanted to go through it all, fully conscious of what was happening. I hope that it will be quick. Goodbye!"[52]

As remarkable as was the courage this woman displayed, Höss chose to recite the story, as he did most events, as a simple matter of fact. He apparently found nothing particularly remarkable about this woman who could have lived, but chose to die while comforting others on their path to death. Höss could not recognize her selfless act. The strength and goodness of this Jew could not be reconciled with his belief that Jews were "untermensch"—inferior to Germans. It seems Höss talked about his experiences in proximity to the deaths of others in the hope he would be commended for his own courage.

Höss said he was compelled to:

watch hour after hour, by day and by night, the removal and burning of the bodies, the extraction of the teeth, the cutting of the hair, the whole grisly, interminable business. I had to stand for hours on end in the ghastly stench, while the mass graves were being opened and the bodies dragged out and burned.... I had to look through the peep-hole of the gas-chambers and watch the process of death itself, because the doctors wanted me to see it.

He acknowledged that he "had to appear cold and indifferent to events that must have wrung the hearts of anyone possessed of human feelings." When asked how he and his men could watch such torment and suffering, he replied that "the iron determination with which we must carry out Hitler's orders could only be obtained by a stifling of all human emotions." He almost came to regard pity as a betrayal of Hitler.[53]

Höss looked with an expressionless face at an old man who passed him and said, "Germany will pay a heavy penance for this mass murder of the Jews." The man's eyes were filled with hatred as he walked into the gas chamber.[54] Höss watched as innocent, helpless children were put to death (Appendix III). He recounted a woman who tried to throw her children out of the gas chamber as the door was closing. Weeping, she cried out, "At least let my precious children live." Of course, Höss did not. One woman approached Höss as she walked past and pointed to her four children. She whispered, "How can you bring yourself to kill such beautiful, darling children? Have you no heart at all?" At the end of his memoirs, Höss wrote:

Let the public continue to regard me as the blood-thirsty beast, the cruel sadist and the mass murderer; for the masses could never imagine the commandant of Auschwitz in any other light.

They could never understand that he, too, had a heart and that he was not evil.

Most people would find it difficult to conceive that any person who is not suffering from significant mental deficits could suppress his emotions to the point he could willingly participate in the mass execution of children.[55] Höss was not crazy.

Death in the Gas Chambers

Joseph Stalin, who knew about mass murder, once said, "The death of one man is a tragedy. The death of millions is a statistic." To understand the tragedy of Auschwitz, it is important to remember that everyone who died there was you, me and our loved ones. The process of death implemented by Höss was not quick and painless, though he liked to think it was. At Nuremberg, Höss was asked by Dr. Goldensohn, "How long did it take for Zyklon B to work?" As if answering a question on an oral examination, Höss responded, "After all of the observations during all of those years, I feel that it depended upon the weather, the wind, the temperature; and as a matter of fact, the effectiveness of the gas itself was not always the same. Usually it took from three to fifteen minutes to extinguish all these people, that is, for no sign of life anymore." While there were no peepholes in the little white house and little red house, once the new crematoria were built, the SS could watch their victims struggle and suffer and "we could ascertain when these people were all dead." Höss never said he and the SS could not bear to look.[56]

In his diary, Johann Paul Kremer said, regarding the gassing he observed on September 2, 1942, "Shouting and screaming of the victims could be heard through that opening and it was clear that they fought for their lives. These shouts were heard for a very short time. I should say for some minutes but I am unable to give the exact span of time." Kremer does not suggest that the screams drove him or other SS men away from the gas chambers or caused them to suffer nightmares. The people closest to the induction vents died at once. One witness recounted what he heard: "After a while I heard the sound of piercing screams, banging against the door and also moaning and wailing. People began to cough. Their coughing grew worse from minute to minute, a sign that the gas had started to act. Then the clamor began to subside and to change to a many-voiced dull rattle, drowned now and then by coughing." One of the Sonderkommandos described what he heard: "For two endless minutes one could hear people beating against the walls. Screams that no longer sounded human. After that nothing." Death is due to suffocation and is accompanied by sensations of fear, dizziness and vomiting.[57]

In his memoirs, Höss refers to the sight of the dead Jews scientifically, as if they were nothing more than experimental lab rats. He states, "There was no noticeable change in the bodies and no signs of convulsions or discoloration.... Soiling through opening of the bowels was also rare. There were no signs of wounding of any kind. The faces showed no distortion." As with other events he describes, Höss refused to recognize the enormous atrocity he had perpetrated. Most likely by design, Höss chose not to see the horrific scene as it truly appeared.[58]

In reality, after the gas chamber had been opened, the sight gave the impression that those locked in it had engaged in a hopeless struggle against death. Entangled corpses full of blood oozed out of the chamber. When the room was particularly crowded, many of the dead were found half-squatting, their skin colored pink with occasional red or green spots. Some foamed at the mouth, others bled from the ears, nose or mouth. Shlomo Venezia, a member of the Sonderkommando, said, "Because of the effect that their fear and the gas had on them, the victims often evacuated everything they had in their bodies. Some bodies were all red, others very pale, as everyone reacted differently. But they had all suffered in death. People often imagine that the gas was thrown in, and there you were, the victims died. But what a death it was!... You found them gripping each other—everyone had desperately sought a little air."[59]

Dr. Miklos Nyiszli, a Hungarian Jew who became Josef Mengele's assistant, worked in the dissecting room in crematorium II. He also provided medical care to the Sonderkommandos and the SS guards who worked in the crematoria. Dr. Nyiszli saw the gas chamber when it opened: "The bodies were not lying here and there throughout the room but piled in a mass to the ceiling. The reason for this was that the gas first inundated the lower layers of air and rose but slowly towards the ceiling. This forced the victims to trample one another in a frantic effort to escape the gas. Yet a few feet higher up the gas reached them. What a struggle for life there must have been!" Contrary to Höss' assertion that Zyklon B offered an easy death, the victims showed the marks of a terrible struggle and incredible suffering.[60]

Inside the gas chamber, people instinctively sought to survive. They trampled each other, including their own loved ones, to get air. Generally, the bodies of the women, the children and the aged were at the bottom of the pile; the strongest were at the top. The bodies were covered with scratches and bruises from the struggle that had set them against each other. Their faces, bloated and blue, were so deformed as to be almost unrecognizable. Nevertheless, the Sonderkommando often discovered their kin among the dead. On December 11, 1942, of the 524 male prisoners who were selected from the transport, several dozen healthy looking men were chosen and assigned to the Special Squad. They were deployed the same day to clear out the gas chambers and recognized among the dead their family members, friends and acquaintances with whom they had arrived. Under the blows of the armed SS men, they carried the bodies of their loved ones out of the bunkers.[61]

About a half hour after the induction of the gas, the ventilation was turned on, the door was opened and Sonderkommando prisoners wearing gas masks began dragging the fresh corpses out of the chamber. SS doctors were present to extend emergency medical assistance to the disinfectors and to assure that the victims were dead. The Nazis were not finished with them. Sonderkommandos with clippers then sheared any hair from the women to be used to make yarn for socks for submarine crews and for German Railroad workers. When Auschwitz was liberated, the Soviet Army found 7.7 tons of human hair packed in bundles, estimated to have come from about 140,000 women. Glasses and artificial limbs were also removed. After shearing, the bodies were carried by elevator up to the ground floor at crematoria II and III. Finally, before incineration, the jewelry and gold fillings of the dead were removed. Each time the gas chambers were emptied, Sonderkommando prisoners whitewashed the walls and washed the floors so the next group would enter unsuspecting.[62]

In his book, *Auschwitz: A Doctor's Eyewitness Account*, Dr. Nyiszli said,

> The Sonderkommando squad, outfitted with large rubber boots, lined up around the hill of bodies and flooded it with powerful jets of water. This was necessary because the final act of those who die by drowning or by gas is an involuntary defecation. Each body was befouled and had to be washed. Once the "bathing" of the dead was finished—a job the Sonderkommando carried out by a voluntary act of impersonalization and in a state of profound distress—the separation of the welter of bodies began. It was a difficult job. They knotted thongs around the wrists, which were clenched in a viselike grip, and with these thongs they dragged the slippery bodies to the elevators in the next room. Four good-sized elevators were functioning. They loaded twenty to twenty-five corpses to an elevator. The ring of a bell was the signal that the load was ready to ascend. The elevator stopped at the crematorium's incineration room, where large sliding doors opened automatically. The kommando who operated the trailers was ready and waiting. Again straps were fixed to the wrists of the dead, and they were dragged onto specially constructed chutes which unloaded them in front of the furnaces.

Shlomo Venezia, a member of the Sonderkommando, recalled that the ones tasked with dragging the bodies out of the gas chamber started by pulling the corpses out with their hands, but in a few minutes their hands were dirty and slippery. Some tried to drag the bodies along with a belt, but this actually made the work even harder. Finally, the simplest thing was to use a walking stick under the nape to pull the bodies along. There was no shortage of walking sticks because of all the elderly people who were put to death.[63]

Venezia related his own experience of meeting a relative. He saw his father's cousin, Leon Venezia, in the undressing room. He had come to Auschwitz on the same transport as Shlomo. He hurt his knee and it was not healing, so he was taken from the hospital to the gas chamber. Leon begged Shlomo to let him join the Sonderkommando. Even though Shlomo knew that would be impossible, he asked; the SS refused. Leon was hungry, so Shlomo brought him some food. Leon wanted to know, "How long does it take to die? Does it really hurt?" Shlomo lied, and they hugged as Leon was the last to go in. When the gas chamber was reopened, Shlomo and his brother, who was also a Sonderkommando, said a prayer over Leon's body before burning it.[64]

Some inmates taken to the crematoria were killed by means other than gassing. Dr. Nyiszli recalled that each evening, 70 men or women were brought to his crematorium and dispatched with a single small caliber pistol shot to the back of the neck. Death was not always instantaneous. This group constituted the daily quota of prisoners from the hospital too "seriously ill" to warrant further food or treatment. On a day Dr. Nyiszli witnessed the slayings, 80 men were taken to the incineration room, where they were undressed by the Sonderkommando. Standing near the ovens, Oberschaarführer Eric Muhsfedlt, wearing rubber gloves, shot the men. Dr. Nyiszli said, "One by one the bodies fell, each yielding his place to the next in line. Within a few minutes he had 'tumbled'—that was the term in general usage—the eighty men. Half an hour later they had all been cremated."[65]

In 1942, approximately 200,000 human beings were gassed in bunkers I and II. The last use of the gas chamber at crematorium I in Auschwitz I occurred near the end of 1942. Its last victims would be several hundred Sonderkommandos who were employed in the killing operations. The life of a Sonderkommando was a terrible one. Though it may be extended, if only temporarily, the price was almost unimaginable. They did not choose to join; they were chosen. If they refused, they were shot in the back of the neck. As witnesses to the worst of Nazi atrocities, few were left alive. In his own non-empathetic way, Höss gave credit to the Sonderkommandos for the work they had to perform:

> They carried out their grisly task with dumb indifference. Their one object was to finish the work as quickly as possible so that they could have a longer interval in which to search the clothing of the gassed victims for something to smoke or eat. Although they were well fed and given many additional allowances, they could often be seen shifting corpses with one hand while they gnawed at something they held in the other. Even when they were engaged in the most gruesome work of digging out and burning the corpses buried in the mass graves, they never stopped eating.
> Even the cremation of their near relations failed to shake them.[66]

Höss could not understand that the Sonderkommandos simply became hardened to the gruesome work they were forced to perform. Shlomo Venezia recalled:

> Your only choice was to get used to it. Very quickly, too. On the first days, I wasn't even able to swallow my bread when I thought of all those corpses my hands had touched. But what could you do? A person had to eat.... After a week or two, you got used to it. You got used to everything. The same way that I'd gotten used to the

sickening smell. After a while, you stopped registering it. You'd gotten onto a treadmill. But you didn't even realize, since, quite simply, you stopped thinking! During the first two or three weeks, I was constantly stunned by the enormity of the crime, but then you stop thinking.

Survival required that the Sonderkommandos learn to feel nothing or at least bury their emotions until it was safe to feel. For the time being, they could not be ordinary human beings. Höss proclaimed he, too, was required to suppress his emotions. There was a difference. He was willingly killing people; the Sonderkommandos were being forced to dispose of the bodies and would have been killed instantly if they failed to perform their task.[67]

Filip Müller was transported to Auschwitz from Czechoslovakia on one of the earliest transports and was thrust into the crematorium as a Sonderkommando. On the first day, three prisoners refused to continue the grisly work and were shot. He had not yet reached that point of despair:

> Of course, I had no illusions: I knew with certainty that a dreadful end awaited me. But I was not yet ready to capitulate. The more menacing death grew, the stronger grew my will to survive. My every thought, every fiber of my being, was concentrated on only one thing: to stay alive, one minute, one hour, one day, one week. But not to die. I was still young, after all. The memory of my parents, my family and my early youth in my home town had faded. I was obsessed and dominated by the determination that I must not die. The heap of dead bodies which I had seen and which I was made to help remove only served to strengthen my determination to do everything possible not to perish in the same way; not to have to lie under a heap of dead bodies; not to be pushed into the oven, prodded with an iron fork and, ultimately, changed into smoke and ashes. Anything but that! I only wanted one thing: to go on living. Sometime, somehow, there might be a chance to get out of here. But if I wanted to survive there was only one thing: I must submit and carry out every single order. It was only by adopting this attitude that a man was able to carry on his ghastly trade in the crematorium of Auschwitz.[68]

Höss' lack of understanding of the impossible position of Sonderkommandos like Müller is further reflected in this statement:

> The attitude of the men of the Special Attachments was also strange. They were well aware that once the actions were completed they, too, would meet exactly the same fate as that suffered by these thousands of their own race, to whose destruction they had contributed so greatly. Yet the eagerness with which they carried out their duties never ceased to amaze me. Not only did they never divulge to the victims their impending fate, and were considerably helpful to them while they undressed, but they were also quite prepared to use violence on those who resisted.

Once again, Höss demonstrates a complete failure to comprehend how the circumstances imposed on the Sonderkommandos affected them. If they did not carry out their duties, they would be shot immediately. As long as they worked, the hope of life continued. Telling the victims about their fate would not change it and would only enhance their anxiety. The Sonderkommandos stayed alive by maintaining the deception.[69]

Hungarians

Hungary, under the leadership of Miklos Horthy, was allied with the Axis Powers in World War II. As a result, while the Nazis pressured Horthy to impose anti–Semitism on Hungarian Jews during the early part of the war, it was not vigorously enforced. In June 1941, Hungary sent troops to invade the Soviet Union but German progress stalled. In January 1943, the Soviets destroyed the Hungarian Army, causing enormous casualties. Hungary decided it was time to reevaluate which side it was on. The Hungarians secretly held talks with the Western Allies and an arrangement was reached whereby the Hungarians would change sides and fight against Germany once Hungarian territory was under threat from an Allied advance.[70]

Hitler discovered the betrayal. On March 18, 1944, Horthy met with Hitler, who, under threat of unilateral military action, compelled Horthy to accept German occupation and set up a pro–German government. The Wehrmacht occupied Hungary on March 19, 1944. Hitler also demanded that 100,000 Jews be delivered "for labor" in Germany. Again, Horthy submitted. Hungarians Jews, who had felt the effects of anti–Semitic legislation, now suffered the full wrath of Hitler and the Final Solution. More than 725,000 Jews lived in Hungary. The very next day, SS-Obersturmbannführer Adolf Eichmann, who was responsible for rounding up the Jews and sending them to the extermination centers, went to Hungary to begin the process of deporting Hungarian Jews. Budapest was less than 500 kilometers from Auschwitz.[71]

In preparation for the massive amount of deportees, leadership changes at Auschwitz had to be made. Since December 1943, Höss had been serving in the Concentration Camp Inspectorate at Oranienberg as the head of Amtsgruppe DI within the WVHA. His expertise in mass extermination was needed back at Auschwitz. In May 1944, SS-Obersturmbannführer Arthur Liebehenschel, who had been serving as the commandant of Auschwitz I, was transferred to Majdanek in the Lublin district. SS-Sturmbannführer Richard Baer took his place. SS-Obersturmführer Friedrich Hartjenstein, who had been appointed as commandant of Auschwitz-Birkenau, was replaced in May 1944 by SS-Hauptsturmführer Josef Kramer. SS-Hauptsturmführer Heinrich Schwarz remained the commandant of Monowitz. While retaining his position in the Inspectorate, Höss returned to Auschwitz as commander of the overall SS garrison to oversee the extermination of the Hungarian Jews. The commandants of both Auschwitz I and Auschwitz-Birkenau were now answerable to him. According to Aleksander Lasik, who wrote a chapter about

Höss in *Anatomy of the Auschwitz Death Camp*, Höss arranged to have Liebehenschel transferred out of Auschwitz to set the stage for his arrival. The massacre of Hungarian Jews at Auschwitz would become known as Aktion Höss.[72]

Höss arrived at Auschwitz on May 8, 1944, and began preparations for the Hungarian extermination. The railway from the main line about two kilometers away was completed so that transports could be delivered into Birkenau, a mere 100 meters from crematoria II and III. Höss reinstated his proven assistants in the key positions of the extermination machinery. He ordered that the furnaces of crematorium V be repaired and, to accommodate the large number of bodies that would need to be incinerated, that five pits be dug nearby for the burning of corpses. Cracks in the brickwork of the ovens were filled with a special fireclay paste. New grates were fitted in the generators, while the six chimneys underwent a thorough inspection and repair, as did the electric fans. The walls of the four changing rooms and the eight gas chambers were given a fresh coat of paint. Crematoria II and III received new elevators connecting the gas chamber with the incineration room, and the gas chambers of crematorium V were equipped with a new ventilation system to speed up the extermination process. Not only were the existing killing and incinerating installations fully repaired, Bunker II was now renumbered Bunker V and brought back into operation. The number of Sonderkommandos was increased from 200 to 900.[73]

Meanwhile hundreds of thousands of Hungarian Jews were being rounded up and forced into ghettoes and camps. Eichmann wanted to send five trains a day into Auschwitz with 40 to 50 cars and up to 100 people per car. Höss traveled to Budapest to tell Eichmann Auschwitz could not handle that many people each day. They settled on two trains, then three trains, on alternate days. The first transport of Hungarian Jews, 1,800 people, arrived in Auschwitz on April 29 and pulled over the new spur through the gate into Birkenau. On May 14, full-scale deportations from the Hungarian provinces to Auschwitz started, at the rate of approximately 12,000 to 14,000 deportees a day. By the end of the first week in July 1944, nearly 440,000 Hungarian Jews had been sent to Auschwitz. Of that number, 394,000 were taken immediately to the gas chambers. During no other similar time period did Auschwitz execute more human beings. In May and June alone, almost 10,000 people per day were being gassed, exceeding the incineration capacity of 132,000 bodies per month.[74]

During this time, Filip Müller said the Sonderkommandos were required to perform what they described as "express work." Bodies were first sorted according to their combustibility. Well-nourished bodies helped burn those that were emaciated. The Sonderkommandos made four stacks: Strong men first, the next group would be the size of women, then children, and

VIII. Crystal Death

Entrance to Auschwitz II–Birkenau through which 400,000 Hungarians passed (author photograph).

finally Musselmänner. Experiments conducted by technicians from Topf and Sons, who manufactured and supplied the cremation ovens, showed what combination of bodies burned best using the least amount of coke as fuel. The goal of the experiments was to find the most economical and fuel-saving procedure.[75]

To help with the Hungarian extermination, Höss promoted Oberschaarführer Otto Moll to be the director of all the crematoria. Dr. Nyiszli described Moll as "the Third Reich's most abject, diabolic and hardened assassin." He witnessed one of Moll's mass pit executions. Nyiszli saw a terrified crowd of about 5,000 Jews, the overflow from the gas chambers, surrounded by SS holding leashed police dogs. The prisoners were led several hundred at a time into the undressing room. Rushed through that process, they left by the door at the opposite side of the house. Once out the door, a Sonderkommando immediately seized their arms and steered them between the double row of SS that ran for 50 yards to the pyre which had been hidden by the trees.[76]

The pyre was a ditch 50 yards long, six yards wide and three yards deep, filled with burning bodies. SS soldiers, stationed at five-yard intervals along the ditch, awaited their naked victims. Each SS man held a small caliber pistol to administer a bullet to the back of the neck. At the end of the pathway two

Sonderkommandos seized the victims by the arms and dragged them for 15 or 20 yards into position before the SS. Their cries of terror covered the sound of the shots. A victim was shot and immediately, even before death, hurled into the flames. During his trial, Höss reported that he put Moll in charge of the crematoria because Moll's predecessor was not able to fulfill the task. The prosecutor asked: "And Moll was able?" Höss replied, "Yes, he was able to do it." The efficient functioning of the extermination process was all that mattered to Höss.[77]

Members of the Sonderkommando who survived also provided testimony about Moll's horrific and bloodthirsty behavior around the pits. Filip Müller stated, "When there was a lot of work, he himself helped to throw the corpses (into the ditches for burning); he rolled up his sleeves and worked as two men." A note hidden by an unknown Sonderkommando member which was found after the war reflected: "Hauptscharführer Mohl [Moll] put four people in a straight line one after the other and shot all four with one single shot. If one bent his head to the side, Moll threw him living into the burning grave of the dead. If someone didn't want to enter the gas chamber, Moll seized him by the hands, twisted them, knocked him down and trampled him to death with his feet." Müller also recalled that Moll was fond of killing babies by flinging them into the boiling human fat on either side of the pits. Hitler was aware of and appreciated the deadly and efficient work that both Moll and Höss were performing in implementing the Final Solution. In April 1943, he decorated both men with the Cross of Merit, First Class, with Swords. Moll would be put on trial by an American Military Tribunal at Dachau in November 1945 and found guilty of war crimes. He was executed by hanging on May 28, 1946.[78]

After the Hungarian Jews were murdered, Höss returned to Berlin on July 29, 1944, but not before arranging the liquidation of the Gypsy camp in August 1944. At that time, about 4,000 Gypsies remained in their separate camp. For Höss, they were a source of great trouble, yet he described them as his "best-loved prisoners." Nevertheless, the decision was made that they, too, must be exterminated. An attempt was made to clear their camp, section BIIe, on May 16, but the Gypsies had been forewarned. They armed themselves with knives, spades, iron pipes, crowbars and stones. When the SS saw that the Gypsies were prepared to fight, they withdrew. The reprieve was short-lived. While some Gypsies were later selected for work or transferred elsewhere, most were successfully executed in the gas chamber in early August 1944.[79]

In his memoirs, Höss noted that, after Hungary, Rumania was the next country whose Jews were due to be deported. Eichmann expected to get 4,000,000 Jews from that country. Bulgaria was to follow with an estimated 2.5 million Jews. Italy had not surrendered its Jews in large numbers. Opposition to their deportation made mass extermination of Italian Jews unlikely. Finally, Spain was on the deportation list. There, also, opponents kept Spanish Jews in relative safety. As Höss put it, "The course taken by the war destroyed these plans and saved the lives of millions of Jews."[80]

"Love from Yana"

In March 1944, as the Theresienstadt family camp was being liquidated in the gas chambers of Auschwitz, Filip Müller, who had survived two years in the Sonderkommando, was with other prisoners in the underground passage between the undressing room and the gas chamber. Müller had no business there, but he and they were Czech Jews:

> In their frightened eyes I could read fear and despair. Young mothers were clasping their little ones to their breast, while older boys and girls clung weeping to their parents' legs.
>
> ...
>
> They began to bid each other farewell. Husbands embraced their wives and children. Everybody was in tears. Mothers turned to their children and caressed them tenderly. The little ones sensed that something frightening was about to happen. They wept with their mothers and held on to them.
>
> The people, crowded together on one side of the room, were shaking with terror. Almost all of them were now sobbing: their weeping sounded like a heart-breaking dirge. Most of them were badly hurt from truncheon blows as well as from the sharp teeth of the dogs.[81]

As the SS forced Müller's countrymen and women into the gas chamber, they began to sing the Czech national anthem and the Hebrew song "Hatikvah." Müller, who knew the fate of the Sonderkommando was always death, had, until then, allowed himself to hope he would survive the hell of Auschwitz. Now, as he watched the brave and strong bearing of these Czech patriots, he feared all was lost and decided to share in their fate:

> In the great confusion near the door I managed to mingle with the pushing and shoving crowd of people who were being driven into the gas chamber. Quickly I ran to the back and stood behind one of the concrete pillars. I thought that here I would remain undiscovered until the gas chamber was full, when it would be locked. Until then I must try to remain unnoticed. I was overcome by a feeling of indifference: everything had become meaningless. Even the thought of a painful death from Zyklon B gas, whose effect I of all people knew only too well, no longer filled me with fear and horror. I faced my fate with composure.
>
> Inside the gas chamber the singing had stopped. Now there was only weeping and sobbing. People, their faces smashed and bleeding, were still screaming through the door, driven by blows and goaded by vicious dogs. Desperate children who had become separated from their parents in the scramble were rushing around calling for them.[82]

Time was moving very slowly for Müller. Some people spoke to him, not comprehending why he had chosen to die with them. He wanted to remain undiscovered. He recounted:

> Suddenly a few girls, naked and in the full bloom of youth, came up to me. They stood in front of me without a word, gazing at me deep in thought and shaking their heads uncomprehendingly. At last one of them plucked up courage and spoke to me: "We understand that you have chosen to die with us of your own free will, and we have come to tell you that we think your decision pointless: for it helps no one." She went on: "*We* must die, but you still have a chance to save your life. You have to return to the camp and tell everybody about our last hours," she commanded. "You have to explain to them that they must free themselves from any illusions. They ought to fight, that's better than dying here helplessly. It'll be easier for them, since they have no children. As for you, perhaps you'll survive this terrible tragedy and then you must tell everybody what happened to you. One more thing," she went on, "you can do me one last favor: this gold chain round my neck: when I'm dead, take it off and give it to my boyfriend Sasha. He works in the bakery. Remember me to him. Say 'love from Yana.' When it's all over, you'll find me here." She pointed at a place next to the concrete pillar where I was standing. Those were her last words.

The girls took Müller and dragged him, protesting, to the door of the gas chamber. A last push caused him to land in the middle of a group of SS. One of them recognized him and began to beat him, "You bloody shit, get it into your stupid head: we decide how long you stay alive and when you die, and not you. Now piss off, to the ovens!"[83]

Müller went to the cremation room, feeling faint. Fellow prisoners helped him get fresh air. He tried to go back to work, once again committed to fight for his life. After the gas had done its deadly work, Müller went back into the gas chamber and found Yana's body near the concrete pillar where they had talked. He took the necklace and left. When he returned to camp, he found Sasha in the bakery and gave him the gold chain and Yana's message. Sasha began to cry and said nothing mattered anymore. Müller had no words of comfort.[84]

Even Miracles Cannot Be Spared

In a place filled with oceans of sadness, perhaps one of the saddest occurred at crematorium II. Dr. Nyiszli recalled that the Sonderkommando were clearing bodies out of the gas chamber when one of them rushed in and yelled, "Doctor, come quickly. We just found a girl alive at the bottom of the pile of corpses." He found her against the wall, near the entrance of the immense room, half covered with other bodies, in the throes of a death rattle, her body seized with convulsions. They removed the still-living body from the corpses pressing against it. Nyiszli carried the girl, no more than 15, into the room adjoining the gas chamber and laid her on a bench. She had not yet recovered consciousness and was breathing with difficulty; Nyiszli administered three intravenous injections.[85]

The girl opened her eyes and looked fixedly at the ceiling. Her breathing became deeper and more and more regular. Within a few minutes she was regaining consciousness; her circulation brought color back into her cheeks, and her delicate face became human again. She looked around with astonishment, still not realizing what had happened to her. The girl's movements became more animated. Eventually, she was able to answer Nyiszli's questions. She told him she had come on a transport with her family from Transylvania.[86]

Oberschaarführer Muhsfedlt arrived to supervise the work and saw the Sonderkommando and Nyiszli gathered in a group around the girl. Nyiszli tried desperately to convince him that her life should be spared. He proposed that she be taken to the gate and allowed to join a kommando of women in camp. He assured Muhsfedlt she would not relate what had happened to her. Muhsfedlt responded that the plan might work if she were three or four years older. An older girl would be wise enough to stay quiet. But, at her age, she would talk and they would pay with their lives. "There's no way of getting around it," he said, "the child will have to die." Within 30 minutes, she was killed with a bullet to the back of the neck.[87]

IX

Property, Corruption and the Inspectorate

In the words of SS-Unterscharführer Pery Broad, "Hitler's plan to exterminate the Jews had not only the aim of achieving his 'ideals of outlook' and of 'cleaning Europe,' but it also served to a great extent to finance and support Germany's war economy." Most people who entered through the gates of Auschwitz were deceived into believing that they were being resettled. Encouraged by the Nazis to bring the belongings they might need to start a new life, deportees carried money and their most precious possessions, including jewelry and family keepsakes. In the first two years of Auschwitz's existence, when most of the prisoners were non–Jewish, personal property was not confiscated. However, that policy changed dramatically when Jewish transports began arriving on a regular basis. At the time Jewish deportees entered Auschwitz, they were deprived of all personal belongings. The property of Jews, whether they were taken immediately to the gas chambers or were found fit for labor, were forfeited and became the property of the Reich. The killing of Jews and plundering of their property in the General Government in Poland were carried out as part of a larger plan code-named "Operation Reinhard" in honor of SS-Obergruppenführer Reinhard Heydrich, the chief of the Reich Main Security Office who had been assassinated in June 1942. The seizure and appropriation of Jewish property at Auschwitz was carried out by Höss under the same code name.[1]

Jews usually arrived at Auschwitz with clothes, food, personal items and assorted household articles, including blankets, sheets, pots, rugs and other necessities. Arriving deportees would be told to leave their luggage at the train—they would collect it later. Almost immediately, work kommandos began the process of gathering the mounds of luggage for transportation to one of many Auschwitz warehouses. Food went to the storeroom near the prisoner kitchen. At the gas chamber, Jews were forced to undress in one room before entering the "bath and delousing room." Compelling them to undress permitted easy assimilation of their clothing and shoes. In addition to their attire, jewelry, watches, eyeglasses, prostheses and any other personal property the arriving victims brought with them would be gathered by prisoners in the work kommandos from the undressing room and removed to the appropriate warehouse.[2]

The amount of property that was confiscated multiplied exponentially over time. Initially, all the clothes and luggage could be stored in one block in the main Auschwitz camp. However, by mid–1942, six barracks were needed near the main camp for storage. These barracks also became inadequate. Eventually, camp officials created an extensive network of storage depots. Prisoner labor squads working in the storerooms were known in the official camp terminology as "order kommandos." The camp prisoners came to refer to the property that was looted from the victims as "Canada," because the amount of the goods and its staggering value symbolized the wealth of the country of Canada. There was Canada I and then Canada II, which began operating in December 1943, both located in Birkenau.[3]

Both Canada I and Canada II were situated in the BIIg sector of the Birkenau camp. Canada I comprised six storage barracks near the main camp. Canada II, which exceeded Canada I in size, comprised 30 barracks. As of October 2, 1944, shortly after conclusion of the extermination of the Hungarian Jews, 815 women were working at Canada II while 250 women were working at Canada I. Prisoners considered the labor squads that worked in Canada to be better kommandos than other labor squads. They had far more chances to "organize" food, clothing and other valued items. Jews hid many precious items in their clothes and shoes, which were confiscated. The Canada inmates were adept at searching for these items and could, when located, secrete them for their own use. They could exchange these valuables for more desirable and necessary products such as food, clothes, shoes, alcohol and cigarettes that were smuggled into the camp by civilian employees and SS men. An inmate who engaged in such "organizing" was instantly recognizable, for he or she was better dressed and better nourished. However, carelessness could be fatal. Should a prisoner be caught taking property that belonged to the Reich by non-cooperating SS or inmate leadership, he or she could be shot on the spot or sent to the gas chamber.[4]

The items confiscated from the Jewish deportees, property which would have gone a long way to mitigating their disastrous living conditions, were reused by the Nazis in various ways. Around Christmas 1942, Himmler ordered that confiscated blankets, sheets and quilts be sent to needy German families, along with coats and clothes for the winter. Tablecloths, towels and other textile items were sent to German settlers. Clothes and shoes were sent to other concentration camps. Wristwatches and fountain pens were distributed to soldiers of the frontline SS divisions, Luftwaffe pilots and submarine crews. Safety razors and blades were delivered to SS infirmaries and sold in SS mess halls. Scissors were sent to SS barbershops. Hard currency, valuables and precious metals were sent directly to the WVHA in Berlin.[5]

In a speech at Posen, Poland, on October 4, 1943, Himmler spoke of the extermination of the Jews to a room of high-ranking SS officers. A lesser known part of the speech concerned the Nazi plunder of Jewish property:

> We have taken away the riches that they had, and…. I have given strict order, which Obergruppenführer Pohl has carried out, we have delivered these riches [carefully] to the Reich, to the State. We have taken nothing from them for ourselves. A few, who have offended against this, will be judged in accordance with an order, [loudly] that I gave at the beginning: he who takes even one Mark of this is a dead man. [less loudly] A number of SS men have offended against this order. They are very few, and they will be dead men [yells] WITHOUT MERCY![6]

Perhaps Himmler pretended not to know the truth. In fact, many SS succumbed to the temptation to take valued Jewish property for themselves knowing it violated the sacred duty owed to assure the Jewish valuables were sent to the Reich. It was simply too tempting and too easy. Members of the SS and inmates often cooperated. Canada workers would bribe an SS man not to watch too closely or search them for stolen goods. An SS guard who wanted to appropriate something in Canada needed the aid of prisoners, since he could not rummage through the mountains of goods and choose a valuable without being noticed. Extensive pilfering prompted Höss to require staff, at the beginning of the Hungarian exterminations, to sign a pledge not to take Jewish property for themselves upon penalty of death. The oath did little to deter theft. The diary of Johann Paul Kremer reflected that he sent parcels from Auschwitz containing property he obtained from Canada. Part of the problem was that property corruption was not limited to low-level SS personnel. Higher-ups were implicated, including the head of the Political Department SS-Unterscharführer Maximilian Grabner and even Höss himself.[7]

Testimony regarding Höss' personal corruption comes from several inmates. Inmate Erich Grönke testified at the 1964 Frankfurt war crimes trial as follows:

> I frequently went to Höss' villa, sometimes twice a day. Höss always had special requests, and this is what I had to do for him: care for the saddlery of his horses and the family shoes, and obtain things that were needed every day. The leather factory housed not only the shoemaker's workshop but also the smithy, the locksmith's shop, the wheelwright's workshop, and eventually also the tailor's shop. Höss wanted something from all these workshops, and he used me as an intermediary.

Stanislaw Dubiel attested that he was a gardener at the Höss home beginning April 6, 1942, until the autumn of 1943. When gathering food rations for the women prisoners, he always took away foodstuffs for the Höss family. Hedwig stressed that no SS men should hear of these transactions. Dubiel

IX. Property, Corruption and the Inspectorate

assured her that he had settled everything with a "friend." Dubiel was organizing the food with Höss' knowledge, but knew Höss would certainly deny everything if Dubiel was discovered. Dubiel took advantage of the situation to smuggle food into the camp to feed those prisoners who needed it most, particularly the sick inmates.[8]

Dubiel took sugar, flour, margarine, various baking powders, condiments for soup, macaroni, oat flakes, cocoa, cinnamon, cream of wheat, peas and other foodstuffs to the Höss house. Hedwig did not make a direct request for the food; she would simply start talking about what she needed for her household. Dubiel then knew what she wanted him to bring. He said the food was not only for the Höss family; some of it was sent by Hedwig to her relatives in Germany. Dubiel provided meat and more than the allotted amount of milk. Höss also obtained large amounts of cigarettes from the prisoners' canteen. Höss never paid for the provisions taken from the prisoners' food stores or from the camp butcher that were used in his household and kitchen. Dubiel stated that Höss was fully aware he was bringing the extra items because Höss often found Dubiel in the kitchen unpacking the things he had brought.[9]

Dubiel provided more than food items for Höss. He supplied shoe polish and shoe brushes. Hedwig often exchanged underwear from Canada taken from Jews sent to the gas chambers and gave it to her domestic servants, who included women prisoners. Dubiel indicated that everything in the Höss house was made by prisoners from camp materials. The rooms were furnished with the most magnificent furniture, the desk drawers were covered with leather from the magazines of the leather factory where there were stores of leather goods looted from the Jewish mass transports. Grönke, who supplied Höss with leather goods, was a former criminal by profession. Höss managed to secure his release and then employed him as manager of the leather factory. Grönke brought leather goods of all kinds, including shoes for men, women and children. All clothes for Höss and his sons were made in Grönke's leather factory. Two Jewish dressmakers were employed in the Höss home for about a year and six months, making dresses for Hedwig and her daughters using materials supplied by Grönke from the stores taken from the Jews.[10]

In his memoirs, Höss provided a detailed explanation about Operation Reinhardt and the seizure of Jewish possessions. He indicated that personal goods worth millions were seized. Höss described how luggage was taken from the train platform to Canada, where the property was sorted and searched for hidden valuables. As Höss learned, not even the threat of a death sentence deterred the SS from taking Jewish property. Höss acknowledged that an "immense amount of property was stolen by members of the SS and by the police, and also by prisoners, civilian employees and railway personnel." He speculated that a great deal of the property remains "hidden and buried in the Auschwitz-Birkenau camp area." Not surprisingly, he omitted any mention of his participation in the theft. In recollecting the confiscation of Jewish property, Höss stated that the "treasures brought in by the Jews gave rise to unavoidable difficulties for the camp itself." He complained that "Jewish gold was a catastrophe for the camp." Höss appears to blame the Jews for the corruption caused by the theft of their property after they were forcibly deported to Auschwitz to be exterminated in the gas chambers![11]

The extensiveness of the corruption at Auschwitz was ultimately too much for Himmler to ignore. He appointed a commission led by SS-Sturmbannführer Konrad Morgen in the latter half of 1943 to investigate the allegations of embezzlement and theft at Auschwitz. Searches were conducted and large amounts of stolen property were found among the belongings of the SS guards. Maximilian Grabner, the sadistic and unscrupulous head of the Political Department known for "dusting out" the cellars of Block 11, was charged with theft. Gerhard Palitzsch and numerous others were also arrested for corruption, but not Höss. The evidence of corruption seized by Morgen was stored in a barrack near crematorium I that belonged to the Political Department. On the night of December 7, 1943, a mysterious fire destroyed all the seized articles and, thus, the evidence of corruption.[12]

When Morgen went to Auschwitz, his mandate was to investigate corruption. However, he was shown the process of extermination from the unloading of Jews at the train platform to the gas chamber. Morgen had just come from Lublin, where Kriminalkommissar Christian Wirth with the Criminal Police told him he was under orders from the Führer to exterminate the Jews. Now, here in Auschwitz, he witnessed murder. Though mass extermination was daily work for Höss at Auschwitz, Morgen was one member of the SS unfamiliar with the Final Solution. Morgen also learned about Grabner's unauthorized killing of prisoners at the Death Wall in the courtyard of Block 11. At Nuremberg, Morgen testified that, under normal circumstances, he would have arrested both Wirth and Höss. Because Germany was at war, Morgen was required to proceed more cautiously. He could do nothing about Hitler, the source of the Final Solution, but he decided to prevail upon his superiors to convince Hitler to withdraw his kill order. He further decided to prosecute Höss for murder. That effort did not get very far.[13]

Grabner was charged and put on trial before an SS court not only for his acts of corruption but also for 2,000 murders. As Morgen expected, Grabner claimed he was only following orders in performing the executions. Grabner indicated Höss was informed about the executions and approved them. When that defense was raised, the SS court suspended Grabner's proceedings and sent investigators to the Reich Main Security Office to determine if,

IX. Property, Corruption and the Inspectorate

in fact, the policy of extermination existed. Morgen testified at Nuremberg that the Reich Main Security Office denied the existence of any general order regarding mass killings in Auschwitz. According to Morgen, proceedings against Höss were begun near the end of 1944, but the advance of Allied troops precluded his arrest. SS-Oberführer Günther Reinecke, chief of the department in the Amstgruppe "SS Courts" and chief judge of the Supreme SS and Police Court, also testified at Nuremberg. He stated that, at the end of 1944, proceedings were begun against Höss for the murder of unknown persons. Additionally, Höss was to be charged for his alleged involvement with Auschwitz prisoner Eleanor Hodys.[14]

Eleanor Hodys came from Austria and was imprisoned at the Ravensbrück concentration camp as a political prisoner. She arrived in Auschwitz on March 26, 1942, in the first transport of women. The story about the relationship between Höss and Hodys is not clear and based to a great extent upon Hodys herself, whose credibility is questionable. Apparently, Hodys worked at the Höss home as an "artistic embroiderer." According to Hodys, Höss found her attractive and tried to kiss her one day when Hedwig was away. Perhaps suspicious that Höss was attracted to Hodys, Hedwig discharged her from household service. Hodys told Konrad Morgen that Höss imprisoned her in a cell in the basement of the administrative building and came to her cell on multiple nights. Again, according to Hodys, they had intercourse on several different occasions. In February 1943, Hodys learned she was pregnant. Höss stopped visiting, and Hodys was taken to Block 11, the punishment block. Some evidence suggests Höss wanted Hodys to be killed. On June 26, she was released into the women's camp, where an abortion was performed. Whether Höss or an inmate was the father is uncertain.[15]

Even though Höss was not prosecuted for the alleged affair with Hodys or his participation in the corruption at Auschwitz, he was tainted by the claims. Either because of the corruption and Hodys investigation, the Grabner murder inquiry, the growing concern about mass extermination of the Jew, or all three, a decision was made that Höss would have to step down as commandant of Auschwitz. At that time, Auschwitz, because of its size, was divided into three components: Auschwitz I (the original camp), Auschwitz II (Birkenau) and Auschwitz III (Monowitz). SS-Obersturmbannführer Arthur Liebehenschel, the head of Amtsgruppe DI within the WVHA, was transferred and became the commandant of Auschwitz I. SS-Obersturmführer Friedrich Hartjenstein became the commandant of Auschwitz II. SS-Hauptsturmführer Heinrich Schwarz became the commandant of Monowitz.

Höss preferred an assignment to the front and twice asked Himmler for a transfer there. Himmler would not allow it. He had no intention of taking the chance that someone with Höss' extensive knowledge of and experience with the Final Solution might fall into the hands of the enemy. Instead, Höss was offered the position as commandant of Sachsenhausen or Liebehenschel's former position in Amtsgruppe DI. Not wanting to be a commandant at another camp, Höss chose the latter. Höss had performed extraordinary service for the Führer and the Reich in his creation of Auschwitz from rundown Polish army barracks into the greatest murder factory the world had ever known. Hitler's close associates, including Himmler and his old friend Martin Bormann, would not let Höss be dragged down by Morgen's commission. The murder inquiry went nowhere.[16]

On March 3, 1942, Himmler entered an order incorporating the Inspectorate of Concentration Camps, headed by Richard Glücks, into the SS Main Economic and Administrative Office (WVHA) led by Oswald Pohl. The Inspectorate of Concentration Camps became Branch or Amtsgruppe D of the WVHA. DI was the central office responsible for matters concerning prisoners, communications, camp security, sentry duty, motor vehicles, weapons and training of the SS; the director of that office had been SS-Obersturmbannführer Arthur Liebehenschel, who now switched jobs with Höss. On November 11, 1943, Höss was appointed chief of Department DI-Central Office within the WVHA and assumed his new post on December 1, 1943. Hedwig and the children remained in the villa at Auschwitz while Höss went to the Inspectorate office at Oranienberg near the Sachsenhausen concentration camp outside Berlin. As the head of Amtsgruppe DI within the WVHA, Höss obtained detailed knowledge of the entire Nazi concentration camp system—its size, administrative methods and decision-making mechanisms—and he became responsible for overseeing supplies, security, transports, arms and punishments for all concentration camps, not just Auschwitz. He coordinated all undertakings within the camp system, had the right to control the activities of camp commandants and could submit proposals for personnel changes in the camps. His immediate supervisor was SS-Gruppenführer Richard Glücks, a man he did not like and who thought no better of him.[17]

Höss said that Glücks' attitude was that of the typical office worker who had no knowledge of practical matters. He only occasionally visited the camps and even then "saw nothing and learnt nothing." According to Höss, Glücks regarded his perpetual worries and complaints about Auschwitz as grossly exaggerated. He blamed Glücks for not removing the officers and junior officers who had become intolerable to Höss in Auschwitz. Höss believed Glücks tried to dismiss him as the commandant because of the number of escapes, but Himmler protected him. Höss remarked that Glücks did not like trouble and would do anything to avoid it. Unfortunately, Auschwitz brought nothing but trouble. Despite the animosity between Höss and his superior, Glücks gave Höss a free hand in his job.[18]

Höss was personally unfamiliar with most of the camps, so, at the sug-

IX. Property, Corruption and the Inspectorate

gestion of Oswald Pohl, the head of the WVHA, much of his initial time as DI chief was spent traveling. He found overcrowded camps and "unrelieved squalor." In the summer of 1944, the SS moved about half of the population of Auschwitz (then a total of about 130,000 inmates) to other camps for armaments labor. Höss said the "prisoners would have been spared a great deal of misery if they had been taken straight into the gas-chambers at Auschwitz. They soon died, without making any substantial contributions to the war effort and often without having done any work at all." Höss said he reported the situation to Himmler, who did nothing.[19]

Unlike the WVHA, Adolf Eichmann's office, Section B4 of Amtsgruppe IV of the RSHA responsible for Jewish affairs, was not interested in preserving Jewish lives for labor, as was Pohl. Eichmann exercised his efforts to assure that the Final Solution was fully implemented. Himmler wanted it both ways. According to Höss, when the RSHA delivered prisoners from the concentration camps for labor, "[i]t was a matter of indifference to them whether this objective was realized straight away by execution or by way of the gas-chambers, or rather more slowly through diseases brought about by the unwarrantable conditions in the concentration camps, which were deliberately not put right." Höss said that "thousands of prisoners died at their work, since virtually all the basic necessities of life for such masses of prisoners were lacking."[20]

In his memoirs, Höss was less than candid about his awareness that slave labor was killing prisoners. He said he "guessed at the time *this* was happening, but was reluctant to believe it" (emphasis added). Having spent years as commandant of Auschwitz, he had now come to realize "the dark shadows that lay behind the concentration camps." Höss concluded that "concentration camps were intentionally, though sometimes unintentionally, transformed into huge-scale extermination centers." Writing his memoirs as he did, immediately after the war, before all the evidence from survivors, documents and Auschwitz itself was known, perhaps Höss hoped people would exonerate him from responsibility for the disaster that befell those who were deported to the camp. He professed that circumstances there were simply beyond his control. Höss found it very difficult to admit any personal fault for the great tragedy at Auschwitz.[21]

Leaving Auschwitz behind in July 1944 did not mean Höss would no longer be involved with the gas chambers. Paul Werner Hoppe was named the commandant of Stutthof concentration camp near Gdansk, Poland, in July 1942. He had been Theodor Eicke's adjutant and spent time at the front prior to becoming the Stutthof commandant. Several months after his appointment, Glücks called Hoppe to Berlin and advised him about the Final Solution. He was told Zyklon B would be sent to Stutthof. Hoppe returned to his camp to make the necessary preparations. In his capacity as Director of

Amtsgruppe DI, Höss visited Stutthof to offer advice and assistance to Hoppe based on his Auschwitz experience.[22]

Having spent years at Auschwitz, where conditions for prisoners were abominable, the reaction of Höss in discovering the state of other Nazi camps is ironic. One of the camps Höss supervised was Bergen-Belsen, about 300 kilometers west of Berlin. According to Höss, the camp, while under the command of SS-Sturmbannführer Adolf Haas, was "a picture of wretchedness." Höss accused Haas of failing to make any attempt to improve the state of the buildings or the grim hygienic conditions prevailing at Bergen-Belsen, a converted prisoner-of-war camp. As Höss saw it, sanitary conditions were far worse than at Auschwitz. Höss relieved Haas of his post in the autumn of 1944 and installed SS-Hauptsturmführer Josef Kramer, who had served under Höss and later been appointed commandant of Auschwitz-Birkenau in his place.[23]

By the end of 1944, according to Höss, it was no longer possible to do much in the way of building; Kramer could only patch up and improvise at Bergen-Belsen. Despite all his efforts, Höss said, Kramer was not able to rectify the results of Haas' negligence. Thus, when Auschwitz was evacuated in January 1945, and a large proportion of the prisoners were forced into Bergen-Belsen, the camp was at once filled to overflowing and a dreadful situation arose. Höss excused Kramer, claiming he was powerless to cope with the tragic situation. Höss and Pohl visited the camp in March 1945 when the population had ballooned from 15,000 in late 1944 to close to 50,000. Inmates from camps in the west and in the east, including Auschwitz, which were evacuated by the Nazis, were sent to Bergen-Belsen. Water was scarce, and disease was rampant. Hundreds of prisoners died each day. In his memoirs, Höss says, "...it was little wonder that the British found only dead or dying or persons stricken with disease, and scarcely a handful of healthy prisoners in a camp that was in an unimaginably disgusting condition." Höss fails to explain why, as the head of Amtsgruppe DI, he permitted prisoners from so many camps to be funneled into Bergen-Belsen when he knew the conditions there were already atrocious.[24]

X

Justice

The Nuremberg trials had been ongoing for four months at the time the British captured Rudolf Höss at Gottrupel in March 1946. Once the four Allied nations—the United States, the United Kingdom, France and the Soviet Union—decided upon a trial for Nazi war crimes, a list of suspected war criminals had been compiled. The most notorious were tried first. Hitler and Himmler had committed suicide. Likewise, Joseph Goebbels, the propaganda minister, had killed himself. Hermann Göring was the lead defendant at Nuremberg. Other defendants in the dock included Albert Speer, Minister of Armaments; Rudolf Hess (not to be confused with the commandant), Deputy Führer until he fled to Great Britain in 1941; Field Marshal Wilhelm Keitel, Chief of the Armed Forces High Command; Admiral Karl Doenitz, Commander-in-Chief of the Navy and brief successor to Hitler as the ruler of Germany; and Hans Frank, who as head of the General Government in Poland remarked, "We must annihilate the Jews wherever we find them and whenever it is possible." The prosecution knew that Rudolf Höss served as the commandant of Auschwitz, and that Auschwitz was a major extermination camp in the Nazi regime. However, at the time the Nuremberg trials started, he remained at large.[1]

Word spread rapidly of Höss' capture. By that time, the prosecution had presented all its evidence, and most of the prosecutors had dispersed. Lieutenant Commander Whitney R. Harris, United States Naval Reserve, a member of the U.S. prosecution team, was one who remained. When he learned that Höss was in custody, he asked the British to send him to Nuremberg, and they promptly complied. Harris spent three days interrogating Höss. He described Höss as a "plain, little man" who was not very impressive. Höss told Harris about the number of persons killed at Auschwitz in the gas chambers and by disease and starvation. He discussed the order to implement the Final Solution, his use of Zyklon B and the burning of bodies. He talked about the improvements he made over the killing system at Treblinka. Höss also mentioned medical experimentation on prisoners.

In addition to Harris, the psychologist, Dr. G. M. Gilbert, and the psychiatrist, Dr. Leon Goldensohn, also interviewed Höss at Nuremberg on various occasions. In his memoirs, Höss refers to the "extremely unpleasant" interrogations he underwent at Nuremberg, not physically, but psychologically. Höss stated, "I cannot really blame the interrogators—they were all Jews."[2]

Harris reduced Höss' testimony into an affidavit which Höss signed on April 5, 1946 (see Appendix II). The Allied countries wanted to get the affidavit into the record, but there was a problem: The prosecution had rested its case, and there was no procedural basis for introducing Höss' affidavit. An unusual opportunity presented itself. Defendant SS-Obergruppenführer Ernst Kaltenbrunner had been appointed Chief of the RSHA to replace Reinhard Heydrich after his assassination in June 1942. According to Kaltenbrunner, when he assumed that post, Himmler assured him he would only be responsible for intelligence, not repressive activities. Himmler indicated he would leave that job to Heinrich Müller of the Gestapo. Kaltenbrunner said he had never been in a concentration camp, a fact Höss could verify.[3]

Dr. Kurt Kauffmann, the attorney for Kaltenbrunner, decided to call Höss as a witness to substantiate this defense. Höss attested, as expected, that Kaltenbrunner had not been to Auschwitz. Dr. Kauffmann also elicited testimony from Höss that Himmler told him the Final Solution was a "secret Reich matter" of which Kaltenbrunner would be unaware. Dr. Kauffmann should have stopped there. Attempting to further strengthen Kaltenbrunner's case, Dr. Kauffmann questioned Höss about the signing of execution orders. Höss testified that almost all execution orders were signed by either Himmler or Gestapo Chief Heinrich Müller. On cross-examination by Colonel John Harlan Amen of the United States, Höss stated that most of the execution orders were not signed by Kaltenbrunner, but some were. Höss also acknowledged that Müller was signing *as the representative* of Kaltenbrunner, who was Chief of the RSHA. In that capacity, Kaltenbrunner was responsible for ordering the executions. Also, the prosecution produced a photograph showing Kaltenbrunner in Mauthausen, undermining his claim that he had never been in a concentration camp. In his memoirs, Höss stated, "I have never been able to grasp, and it is still not clear to me, how I of all people could have helped to exonerate Kaltenbrunner." Clearly, he did not. The Tribunal found Kaltenbrunner guilty, and he was executed on October 16, 1946.[4]

In his interviews with Harris, Höss appeared emotionless and detached. Before the Tribunal, his testimony was also mechanical and matter-of-fact:

> DR. KAUFFMANN: Yes.... From 1940 to 1943, you were the Commander of the camp at Auschwitz. Is that true?
> Höss: Yes.
> DR. KAUFFMANN: And during that time, hundreds of thousands of human beings were sent to their death there. Is that correct?

X. Justice 159

Höss: Yes.

Dr. Kauffmann: Is it true that you, yourself, have made no exact notes regarding the figures of the number of those victims because you were forbidden to make them?

Höss: Yes, that is correct.

Dr. Kauffmann: Is it furthermore correct that exclusively one man by the name of (Adolf) Eichmann had notes about this, the man who had the task of organizing and assembling these people?

Höss: Yes.

Dr. Kauffmann: Is it furthermore true that Eichmann stated to you that in Auschwitz a total sum of more than 2 million Jews had been destroyed?

Höss: Yes.

Dr. Kauffmann: Men, women, and children?

Höss: Yes.

...

Dr. Kauffmann: Is it true that in 1941 you were ordered to Berlin to see Himmler? Please state briefly what was discussed.

Höss: Yes. In the summer of 1941 I was summoned to Berlin to Reichsfuhrer SS Himmler to receive personal orders. He told me something to the effect—I do not remember the exact words—that the Führer had given the order for a final solution of the Jewish question. We, the SS, must carry out that order. If it is not carried out now then the Jews will later on destroy the German people. He had chosen Auschwitz on account of its easy access by rail and also because the extensive site offered space for measures ensuring isolation.

...

Dr. Kauffmann: And after the arrival of the transports were the victims stripped of everything they had? Did they have to undress completely; did they have to surrender their valuables? Is that true?

Höss: Yes.

Dr. Kauffmann: And then they immediately went to their death?

Höss: Yes.[5]

By questioning Höss about matters covered in the April 5, 1946, affidavit, Dr. Kauffmann "opened the door" for the prosecution to cross-examine him directly from the affidavit to assure the accuracy and completeness of the record. Colonel Amen then asked Höss to affirm damaging statements made in the affidavit regarding the number of victims who died in Auschwitz by extermination, as well as by starvation and disease. The affidavit reflected that 70 to 80 percent of all persons sent to Auschwitz as prisoners died there, the remainder having been selected and used for slave labor in the concentration camp industries. Höss admitted that 400,000 Hungarian Jews were executed at Auschwitz in the summer of 1944.[6]

Col. Amen then read from the part of the affidavit in which Höss described visiting the extermination camp at Treblinka. The Tribunal and spectators listened in stunned silence as Höss reaffirmed his statement that the camp commandant at Treblinka related how he had liquidated 80,000 human beings in the course of six months. Those victims came from the Warsaw ghetto. Höss' affidavit reflected that he did not believe monoxide gas, used at Treblinka, was an efficient means of killing people. He noted, proudly, how he improved on this method of destruction by using Zyklon B, which could be dropped into the death chamber from a small opening and could kill in 3 to 15 minutes, depending upon climatic conditions. In Höss' mind, he had made the killing process far more humane. In his affidavit, Höss commented, "We knew when the people were dead because their screaming stopped." Even so, "we usually waited about one-half hour before we opened the doors and removed the bodies." The Tribunal learned that death did not end the desecration. Höss added, "After the bodies were removed our special Kommandos took off the rings and extracted the gold from the teeth of the corpses." Höss testified that the gold was melted down and brought to the Chief Medical Office of the SS at Berlin.[7]

In his interrogation at Nuremberg, Höss was more descriptive of the procedure followed after the gold was extracted.

Q: Will you explain that in more detail?

A: The dentist of the camp at Auschwitz was responsible for the melting of this gold extracted from the teeth, and at the end of each month he personally would take it to the Medical Chief Office in Berlin.

Q: Can you place an estimate, or by any other measure, the value, or the weight, or otherwise, how much gold is collected at Auschwitz during the period of the camps operation?

A: I can give you no figure about that at all. The only thing I learned is from the fact I was in plants where they were burning the bodies, and the gold teeth were collected in tin boxes which had an opening at the top, and they were locked and only the dentist had a key.

Höss indicated the boxes were about eighteen inches long, eighteen inches high and about 12-15 inches long. The dentist would then take the gold to his office where, according to Höss, he "melted it down into gold bars; which he kept locked in his safe, and when he got the right amount, he would take them down to Berlin in that shape." Each bar was about 12-15 inches long, three inches high and three inches thick.[8]

The affidavit further explained that Höss had improved the process employed by by Treblinka by increasing the size of the Auschwitz gas chambers to hold 2,000 people at one time whereas at Treblinka's gas chambers could only accommodate 200 people each. He then described selection based upon fitness for work. Of course, Höss testified, "[c]hildren of tender years were invariably exterminated since by reason of their youth they were unable to work." Still another improvement at Auschwitz was the effort to fool the victims into thinking that they needed to undergo a delousing process. "Very frequently," recalled Höss, "women would hide their children under the clothes, but of course when we found them we would send the children in to be exterminated." Notwithstanding the attempts to deceive the victims and the efforts at secrecy, Höss stated in the affidavit that "the foul and nauseating stench from the continuous burning of bodies permeated the entire area and all of the people living in the surrounding communities knew that exterminations were going on at Auschwitz."[9]

Höss' testimony at Nuremberg stunned and appalled the spectators and the Tribunal. For the first time, the public received indisputable evidence describing the implementation of Hitler's Final Solution. Many could not even conceive that such atrocities had occurred. The impact of the evidence presented by Höss could not be overstated. Prosecutor Harris recounted that Höss was the most critical witness at Nuremberg in establishing the existence of Nazi atrocities and the Final Solution. Early in the trial, the prosecution had shown a film taken in the concentration camps as they had been found when liberated by the Allies. The photographic evidence of emaciated human beings and the charred remains of those who were murdered by the Nazis shocked the courtroom. Most of the defendants feigned ignorance, though defendant Hans Frank, at least, forthrightly said, "Don't let everyone tell you that they had no idea. Everyone sensed that there was something horribly wrong … [e]ven if we did not know all the details. They didn't want to know." According to Harris, "there isn't any question that after the testimony of Rudolf Höss that the Holocaust was completely proved."[10]

Harris described Höss' affidavit of April 5, 1946, as the "most significant document which had been introduced at Nuremberg." In *The Nuremberg Trial*, Ann and John Tusa state that in Höss "were personified all the Nazi virtues of duty, hard work, obedience; and all the worst of Nazi callousness and bestiality." Höss spoke with a sense of pride in achieving the improvements he made at Auschwitz over Treblinka. He probably expected, or at least hoped, that those in attendance, especially the Nazi leaders on trial, would appreciate what he had accomplished. Instead, people listened in shocked silence. To most, his testimony reflected the inconceivable horrors that human beings are capable of inflicting on one another. The only two defendants to comment were Karl Doenitz and Göring, both of whom attributed Höss' behavior at Auschwitz to the fact that he was a southern German.[11]

When Höss stepped down from the witness stand, it is unlikely that anyone was thinking about Kaltenbrunner, who had called Höss as a witness in the first place. The Tribunal, the spectators and the world through the various news organizations who were reporting on the evidence being presented had heard from the mouth of one of the most culpable perpetrators that Hitler and the Nazis had conceived and implemented the most monstrous of crimes against an entire race of people—Jews—as well as hundreds of thousands of others—Poles, Soviet POWs, Gypsies, homosexuals and Jehovah's Witnesses—all because they did not fit into Hitler's vision for the future of Germany. There can be no doubt that Höss' testimony was instrumental in the convictions and death sentences imposed on Göring, Keitel, Frank and a number of other Nuremberg defendants.

After he testified, Höss was interrogated outside the courtroom about SS-Hauptscharführer Otto Moll. By coincidence or fortune, Moll was also in Nuremberg. Apparently aware that Höss had implicated him in the killing and cremation operations at Auschwitz, Moll insisted at his own interrogation that he be allowed to confront Höss. In Moll's presence, Höss repeated his earlier statement that Moll worked in the extermination operations at Auschwitz. Höss also stated that Moll personally shot some of the victims. While admitting to this statement, Moll responded that they were few in number and he "never mistreated any of the prisoners." Despite Moll's efforts to minimize his culpability, Höss insisted that Moll was responsible for assuring people entered the gas chamber and were later cremated.[12]

Höss guarded by American and Polish soldiers prior to his transfer to Poland (courtesy Yad Vashem—the Holocaust Heroes' and Martyrs' Remembrance Authority).

Following his testimony, Höss was taken by Polish authorities from Nuremberg to Warsaw via Berlin on May 25, 1946. When the Polish government learned of his arrest by British authorities, they made a formal request for his extradition. They advised the British that he was at the top of their list of Nazi war criminals and wanted him to answer for Auschwitz, which was described as a "Polish national calamity." In light of the enormous number of victims from Poland compared to other countries, Great Britain readily acquiesced in the request.[13]

An American plane flew Höss and two other Nazis sought by the Polish to Warsaw. He expected a hostile reception. Several officials in the prison came to see him soon after he arrived to show him their Auschwitz tattoo numbers. Nothing was said; Höss believed he knew what they intended. He was kept isolated for nine weeks and was frequently interrogated. At the end of July, he and seven other Germans, including Amon Göth, the commandant of the Plaszow concentration camp at Krakow, were moved to Krakow. A large crowd hurled insults at them at the Krakow train station. Despite the immense horrors inflicted on the Polish people by the Nazis and, in particular, the fact that Auschwitz was the site of such a great number of deportations and deaths, Höss was never physically assaulted while in Polish custody.[14]

Initially, Höss was treated well, but after a few weeks things changed, in his estimation, "completely and overnight." Although he could not understand the conversation of the prison officials, their intent seemed clear: they wanted to take matters into their own hands and kill him in the prison, without a trial. His rations were reduced to a small piece of bread and less than a spoonful of soup, although sufficient food existed for other inmates. Despite having superintended a system at Auschwitz for years in which kapos and blockältesters commanded and abused other prisoners, Höss stated that "[i]t was here that I became acquainted with the power of prisoners in position of authority over their fellows." Psychologically and physically, Höss claims he was almost broken. Then, the public prosecutor's office intervened, no doubt to facilitate its investigation of Auschwitz through Höss' cooperation. From that time on, he received only "decent and considerate treatment" from the Polish, which he never expected and which had a significant impact on the remainder of his life.[15]

Dr. Jan Sehn was a Polish lawyer and a member of the Commission for the Investigation of Nazi War Crimes. In 1945 and 1946, he led the investigations at Auschwitz-Birkenau and prepared the case against Höss. He visited Höss in his cell in Krakow in November 1946 and asked him to list the documents that had been destroyed prior to the liberation of Auschwitz by the Soviet Army in January 1945. Initially, Höss refused the request, then, upon reconsideration, willingly cooperated and provided a wealth of information. He was interrogated 13 times and fully answered all questions. Höss also provided insight into his relationships with Himmler, Eichmann, Maurer, Pohl and Glücks, as well as various other Nazis with whom he interacted during the war. Dr. Sehn was convinced that Höss was being truthful, at least as he saw the truth.[16]

Höss' willingness to cooperate with the investigation and provide evidence that would be used against him at trial may seem perplexing. Several reasons can account for his change of heart. First, he was bored; inactivity tormented him mentally. *Arbeit macht frei* (Work sets you free). As he wrote his memoirs, Höss stated, "In my present imprisonment, I feel the lack of any physical work very much, and I am so thankful that I can do this writing, which I find completely absorbing and satisfying."[17] Second, Höss was proud of his accomplishment. He built Auschwitz from nothing into the largest concentration camp in the Nazi system. No facility served Hitler's goals of destruction of the Jewish race through the gas chambers and slave labor more effectively than did Auschwitz. In his memoirs, Höss recorded his great achievement for future generations to read. Third, though he remained a National Socialist, he became disillusioned with the leaders of the Third Reich and their methods. He wanted the opportunity to distance himself, to an extent, from the crimes of which he and the Nazis now stood accused. Höss explained that everything that went wrong at Auschwitz was the fault of someone else, either his subordinates or his superiors. According to Höss, he was merely an "unwilling cog" in the extermination machine.

Though given the opportunity and time to fully reflect on his years as a Nazi and Auschwitz commandant, Höss was never fully contrite. He had done his best to be a good Nazi and SS man, and this would have to be his legacy. He created Auschwitz from rundown Polish Army barracks. When his complaints to Himmler for aid were rejected, he was forced to build and maintain Auschwitz on his own. When he was directed to exterminate Jews, he did so, trainload after trainload, without complaint and without objection, not because he hated the Jews, but because he was a soldier—at least, that is what he wanted people to believe. As Joseph Tenenbaum noted:

> Höess was perfection itself, a dutiful though unloving son, a perfect soldier, a perfect prisoner, a perfect Nazi and an equally perfect witness on the stand, who told the truth unadorned and unadulterated. His search for perfection drove him to join the racial elite of the SS. He was a criminal, partly because of an aggressive, sadistic guilt complex, but also because of a masochistic sense of duty. But once he set forth on the road of mass homicide, he became the most perfect and precise hangman that has ever appeared in world history.[18]

Höss did not seek absolution, at least not until the end. He wanted everyone to know he did exactly what was expected of him to the best of his ability, and he did an outstanding job.

Höss was charged by Indictment with the following crimes:

(1) That from 1st September 1939, till May 1945, in the German Reich, and from 1st May 1940, till September 1944, on the occupied territory of the Polish State he was a member of the German National Socialist Workers' Party (NSDAP), a criminal organization, which aimed at the subjugation of other nations through planning, organizing and perpetrating crimes against peace, war crimes and crimes against humanity, and also was a member of the SS, a further criminal organization;

(2) That from 1st May 1940, till the end of October 1943, as Commandant of the Auschwitz concentration camp set up

X. Justice

by him, and thereafter from December 1943, till May 1945, as Head of the D.I. Department of the S.S. Central Economic and Administrative Office, as well as in June, July and August 1944, as commander of the SS garrison at Auschwitz, in execution of the Nazi system of persecution and extermination of nations in concentration and death camps organized for the purpose, he supervised the application of that system in the Auschwitz concentration camp against the Polish and Jewish civilian population and against other nationals of the territories occupied by Germany, as well as to Soviet prisoners of war, and thereby acting either himself or through the subordinate camp personnel, he deliberately:

(i) deprived of life: (a) about 300,000 camp registered inmates, (b) about 4,000,000 people mainly Jews brought to the camp from different European countries to be killed upon their arrival, and therefore not included in the register of the camp inmates, (c) about 12,000 Soviet prisoners of war confined in the camp in violation of the Geneva Convention on the treatment of Prisoners of War; all this by asphyxiation in gas-chambers, shooting, hanging, lethal injections of phenol or by medical experiments causing death, systematic starvation, by creating special conditions in the camp which were causing a high rate of mortality, by excessive work of the inmates, and by other methods;

(ii) ill-treated and tortured the inmates physically and morally by various means;

(iii) supervised wholesale robbery of property, mostly jewels, clothes and other valuable articles taken from people on their arrival to the camp, and of gold teeth and fillings extracted from dead bodies of the victims.[19]

The trial against Höss began March 11, 1947, before the Supreme National Tribunal of Poland in Warsaw. Despite the temptation of many to summarily execute Nazi war criminals, the victorious nations sought to provide the accused a measure of due process and separate themselves from the Third Reich which imprisoned and held individuals without cause, then imposed punishment simply because Adolf Hitler and the Nazis summarily determined that the person constituted an "enemy of the State." As the trial against Göring, Speer and the primary Nazi defendants began in Nuremberg in November 1945, Lord Justice Geoffrey Lawrence stated, "The Trial which is now about to begin is unique in the history of the jurisprudence of the world and it is of supreme importance to millions of people all over the globe. For these reasons, there is laid upon everybody who takes any part in this Trial a solemn responsibility to discharge their duties without fear or favor, in accordance with the sacred principles of law and justice." Even more succinctly at the beginning of Höss' trial, the President of the Court, Dr. Alfred Eimer, noted: "Remembering our enormous responsibility before the dead and the living, we do not want to forget the goal for which the freedom loving nations fought: respect for the dignity of every human being; may it include the accused, for it is above all a human being who stands before the court."[20]

The prosecution, led by Dr. Tadeusz Cyprian, presented

Höss on trial in Poland (courtesy Polish Press Agency).

statements from a large number of camp inmates, as well as documentary evidence. Additionally, the case for the prosecution rested on expert evidence submitted to the Tribunal regarding (1) the general Nazi policy and system of extermination of Jews and the organization of the concentration and death camps set up for the purpose by the German authorities in the occupied territories; (2) the general conditions in Auschwitz, in particular as regards health, food, hygiene and the system of treatment; (3) the organization and work of the gas chambers and crematoria; and (4) the medical experiments performed by German doctors on inmates. As regards medical experiments, evidence showed they were performed on men and women of non–German origin, mostly Jews, at Auschwitz and were carried out on orders from the supreme German authorities. Testimony established that the experiments fell into several groups, including: (a) castration experiments by x-ray which caused burning and sometimes death; (b) experiments intended to produce sterilization by injecting a thick white test fluid, with unknown chemical agents, into the uterus and tubes; (c) experiments causing premature termination of pregnancy and carried out on pregnant and childbearing women;

(d) experiments of artificial insemination; and (e) experiments aimed at cancer research, sometimes involving transplanting cancerous bodies to the uterus and cervical channel.[21]

Höss, who was defended by two lawyers appointed by the Tribunal, admitted in substance all the facts alleged against him in the Indictment. In particular, he admitted that he was a member of the NSDAP and the SS, and that in his capacity as commandant of Auschwitz and later as chief of DI Department of the Central Economic and Administrative Office of the SS, he carried out and supervised the extermination of many million Jews and others. Höss also admitted that in the course of this action the victims were robbed of all their possessions and valuables. He denied, however, that he personally committed any acts of ill-treatment or cruelty, and questioned the accuracy of the total number of victims killed in the camp, which according to him was much lower than the four million submitted in the Indictment. All defense questions to witnesses were directed to these points. Neither Höss nor his attorneys introduced any evidence or witnesses, and he relied entirely on those put forward by the prosecution. His whole defense rested on the submission that he was only carrying out orders received from his superiors. He acknowledged his entire responsibility for everything that occurred in the camp whether he personally knew it at the time or not.[22]

Through most of his trial, Höss remained stoic. As he had done at Nuremberg, Höss answered all questions in a brief, precise manner, without emotions. The State Prosecutor, Dr. Cyprian, seized upon Höss' demeanor in his final summation to the court:

> [H]e faces everything with an iron expression and an almost legendary calm. He has no pity for the people; the most horrible descriptions do not move him. So it was, why get excited. But sometimes the stern face of Höss changes. What is painful for him today is having sometimes acted without fulfilling his duties or having exceeded their limits. I am mentioning the fact which caused the most agitation and made him suffer: the reproach that he didn't put enough gas into the gas chambers. He stood up and declared that he put as much gas as necessary since the rules prescribed the exact amount. The accused Höss emphasized constantly that he executed the orders from above without a word of protest and submitted to them because he trusted his superiors blindly. ... Sometimes one got the impression that Höss didn't speak to a Polish tribunal but to the chapter of a High Order by which he had been honored in Germany with the "merit award" [Verdienstkreuz], and that he was legitimizing himself before this chapter of the Order indicating how wonderfully he had fulfilled all his duties.[23]

The trial ended March 29, 1947. On April 2, 1947, Höss was found guilty, as expected, and sentenced to death by hanging. The Tribunal found Höss guilty of the murder of at least 2.5 million people, mainly Jews, at Auschwitz.

In time, the actual number would prove to be less, yet still exceed one million souls. The Tribunal stated:

> The excessive extent of the crime that was put on the scale of justice in this trial, exceeds in its dimensions the person of the accused; it makes his part in the atrocities a small link in the chain of the crimes intended for the living peoples of the world. The individual deeds of Höss are not important, if they have been done at all, or the fact that he wants to shoulder the responsibility for what happened in the camp with or without his knowledge. Important are the deeds of that criminal conspiracy to which Höss belonged and the extent of his participation in it. ... Rudolf Höss wasn't just a blind executioner of the commands of Himmler. In his position as commander of the camp and later as special envoy for the execution of the so-called "Höss Action" he took initiatives of his own which exceeded by far the rules of the camp and the orders and instructions of his superiors. ... Has Höss, the accused, reasons to claim that in regard to all these atrocities he was only the enforcement officer of commands? ... Besides the fact that a command does not exempt oneself from following the law stated in the verdict, it is impossible to invoke the command of a power which itself commits crimes. Such an exit from any responsibility is unacceptable. The accused could only have escaped responsibility if he had separated himself from this criminal conspiracy by leaving. But not only did he remain in it, Höss very much increased its results by his activities. ... Therefore this is not the place to understand his alleged powerlessness toward the commands he had received. Should he be allowed to use the privilege of no punishment because he didn't want to do anything else than follow the commands of the leader of Hitlerism, as, by the way, did all the other members of this criminal group? This would lead to a total exoneration of the conspiracy itself, and instead of a well-deserved punishment for the innumerable crimes committed by this conspiracy all that would remain of the millions of burnt human beings would be their ashes in the wind.[24]

The Tribunal held that whether Höss personally mistreated any prisoner was of no relevance. He voluntarily participated in the vast Nazi conspiracy and took personal initiatives to advance the goals of that evil criminal enterprise. "I followed orders" was no defense. Only by refusing to obey Hitler's command—an action Höss claimed was unthinkable—could Höss have escaped liability. Because he remained a Nazi, he was guilty and must hang. Unsurprised by his sentence, Höss showed no emotion when it was announced. He asked only that he be allowed to write a letter to his wife and that his wedding ring be delivered to her. Höss expressed appreciation to his defense counsel and declined his right to ask for clemency. Nevertheless, the proceedings were sent to the Justice Ministry to be given to the President of the State. Pending the latter's decision, Höss was moved on April 4 to the prison in Wadowice, 22 miles from Auschwitz, to await execution.[25]

XI

Responsibility and Atonement

When the British arrested Höss, they knew, to some extent, about the atrocities that had occurred at Auschwitz. Once it was established that the commandant of Auschwitz was in their custody, his captors hoped he would confess to his role and provide information valuable to an understanding of the working of Nazi concentration camps. As far as his responsibility was concerned, no one needed for Höss to admit what he had done; he was guilty by virtue of the position he held. Interrogation would produce significant details, however, and Höss proved more than willing to provide them. His mistreatment at the hands of the British would cause any competent court to question the accuracy of the eight-page inculpatory statement he gave at Camp Tomato in Minden, except for the fact it proved to be consistent in all material respects with everything Höss repeated later at the trial of the high-ranking Nazi defendants at Nuremberg, in his affidavit of April 5, 1946 and in his memoirs.

Höss was willing, far more than any other Nazi in his position, to admit to and describe the atrocities and horrors in which he participated. However, he accepted personal responsibility only to the extent he happened to be the commandant of Auschwitz. As he stated in his memoirs, "…all these things happened in Auschwitz and so I am responsible. For the camp regulations say: the camp commandant is *fully* responsible for *everything* that happens in his sphere." Höss never admitted that he intentionally inflicted pain on any inmates. He blamed the mistreatment of prisoners on SS men like Karl Fritzsch and Gerhard Palitzsch, who he says taught the prisoner functionaries to be merciless. Höss claimed that, despite his best efforts, he could not stop the abuse. He states that he never mistreated prisoners and "was never cruel" and "never maltreated anyone, even in a fit of temper." He even maintained that he was unaware of much of what occurred at Auschwitz until his trial in 1947.[1]

Höss failed to face up to the reality of the horror he inflicted on the hundreds of thousands of human beings who entered Auschwitz. "Unknowingly," Höss said, "I was a cog in the wheel of the great extermination machine created by the Third Reich." While admitting in his memoirs that he remained a committed National Socialist, he blamed Hitler and Himmler for using their powers "wrongly and even criminally" to plunge the world into war and causing the destruction of Germany. In his last letter to Hedwig, Höss apologized in one breath for inflicting "so much destruction and sorrow upon the Polish people" yet claimed in the same sentence that he "did not do it personally, or by my own free will."[2]

Four days before his execution, Höss finally sought forgiveness for the enormous crime against humanity which he committed and his part in the "horrible human extermination plans of the 'Third Reich.'" However, he directed his plea to the Polish people only; he made no apology for the one million Jews he murdered. At no point did Höss say he should have disobeyed Hitler's and Himmler's order for the Final Solution. He hoped his memoirs would show that the man who the public saw as a "blood-thirsty-beast, cruel sadist and mass murderer" had a heart. Despite his wish that posterity judge him in a more benevolent light, the truth imposes far greater personal responsibility on Höss than he was willing to bear. His omissions of critical facts and events in his memoirs as well as contradictions between his reflections and those of Auschwitz survivors are abundant. The monstrosity that was Auschwitz, over which Höss exercised daily and supreme control, cannot be mitigated with his self-serving autobiography.[3]

Mistreatment of Prisoners

Höss absolved himself from responsibility for the horrendous living conditions which destroyed the body and soul of Auschwitz prisoners. He states that he complained to Berlin and, in particular, Himmler, about the wretched situation and received no help. It was their fault, not his. Höss testified at Nuremberg that conditions in Auschwitz deteriorated when the war began. More prisoners were arriving, and building material was not available to construct adequate living space. Also, according to Höss, Berlin was cutting back on rations for the internees. By necessity, resources, including his efforts, were dedicated to the Final Solution. The welfare of the inmates mattered little and only to the extent it served the German war effort.

The day-to-day circumstances in Auschwitz could hardly escape Höss' notice. He could see the prisoners with his own eyes and had access to records—the Totenbuch—of the number that were dying every day. In his memoirs, for example, Höss observed that "general living conditions in the

XI. Responsibility and Atonement

women's camp were incomparably worse. They were far more tightly packed in, and the sanitary and hygienic conditions were notably inferior." Höss knew that women living in this squalor were becoming ill and dying. As commandant, he had the authority and the power to act. He had done so before. According to Höss, when Auschwitz was being created in 1940, he had been forced to improvise to provide the food and materials the camp needed. He obtained "bread or meat or potatoes" when necessary, he "organized" trucks and fuel and he drove as far as 60 miles to get cooking pots, bed frames and straw mattresses. Determined to show Himmler he had chosen the right man for the job, Höss did whatever was required to establish Auschwitz as a viable concentration camp.[4]

Significantly, there is no evidence that, as Auschwitz grew, Höss made any efforts to mitigate the ever-deteriorating abominable situation. Neither in his testimony at Nuremberg nor in his memoirs did Höss suggest that he made any attempt to improve the deplorable and inhuman living conditions. There is no indication, not even from Höss himself, that he sought more food or food that bore nutritional value for anyone. He did nothing to obtain better shelter, and, while fully aware of the disastrous state of the infirmary, ignored the prisoners' needs for basic medical care. Höss made no effort to improve the appalling sanitary and hygienic conditions. While chief of Amtsgruppe DI from December 1944 to the end of the war, Höss sacked SS-Sturmbannführer Adolf Haas, the commandant of the Bergen-Belsen concentration camp, which Höss described as "a picture of wretchedness." According to Höss, Haas made no attempt to improve the state of the buildings or the grim hygienic conditions. While claiming he never sanctioned the horrors of Auschwitz, Höss himself did nothing to correct the increasingly intolerable living environment.[5]

In his memoirs, Höss was more truthful than he had been at Nuremberg about the existence of prisoner abuse at Auschwitz, but remained reticent about his role in its perpetration:

> I for my part never sanctioned them (the horrors of the concentration camp). I myself never maltreated a prisoner, far less killed one. Nor have I ever tolerated maltreatment by my subordinates. ... I knew very well that prisoners in Auschwitz were ill-treated by the SS, by their civilian employers, and not least of all by their fellow-prisoners. I used every means at my disposal to stop this. But I could not.[6]

Höss was well aware that the SS and prisoner functionaries abused inmates on a daily basis. He fostered this environment by his example and, as necessary, shielded himself and the perpetrators from charges of abuse. When he learned of the massacre of 90 French Jewish women at the Budy penal camp by female German prisoners and the SS, he whitewashed the investigation. Female French witnesses were silenced by phenol injection, and

Höss destroyed the sole set of photographs taken during the investigation. He knew of the torturous roll calls of Auschwitz prisoners twice a day sometimes lasting for hours no matter what the weather or the physical condition of the inmates. Contrary to his claim he never abused prisoners, Höss set the example for this type of mistreatment. As commandant of the protective custody camp at Sachsenhausen on January 18, 1940, Höss was personally responsible for the deaths of more than 150 prisoners when he needlessly ordered a prolonged roll call in freezing weather. Höss made it known that day why he could treat human beings so callously: "Those are not people, they are inmates." With him that day was SS-Hauptscharführer Gerhard Palitzsch, who joined Höss at Auschwitz. Palitzsch learned by Höss' example the propriety and acceptability of cruelty. Palitzsch took that lesson to Auschwitz, where he murdered thousands of inmates, mainly Poles, at the Death Wall in the courtyard of Block 11.

As punishment at Auschwitz, Höss employed standing cells in the basement of Block 11. Records reveal that Höss, on multiple occasions, chose 10 random prisoners who had committed no offense, locked them in a cell in the basement of Block 11 and condemned them to starve to death in retaliation for the escape of a fellow member of their kommando. Following the lead of his commandant, SS-Obersturmführer Karl Fritzsch subsequently inflicted the same punishment on other innocent prisoners. Höss was well aware of the role kapos and block elders played in keeping prisoners subdued and order maintained. He knew the value of the "greens" and brutes like Ernst Krankeman and Vacek—Funktionschäftlings—to serve as prisoner functionaries to beat and randomly kill inmates.[7]

Höss sought to blame "inferior officers" such as Palitzsch and Fritzsch for the mistreatment. He said, "My repeated instructions that Eicke's views (on the treatment of prisoners) be abandoned as hopelessly out-of-date … fell on deaf ears." "For it was not I, but they (Fritzsch and Palitzsch), who ran the camp. It was they who taught the Capos, from the chief block senior down to the last block clerk, how to behave. They trained the block leaders and told them how to treat the prisoners. … Against this passive resistance I was powerless." In fact, Fritzsch, Palitzsch and the other SS personnel operated Auschwitz in the manner encouraged by Höss, which exceeded even Eicke's training. Auschwitz survivor Hermann Langbein stated, "No one influenced the character of the Auschwitz extermination camp so strongly and had such an enduring influence on its guards as Rudolf Höss." SS-Untersturmführer Maximilian Grabner, the head of the Political Department, was known for his sadistic cruelty and unscrupulousness. According to Langbein, Höss equaled or surpassed Grabner as "the most vigorous exterminator of human beings."[8]

Sarah Joskowitz, an Auschwitz survivor, described Höss as "ruthless."

XI. Responsibility and Atonement

She said he was always screaming at the inmates at roll call that "work makes life sweet." He accused the prisoners of not exerting their best effort though they were weak and, in Joskowitz' words, "falling like flies." Survivor Mike Vogel said Höss was the "most cold-blooded animal we ever had." To Höss, "hanging and killing meant nothing." Vogel believed that Höss "loved the sadistic way of killing people." Höss' reputation for violence against prisoners was so well known that, upon his return to Auschwitz in May 1944 to oversee extermination of the Hungarian Jews, the camp resistance movement, which communicated regularly with an underground prisoner organization in Krakow, suggested that an attack be prepared and executed against him as soon as possible.[9]

SS leadership promulgated rules and regulations that governed the treatment of concentration camp inmates. The SS leadership admonished the concentration camp commandants to follow the instructions strictly. Not only were the commandants directed not to inflict cruelty, they were also required to prevent mistreatment. The SS were directed to give decent treatment to inmates and eliminate arbitrary treatment by subordinate SS men. Höss knew the rules well enough that he could remember them, almost verbatim, at his trial in Krakow in March 1947:

> The camp leader is responsible for the entire domain of the inmates of the camp. ... In particular, he has to make sure that the inmates are treated with strictness, but justly. Mistreatments must be reported immediately to the commander of the camp.[10]

According to Höss:

> The SS men of the officer corps of the commander [Kommandanturstab] and of the troop as well as all offices which occupy inmates will be taught constantly, orally and in written form, about the treatment of inmates, in particular about the prohibition of mistreatment of inmates. ... The SS men who supervised and guarded the work details [Arbeitskommando] had to make sure that the inmates worked diligently, but they did not have the right to punish any failures. If an inmate failed the work through laziness, neglect or evil will (!) [he probably means sabotage], it needed to be reported to the camp leader or officer for labor placement at the time of return to the camp. ... After a report for punishment had been made, the inmate was punished by the commander after having been heard by the camp leader with regard to his case. The kind of punishment was to be suggested by the camp leader with a notice about the result of his investigation of the case. The camp commander had the authority to mete out the following punishments: 1. Detention ... 2. Standing in punishment ... 3. Hanging from a post ... 4. Admission into a penal company ... 5. Punishment by flogging [on the order of the Concentration Camps Inspectorate, IKL].[11]

In the winter of 1942, the commandants received the following memorandum:

> The Commander in Chief of the SS and head of the German Police [Heinrich Himmler] has instructed that, in the future, lashing will be the punishment of last

resort. Prior approval to carry out such punishment will be given in the future only in the following cases:

A. When the inmate has been given all other possible punishments in accordance with the camp regulations, such as internal imprisonment, denial of food, or disciplinary labor, and on condition that none of these has been effective. Denial of food will, of course, be imposed only on those inmates who can physically endure this punishment, in accordance with a doctor's certification.

B. As a deterrent in special cases, such as in connection with attempts to escape or attack guards. Care should be taken that the punishment be carried out in a way that makes it a deterrent.

The commandant of the SS has decided that lashings should not be imposed for the convenience of commandants and guards who are too lazy to take upon themselves the effort involved in the education of the prisoners, in order to reform them. If, for example, one inmate is caught stealing food from another—he should be punished by withholding his food, on condition that this is possible from a medical point of view and on condition that this was his first offense of this kind. When, for medical reasons, this is not possible, he should be punished with internal imprisonment for three to five days, and fed only bread and water. Only in cases of repeated offenses should a request for lashing be submitted for prior approval. Lashing is the most severe of punishments. From the requests which have arrived here, it would seem that its purpose was not understood properly. The concentration camp commandants are requested to observe the disciplinary regulations strictly in the future, and restrict lashings to cases in which they are really justified.[12]

Whether Himmler or the SS leadership which generated these regulations sincerely believed they were being applied in Auschwitz is unknown. Any Auschwitz survivor likely would have welcomed their enforcement. In reality, random and arbitrary beatings and whippings were part of everyday life for inmates at Auschwitz, whether they came from SS or prisoner functionaries. As commandant of a camp with tens of thousands of inmates, Höss was fully aware, as he acknowledged, that his prisoners were being cruelly mistreated. In his memoirs, Höss admits he knew that the SS would set their dogs on prisoners, lacerating their skin and tearing their clothes to shreds, but he did nothing about it. Yet, he states, "I was never cruel, and I have never maltreated anyone."[13]

Contrary to his pronouncements of good intent, Höss admitted that his attitude towards conditions in the camp tended towards being cruel. He said that Himmler, at one point, wanted the concentration camps to focus on armaments. Everything else, including the welfare of inmates, became secondary. Höss frankly conceded that, to comply with this mandate, he became "harder, colder and even more merciless. ... I dared not let my feelings get the better of me. Everything had to be sacrificed to one end, the winning of the war. ... By the will of the Reichsführer-SS, Auschwitz became the greatest human extermination center of all time." Höss always remembered the

XI. Responsibility and Atonement

lesson he learned from the execution of his SS associate at Sachsenhausen who showed mercy to his captive friend. He recalled:

> This execution was always before my eyes to remind me of the demand that had been made upon us to exercise perpetual self-mastery and unbending severity.

Höss employed this robotic brutality at Sachsenhausen, qualifying him in Himmler's eyes for the position of commandant of Auschwitz.[14]

In an effort to portray himself as kinder than circumstances made him appear, Höss said it was clear that he was not suited to serve in a concentration camp because he disagreed with Eicke's harsh philosophy. He stated that his "sympathies lay too much with the prisoners." Eicke, who was well aware that Höss had been imprisoned for murder in the early 1920s, proved to be a much better judge of character than Höss. In denying his request for a transfer, Eicke told Höss no one was better qualified than he to serve as a camp guard. Höss learned Eicke's lessons well despite his prior experience as a prisoner himself. In his memoirs, when discussing interactions between prisoners and guards, Höss said, "This is the disadvantage of showing too much kindness and goodwill towards the prisoners. A single gesture of human understanding towards a strong-minded prisoner will often inaugurate a series of lapses from discipline on the part of the guard that can only end in the most severe punishment." His Eicke-trained attitude towards inmates, which he acknowledged was firm and often severe at Sachsenhausen, continued to manifest itself at Auschwitz.[15]

In attempting to shift blame for the brutality of the SS men and women and the prisoner functionaries under his supervision, Höss portrays himself as helpless. He states that despite every means at his disposal, he could not prevent the mistreatment and abuse of prisoners at Auschwitz. He fails to explain what actions he took to prevent any mistreatment. There is no record that any SS personnel at Auschwitz were ever punished for cruelty towards inmates. The Budy massacre resulted in the transfer of two SS staff members, nothing more.

On the other hand, if SS guards were not sufficiently strict, Höss took notice and corrective measures. When a female warden was punished with 25 blows on her buttocks for helping inmates, SS guard Irma Grese was ordered by Höss to deliver the last two blows to make the warden "hard." Former SS technical sergeant Hans Schillhorn testified, "Höss proceeded rigorously against the inmates as well as the SS."[16]

In justifying his implementation of the Final Solution in accordance with the orders of Hitler and Himmler, Höss claimed that refusal to obey an order was unthinkable for the SS. Yet, in absolving himself of responsibility for the systematic abuse inflicted on Auschwitz inmates, Höss failed to acknowledge that the SS men and women who he commanded were also trained to follow orders. Eicke told them on the day the war broke out that every order must be obeyed without hesitation. Certainly, such obedience would include compliance with orders that prisoners not be abused by SS or prisoner functionaries in accordance with SS regulations. If the responsible officers were trained by Eicke and were ordered by Höss not to inflict cruel and inhuman or barbaric punishment on the inmates, they would not have done so or would have faced punishment for their actions. Auschwitz prisoners were constantly beaten and abused by the SS and prisoner functionaries because Höss allowed such mistreatment to occur. It served his purpose of subjugating prisoners and maintaining discipline.[17]

Höss' attempt to minimize or even negate his role in the abuses that plagued the daily lives of inmates also ignores the fact that he was an effective camp commandant. Himmler was so pleased with his efforts at Auschwitz, he promoted him to SS-Obersturmbannführer (Lieutenant Colonel). In May 1943, Himmler sent SS-Obergruppenführer Maximillian von Herff to evaluate Höss and the work he had done at Auschwitz. His report card was exemplary:

> Concentration Camp Auschwitz. Camp commander SS-Obersturmführer Höss. Good soldier by appearance, sportive, a good rider, knows how to behave in every circumstance, calm, modest but determined and matter-of-fact. Does not push himself forward for recognition but lets his performances speak for themselves. H: is not only a good camp commander but he also forged new ways of running concentration camps by his thoughts and educational methods. He is a good organizer, a good agriculturalist and for the Eastern regions the exemplary German pioneer. He is very capable to assume a leadership position in concentration camp management. His particular strength is being practical.

According to Höss, he complained to Himmler early on about his manpower needs. Himmler scoffed and told him that Germany was at war, and Höss must make do with what he had. "As the war went on the Reichsführer-SS was constantly insisting on even greater economies in the manpower employed on guard duties," said Höss, so he left discipline in the hands of his SS subordinates and their prisoner functionaries. Not surprisingly, prisoners were constantly subjected to abuse. If Höss did not always see the mistreatment, it was because he chose not to look.[18]

Höss' cruelty towards the prisoners is clearly evident when compared to the actions of SS-Obersturmbannführer Arthur Liebehenschel, who replaced him in late 1943. Liebehenschel, who served as the commandant of Auschwitz I until May 1944, started a new era in the history of Auschwitz according to survivor Hermann Langbein. He stopped the random and arbitrary killings at Block 11. He ordered the destruction of the standing cells used to punish inmates. Liebehenschel also proclaimed a general bunker amnesty and later had the Death Wall in the courtyard between Block 10 and Block 11 torn

XI. Responsibility and Atonement

down. In addition, he rescinded the order to shoot any prisoner trying to escape.[19]

Jenny Spritzer, who worked in the Political Department, stated: "Everyone felt an enormous relief when one day Höss, the camp commandant, was appointed to a higher position in Oranienburg and replaced by Liebehenschel. The new commandant was aghast at the conditions in Auschwitz and immediately abolished capital punishment. Even the hanging of unsuccessful escapees was prohibited, as was the beating of inmates during interrogations, at work, or anywhere else." It was learned later, after the war, that Liebehenschel even tried to slow down the machinery of extermination. Langbein compared the two commandants in this way: "When technical difficulties threatened the program of extermination, Höss improvised and staked his whole authority on getting his subordinates to act in his spirit, whereas Liebehenschel limited himself to carrying out orders."[20]

Not only did Liebehenschel stop the killings in the courtyard of Block 11, he began an investigation into the Political Department concerning the constant illegal shootings. He noted the curious inconsistency in the Totenbuch, which listed the cause of death for persons who were shot at the Death Wall as illness and the place of death as the infirmary. The Political Department, which was accustomed to Höss' acceptance of the shootings and falsification of records, argued with Liebehenschel that the previous "bloody terror" was necessary. Prisoner Joseph Cyrankiewicz requested to speak to Liebehenschel, who agreed to see him. Cyrankiewicz told the commandant of a plan by a camp informer and a member of the Political Department to blame prisoners for the death of an SS guard during an escape. Liebehenschel advised Cyrankiewicz he would take care of the Political Department informants, who made life miserable for the prisoners, and assured him that there would be no retaliation against the inmates. When Höss was commandant, merely making a request to speak to the commandant could be dangerous.[21]

In *People in Auschwitz*, Langbein quotes Dr. Erwin Valentin, a Jew, as saying on May 16, 1945, "Under Liebehenschel life in Auschwitz changed to such an extent that it can almost be described as relatively bearable. Liebehenschel was especially favorably disposed toward the Jews. He prohibited the beating of Jews in workplaces, dismissed capos and foremen who had administered such beatings, and also accepted complaints from Jews." In his Auschwitz trial in Krakow in 1948, Liebehenschel was convicted of crimes against humanity. Although he was sentenced to death and subsequently executed, the court in its opinion noted, "There is no doubt that after his arrival at the camp the defendant introduced a number of changes in the treatment of the inmates that significantly improved their fate." Liebehenschel's ability to halt the killings at the Death Wall in the courtyard of Block 11 and to control the tenor of the treatment imposed upon Auschwitz prisoners wholly undermines Höss' claim that he was powerless to stop the cruel, systematic and persistent abuse meted out by his SS subordinates and the prisoner functionaries.[22]

Höss said, "Although I became accustomed to all that was unalterable in the camps, I never grew indifferent to human suffering. I have always seen it and felt for it. Yet because I might not show weakness, I wished to appear hard, lest I be regarded as weak, and had to disregard such feelings." In light of the daily horrors and atrocities visited upon the living at Auschwitz, it is difficult to believe that Höss felt compassion for Auschwitz prisoners. At some level, he probably wanted to believe he pitied the victims. Yet, ever since he was a child, Höss had no interpersonal relationships. He felt close to no one—not his mother, not his father, not his siblings, not his wife—save perhaps his children. He had no friends. Höss did not empathize; he did not feel the pain and suffering of the inmates. He shut out feelings. Obedience to Hitler and the Third Reich preempted his soul.[23]

Final Solution

As for his participation in the Final Solution directed by Hitler and orchestrated by Himmler in 1941, Höss repeatedly said that he was given an order, and, as an SS officer, he was compelled to obey it. His memoirs make frequent reference to his obligation to exterminate the Jews, which he called "an extraordinary and monstrous order." When he was summoned to Berlin by Himmler and told of the role he and Auschwitz would play in eliminating Jews from Europe, Höss claims he did not reflect on it. He said, "I had been given an order, and I had to carry it out. Whether this mass extermination of the Jews was necessary or not was something on which I could not allow myself to form an opinion, for I lacked the necessary breadth of view. If the Führer had himself given the order for the 'final solution of the Jewish question,' then, for a veteran National-Socialist and even more so for an SS officer, there could be no question of considering its merits." After his arrest, people repeatedly asked if he could have refused to obey the order or even assassinated Himmler. Höss believed that, of the thousands of SS officers, not one was capable of such a thought. "As Reichsführer-SS, his person was inviolable. His basic orders, issued in the name of the Führer, were sacred."[24]

Although Höss did not think about the mass killings when he was given the order, he insists that he and the other members of the SS who were duty-bound to perpetrate the genocide had their doubts. Höss said the "iron determination" necessary to carry out Hitler's order could only come from the stifling of all human emotions. While his subordinates were free to privately share their doubts, he was not:

XI. Responsibility and Atonement

With very few exceptions, nearly all of those detailed to do this monstrous "work," this "service," and who, like myself, have given sufficient thought to the matter, have been deeply marked by these events.

Many of the men involved approached me as I went my rounds through the extermination buildings, and poured out their anxieties and impressions to me, in the hope that I could allay them.

Again and again during these confidential conversations I was asked: is it necessary that we do all this? Is it necessary that hundreds of thousands of women and children be destroyed? And I, who in my innermost being had on countless occasions asked myself exactly this question, could only fob them off and attempt to console them by repeating that it was done on Hitler's order. I had to tell them that this extermination of Jewry had to be, so that Germany and our posterity might be freed forever from their relentless adversaries.

... we were all tormented by secret doubts.

I myself dared not admit to such doubts. In order to make my subordinates carry on with their task, it was psychologically essential that I myself appear convinced of the necessity for this gruesomely harsh order.

Everyone watched me.

...

I had to appear cold and indifferent to events that must have wrung the heart of anyone possessed of human feelings. ... I had to watch coldly, while the mothers with laughing or crying children went into the gas-chambers.[25]

Höss' assertion that "nearly all" of the SS were deeply affected and tormented by secret doubts about the mass extermination seems not only unlikely but fanciful. Evidence corroborating Höss' statement simply does not exist. Of course, not all of the SS were as brutal as Otto Moll, the sadistic and bloodthirsty pit master who possessed no qualms at throwing living human beings into the fire. However, the extermination of more than a million human beings testifies to the willing participation of the SS guards who abused prisoners and led them to their deaths in the Auschwitz gas chambers. No doubt, the life of the SS who supervised the Sonderkommando as they disposed of the bodies in the cremation pits was difficult. Those guards were given extra rations, including additional liquor, to help them deal with the scenes they witnessed. The stench of burning flesh, the sight of body after body being thrown into the flames and the inevitable human ash deposited on their hands and face would test the fortitude of almost any human being. To say they were traumatized because they participated in the killing of innocent men, women and children, though, is a different matter. There is no testimony from SS or Auschwitz survivors to demonstrate any SS sympathy for the plight of the Jews as they were unloaded from the trains and marched to the gas chambers.

According to SS-Unterscharführer Pery Broad, a member of the Political Department, if one were to ask an SS guard, pointing to the corpses of men and women lying on the ground, together with children, why those people had to be exterminated, then one received as a rule the answer, "It must be so!" And that answer seemed, in his opinion, to be quite conclusive. Broad stated, "Such was the influence of propaganda, finding with them an only too eager acceptance, due also to their sadistic tendencies, to their megalomania and their intellectual limitations." No existing camp document contains evidence that any SS guard was punished for refusing to take part in the Holocaust. In *People in Auschwitz*, Hermann Langbein observed that neither Höss nor other Nazis responsible for implementing the Final Solution defended themselves on the basis that they executed the orders to commit murder out of a fear of punishment. The willingness of so many in the SS to murder hundreds of thousands of human beings without reason is evidence of the diabolical nature of the Nazi philosophy and the SS indoctrination that a person is excused from fault when following an order. It almost defies rational belief that so many agreed to surrender their morality so readily.[26]

Höss seemed unable to describe any sincere or heartfelt feelings when discussing how he felt after participating in killing. He consistently used the term "deeply affected" or "deeply marked" by mass extermination events. Höss used the same phrase when describing the first firing squad he commanded at Sachsenhausen. He stated, "I had to observe every happening with a cold indifference." If Höss was deeply affected, it was not a true sympathy or empathy for his victims. In all likelihood, it arose more from the power he exercised over life and death. Primo Levi, a survivor who wrote the Introduction to *Commandant of Auschwitz*, said that Höss' "statement that his 'stone mask' concealed an aching heart is not only indecent but also a childish lie."[27]

As Höss repeated again and again, "Himmler had ordered [the Final Solution] and had even explained the necessity and I really never gave much thought to whether it was wrong." Although Höss had his orders, he never says he disagreed with them. In fact, in all likelihood, he and most of the SS fully approved of the directive. In his memoirs, Höss acknowledges that, at the time Himmler told him of the Final Solution in the summer of 1941, "the reasons behind the extermination program seemed to be right." As was Höss, the SS had been convinced by Hitler's worldview under National Socialism. The Jewish stereotype was part of that view. In his own words, Höss was a "fanatical National-Socialist" and was firmly convinced that Nazi ideals would prevail throughout the world.[28]

Höss told Dr. Gilbert at Nuremberg that he learned his anti–Semitism from Joseph Goebbels' editorials in *Das Reich*, as well as his books and his various speeches; Alfred Rosenberg's *The Myth of the 20th Century* and some of his speeches; and, of course, Hitler's *Mein Kampf* and his speeches. Höss expounded on what had made an impression:

XI. Responsibility and Atonement

All of these writings and speeches constantly preached the idea that Jewry was Germany's enemy. For me as an old fanatic National Socialist, I took it all as fact—just as a Catholic believes in his Church dogma. It was just truth without question; I had no doubt about that. I was absolutely convinced that the Jews were the opposite pole from the German people, and sooner or later there would have to be a showdown between National Socialism and World Jewry—that was even in peacetime. On the basis of these doctrines, I assumed that other people would sooner or later be convinced of the Jewish danger, and would likewise take a stand against it. All these books and writings and speeches said that the Jewish people were a minority in all countries, but, because their material power was so great, they influenced and controlled people to such an extent that they could maintain their power. It was shown how their control of press, film, radio, and education controlled German life. We assumed it was likewise the case in other countries, and that in time other countries would break their power as we did. And if anti-Semitism did not succeed in wiping out this Jewish influence, the Jews would succeed in bringing about a war to wipe out Germany.[29]

So, if Höss failed to give Himmler's directive any thought in June 1941, it was not simply because it was an order. It was more than SS training; it was indoctrination. Höss acknowledged: "My fanatical love of my fatherland and my greatly exaggerated sense of duty provided a good basis for this indoctrination." Höss recalled, "The Party ruled the State. Its successes could not be denied. The means and the ends of the NSDAP were right. I believed this implicitly and without the slightest reservation." Years of National Socialistic teaching imprinted onto Höss that Jews had cost Germany the First World War, a war in which Höss had fought and seen men die, including his beloved captain.

Hitler, Goebbels and Rosenberg had engrained in Höss the belief that Jews, with their money and influence, controlled and manipulated every aspect of life in Germany to the detriment of ordinary Germans. Although Höss never discussed racial purity, that tenet was central to Nazi philosophy and extermination of the Jews would further that goal. Höss told Dr. Gilbert:

> That was the picture I had in my head, so, when Himmler called me to him, I just accepted it as the realization of something I had already accepted—not only I, but everybody. I took it so much for granted that even though this order, which would move the strongest and coldest nature—and at that moment this crass order to exterminate thousands of people (I did not know then how many)—even though it did frighten me momentarily—it fitted in with all that had been preached to me for years. The problem itself, the extermination of Jewry, was not new—but only that I was to be the one to carry it out, frightened me at first. But after getting the clear direct order and even an explanation with it—there was nothing left but to carry it out.

It was Höss' job and his intent to abolish "Jewish supremacy."[30]

Knowing that Höss held these beliefs about the Jews and had for many years, it is difficult to see where his "secret doubts" crept in. Nothing in his memoirs suggests that he ever changed his view concerning the threat posed by Jews to the world in general and Germany in particular. Höss did address the genocide and conceded in the end it was a bad idea, but not on moral or ethical grounds:

> I also see now that the extermination of the Jews was fundamentally wrong. Precisely because of these mass exterminations, Germany has drawn upon herself the hatred of the entire world. It in no way served the cause of anti–Semitism, but on the contrary brought the Jews far closer to their ultimate objective.

In retrospect, Höss regretted killing the Jews, not because one million human beings had been wiped from the face of the earth but because it had harmed Germany and furthered the goal of world Jewry.[31]

Dr. Gilbert wanted to know why it was "taken for granted that the Jews were to blame for everything." Höss said:

> Well, we just never heard anything else. It was not just newspapers like the *Sturmer* but it was everything we ever heard. Even our military and ideological training took for granted that we had to protect Germany from the Jews.... It only started to occur to me after the collapse that maybe it was not quite right, after I heard what everybody was saying. But nobody had ever said these things before; at least we never heard of it. Now I wonder if Himmler really believed all that himself or just gave me an excuse to justify what he wanted me to do.

As most criminals, only after being caught did Höss take the time to reflect on his wrongdoing. Of course, his failure to think in advance does not excuse his personal responsibility for the atrocities he perpetrated at Auschwitz.[32]

When Höss and other Nazi officials met with Himmler at Flensburg after Hitler's suicide, he was surprised by Himmler's instructions to disguise himself as a common soldier. He said, "With the Führer gone, our world had gone. Was there any point in going on living? We would be pursued and persecuted wherever we went." He and Hedwig each had poison vials to take in case the Soviet advance came too close, but decided not to take them because of their children. Ultimately, Höss did follow Himmler's order, hiding first as a sailor in the Navy, then as a farmer. He changed his name and hoped to escape from Germany with his family. In his memoirs, in justifying his compliance with the extermination order, Höss described himself as "a soldier and an officer." If that is so, why did he and the other Nazis feel the need to hide as criminals?[33]

Höss, as well as all the other Nazis, knew that they were, in fact, criminals. They had fought an unjust war. Germany, led by its beloved Führer, started a world war of aggression by invading Poland without cause. Two years later, they targeted the Soviet Union because Hitler hated Communism and desired territorial expansion. As long as Hitler continued with his successes, Germans followed him wherever he led. Eventually, he marched

XI. Responsibility and Atonement

Germany over the precipice to destruction, resulting in worldwide deaths of more than 60 million people.

Höss was also aware he and the Nazis were mass murderers. At Nuremberg, Höss testified that when he was summoned to Berlin in the summer of 1941 to receive his instructions about implementation of the Final Solution, Himmler stressed that it was a "secret Reich matter." Although Höss said he did not reflect on the order, he was intelligent enough to know that secrecy was mandated by the nefarious nature of the task they would be performing. In his memoirs, Höss noted, "During bad weather or when a strong wind was blowing, the stench of burning flesh was carried for many miles and caused the whole neighborhood to talk about the burning of Jews, despite official *counter-propaganda*" (emphasis added). Höss knew he and the SS were committing mass murder, and they needed to deceive the outside world about their crimes.[34]

Höss was not merely a soldier and an officer, as he portrays himself. He was part of a criminal organization formed at the highest level of government. In its judgment, the Tribunal at Nuremberg declared the SS to be a criminal organization. The Tribunal found that the SS actively participated in the steps leading up to aggressive war, imposed consistently brutal treatment on the inmates of concentration camps and carried out the extermination of the Jews. Höss participated in a conspiracy with other SS knowing full well the crimes he was committing. He *chose* not to think about the monstrosity of exterminating the Jewish race because he agreed with that goal.[35]

Evidence does not support Höss' claim that he "was no longer happy in Auschwitz once the mass exterminations had begun." In May 1943, SS-Obergruppenführer Maximillian von Herff found that Höss had "forged new ways of running concentration camps by his thoughts and educational methods" and was "very capable to assume a leadership position in concentration camp management." His particular strength was being practical. As Laurence Rees noted in *Auschwitz: A New History*, "Höss showed every sign of being keen to return to Auschwitz" to oversee the extermination of the Hungarian Jews in May 1944. His family had remained in the commandant's villa next to Auschwitz I while he was assigned to the Inspectorate of Concentration Camps in Berlin. When Höss returned, he utilized the "pioneer" thinking that had built Auschwitz into the greatest mass killing facility of the Third Reich. He reinstated proven assistants in the key positions of the extermination machinery from which they had been removed by SS-Obersturmbannführer Arthur Liebehenschel. Höss made improvements and repairs on the machinery of death so that Auschwitz could function most effectively as transport after transport of Hungarian Jews entered through the gatehouse into Birkenau. From the end of April 1944 to the first week of July 1944, approximately 394,000 Hungarian Jews were taken immediately from the trains to be executed in the gas chambers under the watchful eye of Rudolf Höss.[36]

Whether or not he was happy, Höss was all business. In supervising the exterminations, Höss said he must abstain from showing the "slightest trace of emotion."[37] Dr. Gilbert and Dr. Leon Goldensohn, the Nuremberg psychiatrist, conducted interviews of Höss and reached a similar conclusion regarding his emotional makeup. In describing Auschwitz, in answering their questions about the mass extermination and in justifying his actions, Höss was completely devoid of emotion.

Dr. Gilbert asked Höss how it was technically possible to exterminate 2.5 million people. "Technically?" he asked. "That wasn't so hard—it would not have been hard to exterminate even greater numbers." To Höss, Dr. Gilbert's inquiries were naïve—posed by someone with no working knowledge of mass extermination. Höss explained that one must figure it on a daily 24-hour basis; it was possible to exterminate up to 10,000 in one 24-hour period. Höss was gassing that many Hungarians each day in the spring and summer of 1944. He informed Dr. Gilbert that there were actually six gas chambers—two large ones which could accommodate as many as 2,000 in each and four smaller ones that would hold up to 1,500. Dr. Gilbert's expressed attempt to understand was not making sense, so Höss redirected him:

> No, you don't figure it right. The killing itself took the least time. You could dispose of 2,000 head in a half hour, but it was the burning that took all the time. The killing was easy; you didn't even need guards to drive them into the chambers; they just went in expecting to take showers and, instead of water, we turned on poison gas. The whole thing went very quickly.

Höss seemed proud of his ability to deceive so many Jews.[38]

Dr. Gilbert stated that in all of his discussions, Höss was quite matter-of-fact and apathetic, showing belated interest in the enormity of his crime only because someone inquired about it. Dr. Gilbert asked Höss about his reaction to the horrendous undertaking Himmler had placed upon him. In the same apathetic tone of voice, Höss stated he had no reaction: "At the moment I could not oversee the whole thing, but later I got some idea of its extent. But I only thought of the necessity of it, as the order was put to me." Again, he insisted disobedience of the order was not an option. He also failed to consider the consequences either for himself or for his victims. Höss believed that he need not worry about responsibility or consequences because, under the prevailing view in Germany at the time, the man who gave the orders was responsible. "But, what about the human–?" Dr. Gilbert started to ask. Höss interrupted, "That just didn't enter into it." By absolving himself of personal responsibility, Höss had justified the murder of more than one million human beings.[39]

XI. Responsibility and Atonement

After several discussions with Höss, Dr. Gilbert made the following assessment:

> There is too much apathy to leave any suggestion of remorse and even the prospect of hanging does not unduly distress him. One gets the general impression of a man who is intellectually normal but with the schizoid apathy, insensitivity and lack of empathy that could hardly be more extreme in a frank psychotic.[40]

Dr. Goldensohn asked Höss similar questions about Auschwitz and received similar answers. When asked what he thought of what happened at Auschwitz, Höss looked "blank and apathetic." He had personal orders from Himmler; he could not protest. If the Jews were not exterminated at that time, then the German people would be exterminated for all time by the Jews, according to Höss. When Dr. Goldensohn asked Höss to explain how the Jews would destroy Germany, he did not know. That is what Himmler told him, and he believed it and "blindly obeyed." Although Nazi propaganda had taught him that Jews controlled German businesses, media and education, Höss most certainly noticed that the Jews who were unloaded from the trains were not all wealthy and powerful. As he watched many middle class and lower class Jews being thrown from the cattle cars, Höss should have wondered how they controlled Germany or constituted a threat to Hitler. "Do you have any feelings of guilt for this?" Dr. Goldensohn wanted to know. "Yes, now naturally it makes me think that it was not right," said Höss, providing the answer he knew Dr. Goldensohn expected someone in Höss' position would give.[41]

Later, Dr. Goldensohn again asked Höss about his personal feelings: "Do you feel guilty, or merely a soldier who has done his duty?" Höss replied in a manner more consistent with the answer he provided Dr. Gilbert, "Up until the capitulation of Germany I believed I carried out orders correctly and acted in the right manner. But after the capitulation, when I read newspaper reports of the trials, et cetera, I came to the conclusion that the necessity for extermination of the Jews was not as they told me—now I am guilty, as are all of the others, and I have to take the consequences." He told Dr. Goldensohn the consequence would be hanging, but that others—those who gave the orders—were more guilty than was he. Höss did not elaborate on what he read that changed his opinion. He said he was "guilty," not that he felt guilt or shame.[42]

One day, Dr. Goldensohn asked Höss for his spontaneous thoughts, hoping to gain a glimpse into the mind of the man who would become known as the greatest mass murderer of all time. Höss had the same puzzled, apathetic expression and gazed from Dr. Goldensohn to the wall and back to the translator in a doleful manner, then answered, "I haven't been thinking of anything in particular." Surprised, no doubt, that Höss was not reflecting on his years at Auschwitz, Dr. Goldensohn asked Höss what he thought of what he had done and his desire for inner peace. As Dr. Goldensohn expected of someone who had been the commandant of Auschwitz, he wondered if Höss suffered any emotional disturbance. Höss responded, "Just that my feet ache and that I am more concerned with my family's welfare than with my own."[43]

Finally, Dr. Goldensohn and Höss entered into the following exchange:

> DR. GOLDENSOHN: Does the fact that you put the phenomenal number of 2.5 million men, women, and children to death, not to mention your supervision of exterminations and excursions in all of the other camps that you supervised since 1943—does that fact not upset you a little at times?
>
> HÖSS: I thought I was doing the right thing, I was obeying orders, and now, of course, I see that it was unnecessary and wrong. But I don't know what you mean by being upset about these things because I didn't personally murder anybody. I was just the director of the extermination program in Auschwitz. It was Hitler who ordered it through Himmler and it was Eichmann who gave me the order regarding transports.
>
> DR. GOLDENSOHN: Do you ever have any thoughts of these executions, gassings, or burning of corpses—in other words, do such thoughts come upon you at times and in any way haunt you?
>
> HÖSS: No. I have no such fantasies.[44]

These exceptional interviews with Höss at Nuremberg by Drs. Gilbert and Goldensohn provide extraordinary insight into the mind of the man who was more responsible than any other for the effective execution of the Final Solution. He related the massacre of men, women and children with no emotion. It was everyday work to him, nothing more. As Dr. Gilbert noted, Höss would not even begin to grasp the enormity of Auschwitz had someone not asked him. Nothing about the suffering he caused or the lives he destroyed bothered him in the least. He absolved himself of all personal responsibility.

On one occasion, Höss observed two small children playing so intently that they simply refused to let their mother tear them away. Höss recalled, "The imploring look in the eyes of the mother, who certainly knew what was happening, is something I shall never forget." People already in the gas chamber were becoming restless, so Höss acted. He nodded to the SS officer on duty who picked up the children and carried them into the gas chamber, accompanied by their mother, who, according to Höss, "was weeping in the most heart-rendering fashion." He can relate that story yet still say, "I didn't personally murder anybody." Höss also told Dr. Goldensohn he was not a sadist because he had never struck any internee in the entire time he was commandant.[45]

On April 12, 1946, at Nuremberg, Höss, following some testing, asked Dr. Gilbert an interesting question: "I suppose you want to know in this way if my thoughts and habits are normal?" Dr. Gilbert wanted to know what Höss thought. Höss responded, "I am entirely normal. Even while I was doing this extermination work, I led a normal family life, and so on." Höss was raised in a loving family even if he never experienced closeness to his parents or sisters. He knew right from wrong and good from bad. Höss said he had a very good, happy childhood. He asserts that he suppressed his feelings deliberately to fulfill Hitler's and Himmler's directive.[46]

As noted by the Polish prosecutor, Dr. Cyprian, at his trial, Höss faced everything with an "iron expression" and "legendary calm." He showed no pity for the people and became agitated only when evidence suggested he failed to fulfill his duties. At the end of his memoirs, having shifted blame to Hitler and Himmler for wrongfully misleading him and Germany, Höss concludes, "Unknowingly I was a cog in the wheel of the great extermination machine created by the Third Reich." Dr. Jan Sehn, the Polish prosecutor who met with Höss on numerous occasions and who was instrumental in motivating Höss to write his memoirs, provides a strikingly accurate estimation of the commandant of Auschwitz: "What is truly missing in all his apathy and memories is an authentic depression. Formally, so to speak, Höss acknowledges the accusations of the prosecution against him, but his report remains the confession of a person completely disinterested, who comes at the end to the conclusion that his fate was tragic."[47]

In his memoirs, Höss references the "tricks" fate played on him. He notes how close he came to death several times in his life—in World War I, in the Freikorps, in a 1941 automobile accident on the autobahn, a riding accident in 1942 and other incidents. As Höss concluded his memoirs in February 1947, he lamented, "On every occasion fate has intervened to save my life, so that at last I might be put to death in this shameful manner." Despite the time given him to reflect on his actions, he could not bring himself to freely admit his guilt.[48]

Viktor Frankl wrote of his concentration camp experiences in *Man's Search for Meaning*. He had lived since September 1942 with his wife and his parents in the Theresienstadt Ghetto in Czechoslovakia. His father died at Theresienstadt. In October 1944, he and his wife were deported to Auschwitz. She would be sent to Bergen-Belsen and die there. Frankl's mother and brother would be killed at Auschwitz. Frankl was transferred to camps near Dachau, finishing the war at Turkheim. When Frankl's camp was liberated, some of the Jews hid the commandant in the forest. The commandant had spent a considerable amount of his own money to buy medicine for the prisoners. They made the American officer searching for him promise the commandant would not be harmed before disclosing his location. No Auschwitz inmate would seek to protect Höss or aid him in his effort to remain hidden from the Allies after the war.[49]

XII

Execution

No one would question the propriety of the site chosen for the execution of Rudolf Höss—Auschwitz I, where it all began seven years before. Next to the crematorium where Russian POWs and Jews were first murdered with Zyklon B and a short walk from the villa where Höss and his family lived their happy lives, a simple wooden gallows had been erected. Only Höss knows what he was thinking as he awaited his execution. Ever since he was a child, he was more comfortable alone—why should he look for solace from anyone now? Outwardly, he appeared supremely calm.

Professor Dr. Stanislaw Batawia, a criminologist and psychiatrist who interviewed Höss numerous times both before and after his conviction, described Höss as follows:

> One has to imagine a man of more than 40, of medium height, normal body and an insignificant appearance. The former commander of Auschwitz had always a concentrated, serious face during this last phase of his life in prison; one could detect distress and sorrow; he always had a sad face with harsh furrows in his brows; his eyes, besides sadness, sometimes also showing anxiety, shame and embarrassment, were looking at the interlocutor in a penetrating manner. Generally, his face was motionless, the rest of the body more or less stiff and rigid; the small hands with thin, delicate fingers, never made any gestures. When his cell was opened he stood up straight, then he remained for a long time totally immobile, resembling more a statue hewn of stone than a living human being.

To Dr. Batawia, Höss appeared reserved and was not talkative but felt the need to explain to the public the reason for his participation in the execution of more than one million human beings. Although most people would certainly see him as evil and sadistic, Höss wanted the opportunity to "justify" his actions, to the extent this was possible, in light of his indoctrination as an SS man and the obligations and burdens imposed upon him by Hitler and Himmler. Dr. Batawia observed that "the shyness he sometimes showed, the visible sensibility, the manner in which he reacted immediately, with darting eyes but reserved mien, to a word that could be interpreted as a disapproval of

XII. Execution

his utterance, all this did not fit the typical figure of the commander of a Nazi concentration camp which we associate with the word 'Auschwitz.'"[1]

Dr. Batawia found nothing abnormal in Höss' psychological makeup. He was not an unfeeling psychopath nor was he a human being who ever showed criminal inclinations or sadistic tendencies. He was a person of very mediocre intelligence and tended, from childhood, to subordinate himself to every kind of authority. He was reserved and sensitive, although he did not show his feelings. Since his youth, Höss took his duties very seriously and fulfilled them conscientiously and eagerly. He demonstrated strength and unusual willpower. Dr. Batawia attributed Höss' criminal development to the sociological framework of his life and the particular historical events of his time which transformed Höss into "more a robot than a living human being, the ideal citizen of the Third Reich and of an SS man." Only at the end of his life did Höss actually *think* about what he had done and what was right and wrong outside of the context of the SS.[2]

Four days before his death, Höss wrote his final letters to his wife and children. The apathy and lack of emotion observed by Drs. Gilbert and Goldensohn in Nuremberg and by Dr. Cyprian at his trial in Warsaw were replaced by an outpouring of heartfelt love and affection. Höss' letter to Hedwig included the reference to himself as an unknowing "cog in the terrible German extermination machine." Höss also told Hedwig, not surprisingly, he only learned about many of the atrocities at Auschwitz during his trial. Understandably, Höss wanted to protect the image of her husband that Hedwig would carry with her after his death. The letters to his family, far more than his testimony about life and death at Auschwitz, reveal the heart in Höss that one million souls wish would have manifested itself sooner.[3]

The two driving principles in Höss' life were love of country and love of family.[4] Höss believed he had displayed his love of country by unbending obedience to Hitler and the SS in his role as Auschwitz commandant. He built the largest concentration camp in the Third Reich that either immediately killed "enemies of the State" (mainly Jews) in the gas chambers or imprisoned them in inhuman living conditions. By his own admission, Höss showed no emotion as he fulfilled these duties. The outward appearance of insensitivity and apathy that Höss portrayed to strangers belied the emotion that he held inside for his family. From his childhood, Höss had been reserved and emotionally isolated. It is fair to say even his family never saw the side of Höss expressed in these words:

11 April 1947

You, my dear, good children!

> Your daddy has to leave you now. For you, poor ones, there remains only your dear, good Mommy. May she remain with you for a good long time yet. You do not understand yet what your good Mommy really means to you, and what a precious

possession she is to you. The love and care of a mother is the most beautiful and valuable thing that exists on this earth. I realized this a long time ago, only when it was too late; and I have regretted it all my life.

To you, my dear, good children, I address therefore my last (beseeching) request: Never forget your dear, good mother! She has constantly taken care of you with such sacrificing love. Her life concerned only you. How much of the good things in life has she sacrificed for your sake. How she feared for you when you were ill and how painfully and untiringly did she nurse all of you. She was never at ease when all of you were not around her. Only for your sake must she suffer now all of the bitter misery and poverty. Don't ever forget this throughout your whole life.

Help her now to carry her painful fate. Be loving and good to her. Help her as well as you can with your limited strength. In this manner pay her part of the thanks for the love and care she gave you during the days and nights.

Klaus, my dear, good boy!

You are the oldest. You are now going out into the world. You have to now make your own way through life. With your own strength you must now shape your life. You have good aptitudes. Use them! Keep your good heart. Become a person who lets himself be guided primarily by warmth and humanity. Learn to think and to judge for yourself, responsibly. Don't accept everything without criticism and as absolutely true, everything which is brought to your attention.

Learn from life. The biggest mistake of my life was that I believed everything faithfully which came from the top, and I didn't dare to have the least bit of doubt about the truth of that which was presented to me.

Walk through life with your eyes open. Don't become one-sided; examine the pros and cons in all matters.

In all your undertakings, don't just let your mind speak, but listen above all to the voice in your heart. Much, my dear boy, will not be understood by you as yet. But always remember my last advice.

I wish you, my dear Klaus, all the luck in your life. Become a competent, straightforward person who has his heart in the right place.

The letter to his eldest son Klaus reflects a truth Höss realized only at the end of his life after many years in the SS. Höss was taught by his father to obey the rules and regulations of the State unconditionally. Now, he warned his own son against blind faith into what someone professes to be absolute truth. Höss sought to pass on to Klaus the value of being a thinking human being, to question authority and to doubt if necessary. He wanted his son to keep his eyes open at all times—to think with his heart as well as his mind.

Kindi and Püppi.

You, my big girls!

You are yet too young to learn the extent of the hard fate dished out to us. But you especially, my dear, good girls, are specially obligated to stand at your poor unfortunate mother's side and with love assist her in every way you can. Surround her with all your childlike love from your heart and show her how much you love her and show her how much you want to help her in her need. I can only beseech you, listen to your dear, good mother! She will now in her devoted love and care show you the right way and will bestow on you those lessons you will need for life in order to become good and capable human beings.

As fundamentally different as you two are in your character, you both, my dear [Püppi], and you, my dear Hausmütterle, have, however, soft and feeling hearts. Retain these throughout your later life. This is the most important thing. Only later will you understand that and will you remember my last words.

My Burling, you dear little guy! Hang on to your happy child disposition. The cruel life will tear you, my dear boy, soon enough away from your child's world. I was happy to hear from your dear mother that you are progressing so well in school.

Your dear father is unable to tell you anything more. You poor little guy have now only your dear, good Mommy left who will care for you. Listen to her with love and kindness and so remain "Daddy's dear Burling."

My dear Annemäusl.

How little was I permitted to experience your dear little personality. Your dear, good Mommy will have to take you, my dear Mäusl, for us into her arms and tell you of your daddy, and how very much he loved you.

May you be for a long time Mommy's little ray of sun and continue to give her much joy. May you, with your sunny ways, help your poor, dear Mommy through all the dreary hours.

Once more from my heart I ask you all, my dear, good children, take to heart my last words. Think of them again and again.

Keep in loving memory,
Your Dad[5]

And in the final letter to his wife, Höss wrote:

11 April 1947

My dear, good Mutz!

My path through life is now coming to a close. Fate has worked out a truly sad ending for me. How fortunate were the comrades who were allowed to die an honest soldier's death.

Calmly and composed I look toward the end. From the beginning I was completely clear about the fact that I would perish with the world to which I had pledged myself with all my body and soul when that world was shattered and destroyed. Without realizing it, I had become a cog in the terrible German extermination machine. My activities in performing my task were out in the open. Since I was the Kommandant of the extermination camp Auschwitz I was totally responsible for everything that happened there, whether I knew about it or not. Most of the terrible and horrible things that took place there I learned only during this investigation and during the trial itself. I cannot describe how I was deceived, how my directives were twisted, and all the things they had carried out supposedly under my orders. I certainly hope that the guilty will not escape justice.

It is tragic that, although I was by nature gentle, good-natured, and very helpful, I became the greatest destroyer of human beings who carried out every order to exterminate people no matter what. The goal of the many years of rigid SS training was to make each SS soldier a tool without its own will who would carry out blindly all of Himmler's plans. That is the reason why I also became a blind, obedient robot who carried out every order.

My fanatic patriotism and my most exaggerated sense of duty were good prerequisites for this training.

At the end it is difficult to have to admit to myself that I have chosen a very wrong path and, because of it, I have brought about my own destruction.

But what good does all the weighing and balancing do? Was it right or was it wrong? In my opinion all our paths through life are predestined by fate and a wise providence, and are unchangeable.

Painful, bitter, and heavy-hearted is the separation from all of you, from you, dearest, best Mutz, and from all of you, my dear, good children, and that I have to leave you behind, poor unfortunates, in poverty and misery.

On you, my poor unfortunate wife, destiny has put the heaviest burden on us through our sad fate. For in addition to our unlimited pain of being torn apart, there is the burdensome worry about your future life and the worry about the children. But dearest, be consoled! Don't despair!

Time has a way of healing even the deepest, most serious wounds, which you cannot believe you can survive in the first painful moments. Millions of families have been torn apart or have been destroyed by this wretched war.

But life goes on. The children grow up. I only hope that you, dearest, best Mutz, may be given the strength and health so that you can care for all of them until they all can stand on their own two feet.

My misspent life places on you, dearest, the holy obligation to educate our children so that they have, in their deepest heart, a true humanity. Our dear children are all naturally good-natured. Nurture all of these good impulses in their hearts in every way. Make them sensitive to all human sorrow. What humanity is, I have only come to know since I have been in Polish prisons. Although I have inflicted so much destruction and sorrow upon the Polish people as Kommandant of Auschwitz, even though I did not do it personally, or by my own free will, they still showed such human understanding, not only by the higher officials, but also by the common guards, that it often puts me to shame. Many of them were former prisoners in Auschwitz or other camps. Especially now, during my last days, I am experiencing such humane treatment I never could have expected.

In spite of everything that happened, they still treat me as a human being.

My dear, good Mutz, I beg you, don't become hardened by the heavy blows fate has dealt us! Keep your good heart for yourself! Don't be led astray by troubles or hardship and misery through which you are forced to endure! Don't lose your faith in humanity.

Try, as soon as possible, to get away from those dreary surroundings.

Start the proceedings to change your name. Take back your maiden name again. Now there should not be any more difficulties about that! My name is now disgraced throughout the whole world, and you, my poor ones, have suffered unnecessary problems time and again because of my name, especially the children, who will be held back from future advancement. Certainly Klaus would have had an apprenticeship long ago if his name had not been Höss. It is for the best that my name disappears with me.

I also received permission to enclose my wedding ring in this letter to you.

With sadness and happiness I think of that time in the spring of our life when we exchanged the rings. Who could have guessed this kind of end of our life together.

"Days in the sun" were not granted us, but instead there were difficult toils,

XII. Execution

much sorrow, and worry. Only step by step did we get ahead. How happy we were through our children, whom you, dearest, best Mutz, happily bore for us time and again. In our children we saw our life's task. Our constant concern was to create a home as a steady foothold for them, and to raise them to be useful human beings. Time and again during my imprisonment I have gone back over our life together, remembering all the events and happenings, over and over. What happy hours we were allowed to experience, but we also had to suffer a great deal of deprivation, illness, grief, and heartbreak.

I thank you with all my heart, my dear, good friend, for all the goodness and beauty you brought into my life, and which you, at all times, shared bravely and faithfully with me, and also for your endless love and care for me. Forgive me, you good woman, if I have ever offended you, or hurt you.

How deeply and painfully I regret every hour that I did not spend with you, dearest and best Mutz, and the children because I believed duty would not allow it, or there were other commitments which I thought were more important.

A kind fate has allowed me to hear from you, dear ones. I received all eleven letters dated from December 31 to December 16. How happy I was therefore, especially during the days of the trial, to read your dear lines. Your care and love for me and the dear small talk of the children gave me new courage and strength to withstand everything. I am particularly grateful, my dearest, for the last letter, which you wrote Sunday during the early hours. It was as if you had a premonition that these would be the very last words that reached me. How bravely and clearly you write about everything. But what bitter sorrow, what deep pain can be found between the lines. I do know how intimately both our lives are intertwined, how hard this having to leave one another is.

I wrote to you, my dear, good Mutz, on Christmas, on January 26, and on March 3, and March 16, and hope you have received these letters. But how little can be said in writing, and especially under these circumstances. How much has to be left unsaid, which cannot be done in writing. But we have to make the best of it. I am so grateful that I could learn even a little about you, and that I could still tell you, dearest, essentially what moved me.

All my life I have been a reserved person. I never liked to let anyone look into me, to see what moved me in my innermost soul, and I always settled everything inside myself.

How often have you, dearest, regretted that, and found it painful, that you yourself, who stood nearest me, could be only such a small part in my inner life. And so I dragged with me all my doubts and depressions for many years about whether what I was doing was right or wrong and whether the harsh orders given to me were necessary. I could not and was not allowed to express my opinions to anyone. You, dearest, good Mutz, can now understand why I became more and more reserved, and more and more unapproachable. And you, dearest Mutz, and all of you loved ones, inadvertently had to suffer from that, and could not explain to yourselves my discontent, my absentmindedness, and my often grumpy manner. But that's the way it was; I regret it painfully. During my long and lonely imprisonment I've had enough time on my hands to think exhaustively about my life. I have thoroughly reviewed every aspect of my actions. Based on my present knowledge I can see today clearly, severely and bitterly for me, that the entire ideology about the world in which I believed so firmly and unswervingly was based on completely wrong premises and had to absolutely collapse one day.

And so my actions in the service of this ideology were completely wrong, even though I faithfully believed the idea was correct. Now it was very logical that strong doubts grew within me, and whether my turning away from my belief in God was based on completely wrong premises. It was a hard struggle. But I have again found my faith in my God. Dearest, I cannot write more about these things. It would just lead to too much.

Should you in your misery, my dear, good Mutz, find through the Christian faith strength and consolation, then follow the urge of your heart. Don't be led astray by anything. Also, you don't have to do what I have done. You should make your own decision about your Lord. The children will in any case, because of school, walk a different path than the one we have taken. Klaus may later wish to decide for himself, after he has matured, and maybe find his own way.

And so there is only a pile of rubble left from our world from which the survivors have to build a new and better world with great difficulty.

My time has come.

Now it is time to say the final goodbyes to you loved ones, you who were dearest to me in all the world!

How hard and painful this parting is.

You, dearest, best Mutz, I thank with all my heart once more for all your love and care and for all that you brought into my life! Through our dear and good children I will always be with you, you my poor, unfortunate wife. I leave with confident hope that after all the difficulty and sadness, you, my loved ones, will be allowed to find a small spot on the sunny side of life, and that you will find a modest chance at life and that you, my dear, good Mutz, will be accorded through our children a quiet and content happiness.

All my intimate good wishes accompany all of you dear ones on your life's journey to come. I thank with all my heart all of the dear, good people who stood by you in your hour of need and helped you, and I send my best regards.

My last dear greetings go to my parents, to Fritz and to all our dear old friends.

For the last time I send to you loved ones my regards, to you all, my dear, good children, my Annemäusl, my Burling, my Püppi, my Kindi and my Klaus, and to you, my dearest, best Mutz.

Oh you, my poor, unfortunate wife, most, most dear and with a heavy heart.

Keep me in loving remembrance.

Until my last breath, I remain with all my loved ones.

Your Daddy[6]

Höss' letter to Hedwig reveals a sincere sorrow at the loss of love, not only in the past but in the future. While busy with his administration of Auschwitz, Hedwig had asked Höss to remember his life was duty to family, not just duty to country. He apologized for the time he should have spent with her and the children when he believed, wrongly, that other commitments were more important. Höss acknowledged his lifelong failure to express emotion to Hedwig who nevertheless always stood by his side. He recognized the burden imposed upon her and thanked her for the "endless love and care" she had shown him. Undoubtedly, in this dying declaration, Höss poured out more emotion to Hedwig than she had ever heard from her husband. He realized that "millions of families have been torn apart or have been destroyed by this wretched war."

As the date of his execution approached, Höss reflected more deeply on his actions. Dr. Batawia suggested that Höss might want to speak to a priest. Had anyone proposed this course earlier, while Höss was the Auschwitz commandant or the Director of the DI Department of the WVHA, the idea, no doubt, would have been rejected outright. Höss' reasons for turning away from the Catholic Church in 1922 and replacing it with the idealism of the Nazi Party and the SS had not changed. Now, at life's end, his own mortality stared him in the face. When he arrived in Wadowice on April 4 after his trial in Warsaw, Höss asked to see to a priest.[7]

Initially, Höss' request was ignored. On April 7, he stated in writing his wish to "return to the Catholic Church" and sought to be visited by a priest. Arrangements were made for Father Wladyslaw Lohn of the Society of Jesus, a Jesuit priest who spoke German, to attend to Höss. On April 10, Father Lohn spoke for several hours with Höss, after which he "rejoined" the Catholic Church and confessed. Höss was noted to be very remorseful. The next day, Father Lohn returned to Höss' cell and administered the sacrament of communion as Höss knelt and cried.[8]

Finally, four days before his execution, Höss sent a statement to the public prosecutor:

> My conscience forces me to make the following declaration: in the seclusion of my detainment I arrived at the bitter knowledge of how enormous my crime against humanity has been. As commander of the Auschwitz extermination camp I executed part of the horrible human extermination plans of the "Third Reich." Thereby I caused the greatest harm against humanity and human solidarity. In particular, I caused incredible suffering to the Polish people. I am atoning for my responsibility with my life. May God forgive me my actions one day. I ask for pardon from the Polish nation. In the Polish prisons I first experienced what human compassion means. In spite of all that had happened I was shown a human compassion that I never expected and which shamed me profoundly. May the revelations and descriptions of the enormous crimes against humanity lead to the fact that in the future all prerequisites for such atrocious events will be prevented in advance!
>
> Rudolf Franz Ferdinand Hoss, Wadowice, April 12, 1947[9]

His last-minute readmission to the Catholic Church and the unexpected compassion shown him by his Polish jailers prompted Höss to seek the forgiveness of Poland, but his nearly lifelong belief in National Socialism was simply too strong to permit him to admit that he had wronged the worst "enemies of the State," the Jews. He acknowledged his participation in the "horrible human extermination plans of the 'Third Reich,'" yet he could not ask forgiveness for the murder of almost one million Jewish men, women and children. Even as the hangman was tying his noose, Höss could not see the wrong in the Final Solution. As Father Manfred Deselaers noted in *And Your Conscience Never Haunted You?*, "In spite of the impressive evidence for a true conversion of Höss, he didn't really comprehend it's full meaning." The "evil" which concerned Höss was his own demise, not the terror and death he imposed upon his victims. They were prisoners and Jews. As Höss told his brother-in-law, Fritz Hensel, who asked about the term "untermensch," "Look, you can see for yourself. They are not like you and me. They are different. They look different. They do not behave like human beings. They have numbers on their arms. They are here in order to die."[10]

The execution was initially set for April 14. Thousands of people had come to the Auschwitz death camp to witness the hanging of the commandant of Auschwitz. They left disappointed. An officer announced the execution had been postponed. Officials feared emotions in the crowd would flare up and the planned state-conducted execution would become a mob lynching. Two days later, Höss was driven from the jail at Wadowice to Block 11, where so many Auschwitz horrors occurred, and placed in a cell. Höss was asked if he had any last requests; he requested a priest and a cup of coffee. He was attended this day by Father Tomasz Zaremba from Oświęcim. Father Zaremba offered to hear confession but Höss declined, citing the confession he gave Father Lohn in Wadowice. One confession was apparently enough to relieve Höss' conscience of whatever guilt he felt for the years of torment, torture and murder he committed as the commandant of Auschwitz. When the judge asked if there was anything else that he would like, Höss answered, holding back his tears, "Yes, I would like to send my kindest regards to my wife and children. I also ask the Polish people to forgive me for what I have done to them." Once again, even at the threshold of death, Höss could not bring himself to apologize for his extermination of Jews.[11]

Höss indicated he was ready. The time was about 10:00 a.m. on April 16, 1947. The officer in charge led Höss towards the gallows near the old crematorium and within sight of the villa where he and his family had spent their "beautiful" life. Little more than 200 witnesses were present that day. Only persons with special passes were permitted entry. As they proceeded to the gallows, Höss walked past the Block 11 courtyard where thousands of Poles were murdered and Block 10 where Drs. Clauberg and Schumann conducted their medical experiments on the prisoners. Photographers captured the scene at the gallows. Höss, his emotions under control, climbed the four steps up the platform and onto a stool. The hooded hangman reached to place the crudely fashioned noose around his neck. As he did, a photographer caught Höss leaning backwards. Victor Frankl, a psychiatrist and an Auschwitz survivor, described a condition known as the "delusion of reprieve," when a condemned man, immediately before his execution, gets the illusion that he might be saved at the last minute. Perhaps that hope prompted Höss to lean

XII. Execution

Höss on the gallows (courtesy Polish Press Agency).

away. There would be no last-minute reprieve for Rudolf Höss. The noose was placed over his neck and tightened—no final words, no expressions of emotion. When the trap door sprung open, Höss was sent to his death—one life for 1.3 million. As one Auschwitz survivor, Stanislaw Hantz, who was present to witness the execution, said, "And during the execution you thought: One life for so many millions of people, is that not too little?" Höss' body was cremated and his ashes scattered.[12]

XIII

Conclusion

Stepan Michael Winternitz was born October 13, 1935, in Prague, Czechoslovakia, to Rudolf and Lore Winternitz. Stepan's father was a chemist (see Appendix III). Lore was a native German born in Hanover on May 13, 1904. On November 20, 1942, Lore and Stepan, her only child, were taken from their home and transported 63 kilometers from Prague to the Theresienstadt concentration camp. Rudolf Winternitz was not with them. On October 4, 1944, just short of his ninth birthday, Stepan and his mother were among 1,500 Jews taken from Theresienstadt to Auschwitz and murdered, most likely in the gas chamber. As Himmler soon thereafter directed that the gassing of the Jews be stopped and the Auschwitz gas chambers be destroyed, Stepan and his mother would be among the last victims to die in Höss' extermination machine.[1]

Höss was no longer in Auschwitz when Stepan and Lore Winternitz were executed. In July, he successfully completed the annihilation of almost 400,000 Hungarian Jews and returned to his post in Berlin. Yet he bore responsibility for the deaths of Stepan, Lore and every human being who perished in the mechanism he created. Höss had come so far from the solitary boy in Baden-Baden and the young soldier in Palestine. While tragedy begs for answers, the precise reason why Höss became a mass murderer is difficult to know. Höss' parents did not teach him to hate, and, while anti–Semitism was not new in Germany, there is no indication Höss ever held strong feelings against the Jews. After his release from prison in 1928, he was encouraged by old comrades to work actively with the Nazis but chose not to. He had been a Nazi since 1922 and fully agreed with the Party's aims, but he objected to their use of mass propaganda and the way they appealed to the lowest instincts of the masses. Even when Höss was induced by Himmler to join the SS, he had his doubts. Throughout his career, Höss did not aspire to be a high-ranking Nazi.

Lt. Commander Whitney Harris, the American prosecutor at Nuremberg who interviewed Höss, commented that, in appearance, Höss did not impress him as someone who murdered or could murder a million people.

XIII. Conclusion

Throughout his imprisonment, Höss seemed apathetic and imperturbable. Drs. Goldensohn and Gilbert, who questioned Höss about the extermination of the Jews, hoped to gain insight into how Höss or anyone could perpetrate the monstrous deeds he committed. He gave them clues, but they were more like excuses. In answering their questions, Höss responded with straightforward answers and appeared perplexed when his interrogators could not understand the simplicity of his responses. "I love my country. The Jews were untermenschen—sub-human. They were the enemy of my country. I was ordered to destroy the enemies of my country." His simplistic answer is far from satisfactory.

Though his actions are difficult to understand, Höss provided a wealth of information regarding his background, the SS and events at Auschwitz. The significance of Höss' testimony and memoirs cannot be overstated. Even in Palestine immediately after the war, Jews doubted the stories of Holocaust survivors because the horrors of Auschwitz and other camps were too incredible to believe. Many Holocaust survivors refused even to speak about their appalling experiences until the monstrous atrocities were made public during the trial of Adolf Eichmann in Israel in 1961. As the commandant of Auschwitz, Höss' admissions provide undeniable proof of the Final Solution and its implementation at the most notorious of the Nazi death camps. He clearly acknowledges that his memoirs were written "voluntarily and without compulsion." As Lt. Commander Harris noted, Höss' testament eliminated any doubt that the Holocaust had occurred. Höss left unequalled historical testimony which informs about Auschwitz, personal responsibility and the dangers of racial hatred.

Yet, for all his admissions, Höss fails to tell the whole truth. While acknowledging the magnitude of the deaths in the gas chambers at Birkenau, he neglects to mention the numerous murders of inmates by injections to the heart and by shooting at the Death Wall of Block 11. Höss does not even begin to adequately describe the intolerable living conditions imposed on those from whom the Third Reich sought to extract the last breath of life in furtherance of the German war effort. He ignores the torture and death inflicted by SS doctors through medical experimentation. In writing his memoirs, Höss was more concerned that the world know, no matter how monstrous the atrocities, he was not responsible. At the end of his life, as he faced death by hanging, Höss apologized to the Polish people for his enormous crimes against humanity. Perhaps his contrition and his last-minute profession of faith gave him a measure of personal relief. Yet his letter of apology was strikingly incomplete in his failure to describe any remorse for killing the Jews. No apology to the Jews would be made. Even by the standards of his faith, Höss started on the road to repentance but did not finish the journey.[2]

When Höss went on trial in Poland in March 1947, he challenged the accusation that he killed four million people at Auschwitz not because he was innocent of the crime but because the number was too high. For Höss, who testified to the extermination of human beings with no emotion or regret, it should hardly have mattered whether 1.1, 2.5 or 4 million people were killed. He was fixated on telling the court and the world he had not personally mistreated any inmates. For Höss, working each day to assure that Jewish men, women and children were murdered in the Auschwitz gas chambers did not constitute cruelty. As the Polish Tribunal noted, whether Höss had personally beaten or tortured any inmates was not the question. He willingly participated in an evil criminal enterprise which he furthered by his own ideas and initiatives that exceeded the orders and instructions of his superiors. Having chosen to remain as the Auschwitz commandant and then the head of Amtsgruppe DI until the end of the war, Höss could not be excused from the terrible crimes he committed on behalf of the Third Reich.

Without doubt, Hitler and SS indoctrination were significant factors that led Höss to commit genocide. As a child, he could not satisfy the standards of his strict father. As a young soldier, Höss' captain stepped in to fill that role. Then, as an adult, Höss needed another authority figure to please. Höss wanted desperately to do a good job for Hitler and Himmler. They had conferred on him the power of life and death and a responsibility to protect the Third Reich. Motivated by an indomitable will to serve his Nazi masters, Höss wielded that power without consequence, mercilessly and without emotion. When Höss appeared at Nuremberg before Göring and the Nazi leadership, he testified that he had done exactly as he was told. He wanted the defendants to know it. Richard Sonnenfeldt, born in Berlin, was a frontline soldier in the United States Army in World War II and later served as an interpreter for war crimes investigators. After interviewing and interrogating Höss at Nuremberg, he concluded that he was "the most efficient, cold-blooded, mass killer that humanity had ever known."[3]

Höss lived the Nazi lie. He willingly chose to buy into the racial purity, Germans-are-better-than-everyone-else and Jews-are-to-blame-for-everything philosophies. It served him and his family well. Fear of reprisal by his Nazi masters did not motivate Höss to engage in his bestial behavior. Not once did Höss say that he was afraid of the personal consequences to himself or his family if he did not comply with the order to execute the Final Solution. If he was blind to the fanaticism and evil of Hitler and Himmler, it was because he chose to be. Primo Levi, who wrote the Introduction for *Commandant of Auschwitz*, noted, "It is always bad to espouse an ideology even if it is cloaked with respectable words such as 'Country' and 'Duty.'" Eicke taught that an SS man must be able to destroy even his closest dependents should they commit an offense against the State or the ideals of Adolf Hitler. Fortunately for Höss, he was never forced to choose between his family and Hitler.[4]

XIII. Conclusion

Höss and the Nazis were nothing more than bullies with power. They had no moral courage. Hitler was a formidable orator because he believed the nonsense he espoused. That did not make him right. Hitler was powerless alone. He needed the support of the German people and the resolve of individuals to carry out his plans. Though responsible for the deaths of millions of people, Hitler never personally killed anyone. Höss and millions of other Germans willingly chose to follow their Führer and to execute his will. In difficult times and sometimes in good, people will attach to someone who is convinced of his own righteousness, his own superiority and his own invincibility. It saves them from having to think and make tough decisions for themselves. Obedience to Hitler allowed Höss to act without questioning the morality of his actions.

Hitler and Himmler empowered Höss and the SS, making "ordinary" people feel important. The power to dominate others instilled a sense of superiority in Höss and his SS colleagues. They maintained that dominance by constantly reminding themselves, as Hitler taught them, they were better than everyone else, especially the Jews. Destruction of anyone who disagreed with Hitler was necessary to protect the State. Pity was unacceptable. Anything less than cold, hard, ruthless subjugation of the "lesser" people rendered them unworthy of Hitler's blessing. In reality, it requires no courage or strength to step on the downtrodden. The woman who voluntarily chose to enter the gas chamber so she could comfort others on their way to die was far more courageous and righteous than was Hitler, Höss and the SS. Ironically, the Nazis and the SS would be remembered as untermensch, not the Jews.

Höss said that conscience was never an issue because he was ordered to exterminate the Jews and that was the only thing that mattered. He makes a vain effort to convince others he never made a moral judgment. In his heart, though, Höss knew what he was doing was wrong. No human being on this side of sanity can destroy one million men, women and children and believe it is justifiable. Höss was not insane. In William Styron's novel *Sophie's Choice*, Sophie is forever haunted when a Nazi doctor at Auschwitz forces her to choose between her son and daughter—one could live, but one must die. Styron's main character noted that the most profound statement yet made about Auschwitz was not a statement at all, but a response: "At Auschwitz, tell me, where was God?" And the answer: "Where was man?" Höss knew that the Final Solution was a "monstrous order," and he carried it out anyway. Legalistically, he believed he could shift the blame to Hitler and Himmler. At a more basic, more human level, that was nonsense, and Höss knew it. He simply disregarded his moral compass.[5]

The photographs of Höss after his arrest and at his trial and even the ones of Höss at Auschwitz walking to the gallows and standing on a stool moments before his death are remarkable for their similarity. In all of them, he could not, he would not, betray any of his doubts or feelings. He was not angry or bitter for being punished. He accepted that decision. Höss could not show emotion or apologize for the extermination of a million human beings without facing an unthinkable reality and unbearable guilt.

In his "death bed" apology to the Polish people of April 12, 1947, which in all respects appears sincere, Höss demonstrates he had a conscience. There was more to Höss than an apathetic, uncaring monster. The letters he wrote to his family were not written by a man with no heart. He poured out emotion to each of his children, telling them the "love and care of a mother is the most beautiful and valuable thing that exists on this earth" and expressing how much Hedwig had loved and sacrificed for them. Höss thanked Hedwig for all the "goodness and beauty" she brought to him and for the "endless love and care" she gave him. He asked her forgiveness for the pain he inflicted on her and expressed his regret for so often putting his job before her. Anyone capable of loving as Höss loved his family had to know what it would feel like to be wrenched involuntarily from the safety of home and separated from family. Watching the trains unload and the Jews walk to their deaths, Höss certainly was aware of the anguish and fear suffered by his victims. It is remarkable to think that a human being, any human being, is capable of ordering, participating in, watching and not doing everything within his or her power to stop the execution of a child.

In the book she wrote about her experiences, *Return to Auschwitz*, Kitty Hart said that many people told her it could only happen in Germany. She warned:

> That's not true. It could have happened anywhere. It can still happen anywhere if conditions are right. ... When you hear someone speak slightingly of "That Jewish lot down the road" or rant "It's high time those bloody blacks were rounded up and sent back where they belong," you are listening to the very people whose prejudices can so readily be inflamed by cunning propaganda at the right moment. And, just as guilty as their predecessors in Hitler's day, there will be those who take no active part, yet allow it all to happen through selfish indifference.[6]

The tragedy that befell the world in the 1930s and 1940s was not caused by something unique to Germans. As long as human frailty and weakness exist, someone somewhere will prey upon the masses to gain and hold power.

According to Father Manfred Deselaers, the real defeat of Höss' ideology was not provoked by its final collapse but by the humanity he experienced at the hands of his jailers, those who he had offended. His apology to the Polish people (but not the Jews) for his crimes against humanity and for causing them "incredible suffering" undoubtedly has foundation in the compassion he was shown while in Polish prisons. Yet, in my experience as a judge, many prisoners, as did Höss, find God in jail. They are remorseful only because they were caught and face consequences for their behavior. It is highly unlikely

XIII. Conclusion

that Höss would have found error in Hitler, Himmler and the Third Reich if Germany had won the war.[7]

Höss wisely instructed his oldest son Klaus, four days before he was executed, to think for himself, be critical and doubt. He told Klaus to listen to the "voice in your heart." The compassion shown Höss by his Polish jailers helped him relearn this last lesson. But he always knew he possessed the power and responsibility to think for himself. He simply chose not to do so when following the Führer's will served his purpose.

For those who still ask why Rudolf Höss committed mass murder, no answer acceptable to everyone is possible. Mental health professionals, like Drs. Gilbert, Goldensohn and Batawia, were only provided some oral history. Auschwitz survivors have expressed multiple opinions about Höss based on the atrocities he committed. Perhaps Hans Huttig, one of the commandants of the Natzweiler concentration camp, who was interviewed by Tom Segev in April 1975 for *Soldiers of Evil*, provides the simplest, most direct answer: "Today it seems so cruel, inhuman, and immoral. It did not seem immoral to me then: I knew very well what I was going to do in the SS. We all knew. It was something in the soul, not in the mind. ... "When it comes down to it, it is a very simple story," the elderly Huttig told Segev, "I was a Nazi."[8]

Appendix I
Höss Statement of March 14, 1946

I, Rudolf Franz Ferdinand Höss, alias Franz Lang, hereby declare, after having been warned accordingly, that the following statement is true:

In 1933 I formed a squadron of horse SS on the farm Sallentin in Pommern. I was detailed by the Party and by landowners to do this as I have been in the cavalry. My party number is 3240.

Himmler noticed me during an inspection of the SS in Stettin—we knew each other from the Bund der Artamanen—and he arranged that the administration of a Concentration Camp was given me.

I came to Dachau in November 1934 where, after additional military training, I was employed as a Blockfuhrer in the Schutzhaftlager. Later on I did the job of a Rapportfuhrer and Gefangenenigentumsverwalter. When I came to Dachau I held the rank of Scharführer SS and was promoted, in 1935, SS Untersturmfuhrer. In 1938 I was sent, as Adjutant, to the Camp Commandant of Sachsenhausen, Oberführer Baranowski. In November 1938 I was made Schutzhaftlagerfuhrer holding the rank of a SS-Hauptsturmführer until my transfer to Auschwitz on the 1 May 1940. I was given the order by a higher authority, to transform the former Polish Artillery Barracks near Auschwitz into a quarantine camp for prisoners coming from Poland.

After Himmler inspected the camp in 1941 I received the order to enlarge the camp and to employ the prisoners in the to be developed agricultural district, and to drain the swamps and inundation area on the Weichsel. Furthermore he ordered to put 8–10,000 prisoners at the disposal of the building of the new Buna Works of the I.G. Farben. At the same time he ordered the erection of a POW Camp, for 100,000 Russian prisoners, near Birkenau.

The number of prisoners grew daily in spite of my repeated interventions that billets were not sufficient, and further intakes were sent to me. Epidemic diseases were unavoidable because medical provisions were inadequate. The death rates rose accordingly, as prisoners were not buried, crematoriums had to be installed.

In 1941 the first intakes of Jews came from Slovakia and Upper Silesia. People unfit to work were gassed in a room of the crematorium in accordance with an order which Himmler gave me personally.

I was ordered to see Himmler in Berlin in June 1941 and he told me, approximately, the following:

The Fuhrer ordered the solution of the Jewish question in Europe. A few so called Vernichtungslager (extermination camps) are existing in the General Government.

Belzec near Rawa Ruska Ost Polen
Treblinka near Malkinia on the River Bug
Wolzek near Lublin

These camps come under the Einsatzkommando of the Sicherheitspolizei under the leadership of high SIPO officers and guard companies. These camps were not very efficient and could not be enlarged. I visited the camp Treblinka in spring 1942 to inform myself about the conditions. The following method was used in the process of extermination. Small chambers were used equipped with pipes to induce the exhaust gas from car engines. This method was unreliable as the engines, coming from old captured transport vehicles and tanks, very often failed to work. Because of that the intakes could not be dealt with according to the plan, which meant to clear the Warsaw Ghetto. According to the Camp Commandant of Treblinka, 80,000 people have been gassed in the course of half a year.

For the above mentioned reasons Himmler declared the only possibility to extend this camp, in accordance with this plan, was Auschwitz, as it was a railway junction of four lines and, not being thickly populated, the camp area could be cut off completely. This is the reason why he decided to do the mass exterminations in Auschwitz and I had to make the preparations at once. He wanted the exact plan in accordance with this instruction in four weeks. Furthermore he said this task is so difficult and important that he cannot order just anybody to do it and he had the intention to give this task to another high ranking SS officer but he did not consider it advisable to have two officers giving orders whilst on a construction job. I was then given the definite order to carry out the destruction of the intakes sent from RSHA. I had to get in touch with SS Obersturmbannfuhrer Eichmann of Amt 4 (Dienststelle commanded by Gruppenfuhrer Müller) concerning the sequence of incoming transports.

At the same time transports of Russian POW arrived from the area of the Gestapo Leitstelle Breslau, Troppau, and Kattowitz, who, by Himmler's written order to the local Gestapo leaders, had to be exterminated. As the new crematoriums were only to be finished in late 1942, the prisoners had to be gassed in provisionally erected gas-chambers and then had to be burned in pits. I am now going to explain the method of gassing.

The sick and people unfit to walk were taken there in lorries. In front of the farmhouses everybody had to undress behind walls made from branches. On the door was a notice saying "Disinfectionsraum." The Unterführer on duty had to tell the prisoners to watch their kit in order to find it again after having been deloused, this prevented disturbances. When they were undressed, they went into the room according to size, 2–300 at a time. The doors were locked and one or two tins of zyklon B were thrown into the room through holes in the wall. It consisted of a rough substance of Prussic acid. It took, according to the weather, 3–10 minutes. After half an hour the doors were opened and the bodies were taken out by the commando of prisoners, who were permanently employed there, and burned in pits. Before being cremated, gold teeth and rings were removed.

Firewood was stacked between the bodies and when approximately 100 bodies were in a pit, the wood was lighted with rags soaked in paraffin. When the fire had started properly more bodies were thrown on to it. The fat which collected in the bottom of the pits was put into the fire with buckets to hasten the process of burning when it was raining. The burning took 6–7 hours. The smell of the burned bodies was noticed in the camp even if the wind was blowing from the west. After the pits had been cleaned the remaining ashes were broken up. This was done on a cement platter where prisoners pulverised the remaining bones with wooden hammers. The remains were loaded on lorries and taken to an out of the way place on the Weichsel and thrown into the river.

After the erection of the new big crematorium, the following method was used. After the first two big crematoriums were finished in 1942 (the other two were finished half a year later) mass transports from Belgium, France, Holland, and Greece started.

The following method was used:

The transport trains ran alongside an especially built ramp with three lines which was situated between the crematorium, store and camp Birkenau. The sorting out of the prisoners and the disposing of the luggage was done on the ramp. Prisoners fit to work were taken to one of the various camps, prisoners to be exterminated were taken to one of the new crematoriums. There the first went to one of the big underground rooms to undress. This room was equipped with benches and contraptions to hang up clothing and the prisoners were told by interpreters that they were brought here to have a bath and be deloused and to remember where they put their clothing. Then they went on to the next room which was equipped with water pipes and showers to give the impression of a bath. Two Unterführers remained in the room until the last moment to prevent unrest.

Appendix I

Sometimes it happened that prisoners knew what was going to be done. Especially the transports from Belsen knew, as they originated from the East, when the trains reached Upper Silesia, that they were most likely taken to the place of extermination. When transports from Belsen arrived safety measures were strengthened and the transports were split up into smaller groups which we sent to different crematoriums to prevent riots. SS men formed a strong cordon and forced resisting prisoners into the gas-chamber. That happened very rarely as prisoners were set at ease by the measures we undertook.

I remember one incident especially well. One transport from Belsen arrived, approximately two-thirds, mostly men were in the gas-chamber, the remaining third was in the dressing room. When three or four armed SS Unterführers entered the dressing room to hasten the undressing, mutiny broke out. The light cables were torn down, the SS men were overpowered, one of them stabbed and all of them were robbed of their weapons. As this room was in complete darkness wild shooting started between the guard near the exit door and the prisoners inside. When I arrived I ordered the doors to be shut and I had the process of gassing the first party finished and then went into the room together with the guard carrying small searchlights pushing the prisoners into a corner from where they were taken out singly into another room of the crematorium and shot, by my order, with small calibre weapons.

It happened repeatedly that women hid their children underneath their clothing and did not take them into the gas chamber. The clothing was searched by the permanent commando of prisoners under the supervision of the SS and children who were found were sent into the gas-chamber.

After half an hour the electric air conditioner was started up and the bodies were taken up to the cremating stove by lift. The cremation of approximately 2,000 prisoners in five cremating stoves took approximately 12 hours. In Auschwitz there were two plants, each of them had five double stoves. Furthermore there were another two plants, each having four bigger stoves and provisional plants as described above. The second provisional plant had been destroyed. All clothing and property of prisoners was sorted out in the store by a commando of prisoners which was permanently employed there and was also billeted there.

Valuables were sent monthly to the Reichsbank in Berlin. Clothing was sent to armament firms, after having been cleaned, for the use of forced labour and displaced persons. Gold from teeth was melted down and sent monthly to the medical department of the Waffen–SS. The man in charge was Sanitaetsfeldzeugmeister SS—Gruppenfuhrer Blumenreuter.

I personally never shot anybody or beat anybody.

Owing to the mass intakes, the number of prisoners fit to work grew immensely. My protests to the RHSA to slow down the transports, which means to send fewer transports, was rejected every time. The reason given was the

Reichsfuhrer SS had given an order to speed up extermination and every SS Fuhrer hampering same will be called to account. Owing to the immense over-populating of existing barracks and owing to the inadequate hygienic installations, epidemic diseases like spotted fever, typhus, scarlet fever and diphtheria, broke out from time to time, especially in the camp Birkenau.

Doctors came under the camp commandant from a military point of view. As far as medical decisions went, they had their own routine and came under the Chef des Sanitatswesens des WVHauptamtes Standartenfuhrer Dr. Lolling, who again came under Reichsarzt Dr. Gravitz.

In one respect the above mentioned rule has been broken—local Gestapo leaders were given orders by RHSA to get in touch with me. Prisoners which were kept in concentration camps for the Gestapo and who have not been sentenced out of political reasons were allowed to be removed by any other means. I received the names of the persons, personally, from the leader of the Gestapo and I passed them on again to the respective doctor for finishing off. This, usually was an injection of petrol. The doctor had orders to write an ordinary death certificate. Regarding the reason of the deaths, he could put any illness.

During the time as Commandant we made the following experiments:

Professor Clauberg, chief of the Women's Hospital, Konigshutte, in Upper Silesia, made sterilisation experiments. This was done as follows. He got in contact with the doctor of the women's camp to find him suitable persons. They were put in a special ward of the hospital. Under a special x-ray screen he gave them a syringe with a special liquid, which went through the womb into the ovary. This liquid, as he said, definitely blocked the ovary and caused an inflammation. After a few weeks he gave them another injection which could tell him that the ovary was definitely blocked. These experiments were made by order of the Reichsfuhrer SS.

Rudolf Franz Ferdinand Höss[1]

Appendix II
Höss Affidavit of April 5, 1946

OFFICE OF US CHIEF OF COUNSEL
FOR THE PROSECUTION OF AXIS CRIMINALITY
APO 124A, US ARMY
INTERROGATION DIVISION

AFFIDAVIT.

I, RUDOLF FRANZ FERDINAND HOESS, being first duly sworn, depose and say as follows:

1. I am forty-six years old, and have been a member of the NSDAP since 1922; a member of the SS since 1934; a member of the Waffen-SS since 1939. I was a member from 1 December 1934 of the SS Guard Unit, the so-called Deathshead Formation (Totenkopf Verband).
2. I have been constantly associated with the administration of concentration camps since 1934, serving at Dachau until 1938; then as Adjutant in Sachsenhausen from 1938 to May 1, 1940, when I was appointed Commandant of Auschwitz. I commanded Auschwitz until 1 December 1943, and estimate that at least 2,500,000 victims were executed and exterminated there by gassing and burning, and at least another half million succumbed to starvation and disease, making a total dead of about 3,000,000. This figure represents about 70% or 80% of all persons sent to Auschwitz as prisoners, the remainder having been selected and used for slave labor in the concentration camp industries. Included among the executed and burnt were approximately 20,000 Russian prisoners of war (previously screened out of Prisoner of War cages by the Gestapo) who were delivered at Auschwitz in Wehrmacht transports operated by regular Wehrmacht officers and men. The

remainder of the total number of victims included about 100,000 German Jews, and great numbers of citizens, mostly Jewish from Holland, France, Belgium, Poland, Hungary, Czechoslovakia, Greece, or other countries. We executed about 400,000 Hungarian Jews alone at Auschwitz in the summer of 1944.

3. WVHA (Main Economic and Administration Office), headed by Obergruppenführer Oswald Pohl, was responsible for all administrative matters such as billeting, feeding and medical care, in the concentration camps. Prior to establishment of the RSHA, Secret State Police Office (Gestapo) and the Reich Office of Criminal Police were responsible for arrests, commitments to concentration camps, punishments and executions therein. After organization of the RSHA, all of these functions were carried on as before, but, pursuant to orders signed by Heydrich as Chief of the RSHA. While Kaltenbrunner was Chief of RSHA, orders for protective custody, commitments, punishment and individual executions were signed by Kaltenbrunner or by Mueller, Chief of the Gestapo, as Kaltenbrunner's deputy.

4. Mass executions by gassing commenced during the summer 1941 and continued until Fall 1944. I personally supervised executions at Auschwitz until the first of December 1943 and know by reason of my continued duties in the Inspectorate of Concentration Camps WVHA that these mass executions continued as stated above. All mass executions by gassing took place under the direct order, supervision and responsibility of RSHA. I received all orders for carrying out these mass executions directly from RSHA.

5. On 1 December 1943 I became Chief of AMT I in AMT Group D of the WVHA and in that office was responsible for coordinating all matters arising between RSHA and concentration camps under the administration of WVHA. I held this position until the end of the war. Pohl, as Chief of WVHA, and Kaltenbrunner, as Chief of RSHA, often conferred personally and frequently communicated orally and in writing concerning concentration camps. On 5 October 1944, I brought a lengthy report regarding Mauthausen Concentration Camp to Kaltenbrunner at his office at RSHA, Berlin. Kaltenbrunner asked me to give him a short oral digest of this report and said he would reserve any decision until he had had an opportunity to study it in complete detail. This report dealt with the assignment to labor of several hundred prisoners who had been condemned to death—so-called "nameless prisoners."

6. The "final solution" of the Jewish question meant the complete

extermination of all Jews in Europe. I was ordered to establish extermination facilities at Auschwitz in June 1941. At that time there were already in the general government three other extermination camps: BELZEK, TREBLINKA and WOLZEK. These camps were under the Einsatzkommando of the Security Police and SD. I, visited Treblinka to find out how they carried out their exterminations. The Camp Commandant at Treblinka told me that he had liquidated 80,000 in the course of one-half year. He was principally concerned with liquidating all the Jews from the Warsaw Ghetto. He used monoxide gas and I did not think that his methods were very efficient. So when I set up the extermination building at Auschwitz, I used Cyclon B, which was a crystallized Prussic Acid which we dropped into the death chamber from a small opening. It took from 3 to 15 minutes to kill the people in the death chamber depending upon climatic conditions. We knew when the people were dead because their screaming stopped. We usually waited about one-half hour before we opened the doors and removed the bodies. After the bodies were removed our special commandos took off the rings and extracted the gold from the teeth of the corpses.

7. Another improvement we made over Treblinka was that we built our gas chambers to accommodate 2,000 people at one time: whereas at Treblinka their 10 gas chambers only accommodated 200 people each. The way we selected our victims was as follows: we had two SS doctors on duty at Auschwitz to examine the incoming transports of prisoners. The prisoners would be marched by one of the doctors who would make spot decisions as they walked by. Those who were fit for work were sent into the Camp. Others were sent immediately to the extermination plants. Children of tender years were invariably exterminated since by reason of their youth they were unable to work. Still another improvement we made over Treblinka was that at Treblinka the victims almost always knew that they were to be exterminated and at Auschwitz we endeavored to fool the victims into thinking that they were to go through a delousing process. Of course, frequently they realized our true intentions and we sometimes had riots and difficulties due to that fact. Very frequently women would hide their children under the clothes but of course when we found them we would send the children in to be exterminated. We were required to carry out these exterminations in secrecy but of course the foul and nauseating stench from the continuous burning of bodies permeated the entire area and all of the people living in the

surrounding communities knew that exterminations were going on at Auschwitz.
8. We received from time to time special prisoners from the local Gestapo office. The SS doctors killed such prisoners by injections of benzene. Doctors had orders to write ordinary death certificates and could put down any reason at all for the cause of death.
9. From time to time we conducted medical experiments on women inmates, including sterilization and experiments relating to cancer. Most of the people who died under these experiments had been already condemned to death by the Gestapo.
10. Rudolf Mildner was the chief of the Gestapo at Kattowicz and as such was head of the political department at Auschwitz which conducted third-degree methods of interrogation from approximately March 1941 until September 1943. As such, he frequently sent prisoners to Auschwitz for incarceration or execution. He visited Auschwitz on several occasions. The Gestapo Court, the SS Standgericht, which tried persons accused of various crimes, such as escaping Prisoners of War, etc., frequently met within Auschwitz, and Mildner often attended the trial of such persons, who usually were executed in Auschwitz following their sentence. I showed Mildner throughout the extermination plant at Auschwitz and he was directly interested in it since he had to send the Jews from his territory for execution at Auschwitz.

I understand English as it is written above. The above statements are true; this declaration is made by me voluntarily and without compulsion; after reading over the statement, I have signed and executed the same at Nurnberg, Germany, on the fifth day of April 1946.

Rudolf Hoess
RUDOLF FRANZ FERDINAND HOESS

Subscribed and sworn to before me this 5th day of April, 1946, at Nurnberg, Germany.

Smith W. Brookhardt, Jr.
SMITH W. BROOKHARDT, JR., LT COLONEL. IGD.[1]

Appendix III
Photos of Child Victims

All images in this section are courtesy Yad Vashem—
the Holocaust Heroes' and Martyrs' Remembrance Authority.

Arthur Bachner, Bielsko, Poland

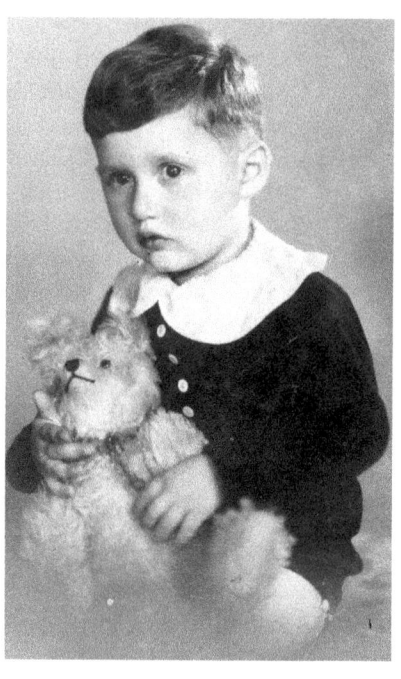

Dushko Cohen, Novisad, Yugoslavia

Photos of Child Victims

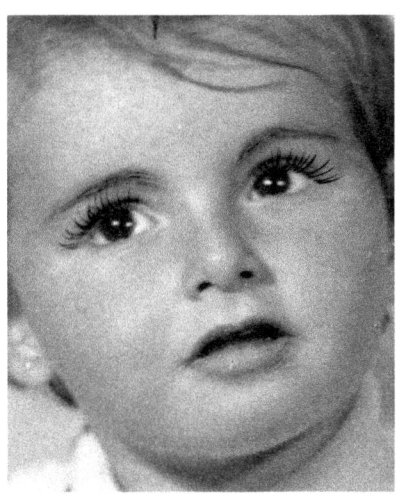

Lya Markovicz, Surduc, Romania

Katy Besnyo, Hungary

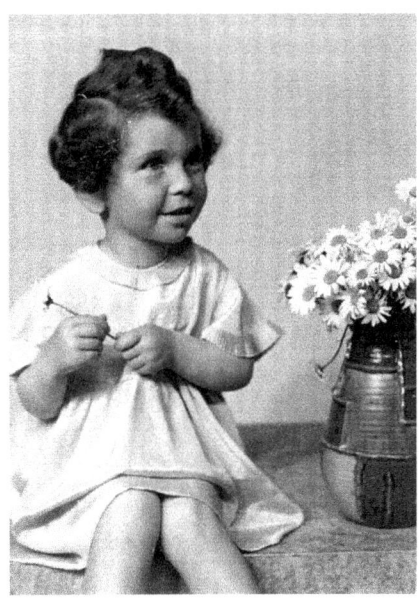

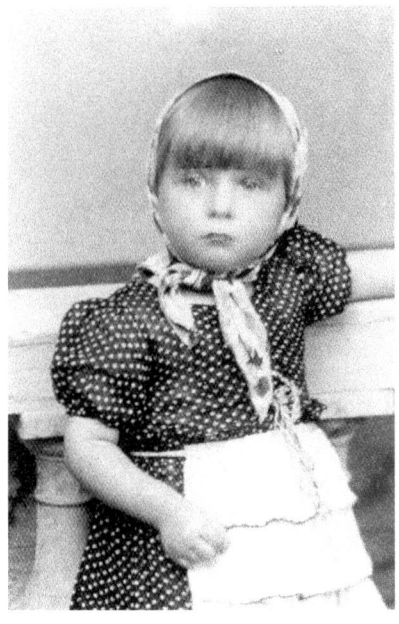

Blanka Herman, Votice, Czechoslovakia
(1933–1942)

Mania Feder, Sosnovice, Poland
(1940–1942)

Appendix III

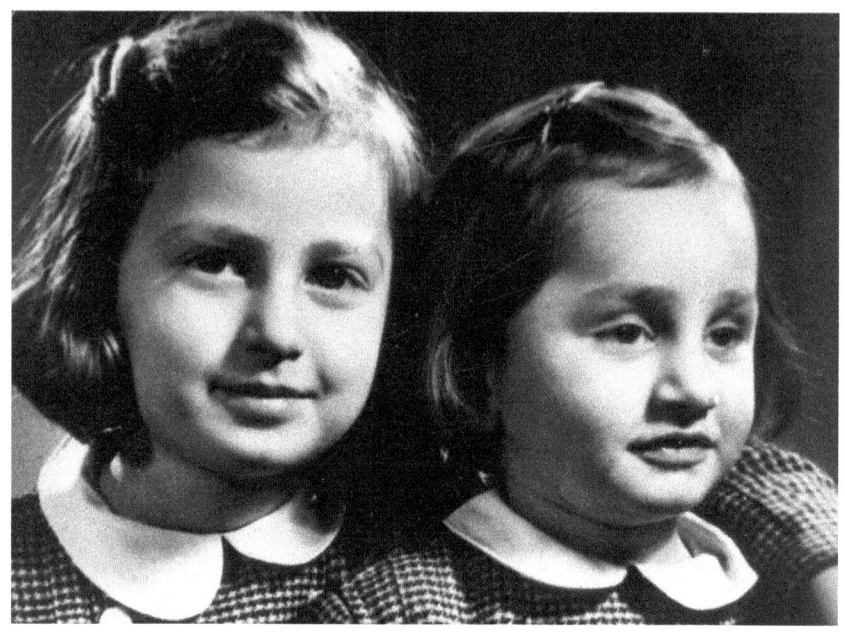

Irene and Sylvia Hahn, Hungary

Stepan Michael Winternitz, Prague, Czechoslovakia (1935–1944)

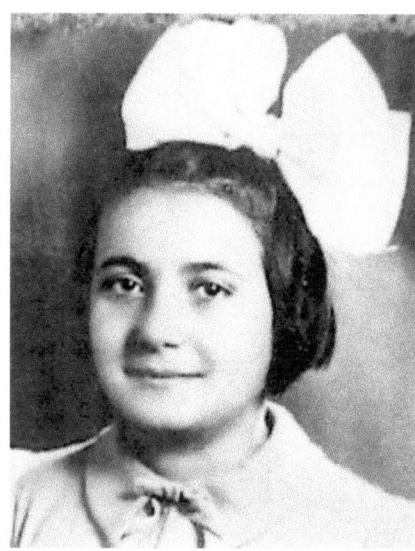

Romcia Dawidowicz, Lodz, Poland (1930–1943)

Photos of Child Victims

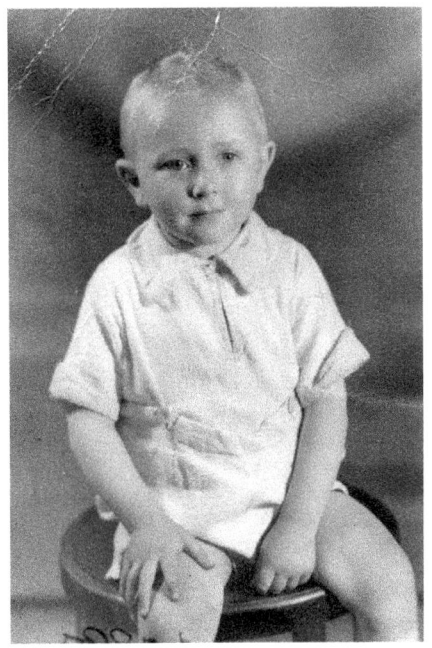

Unnamed boy (burned alive)

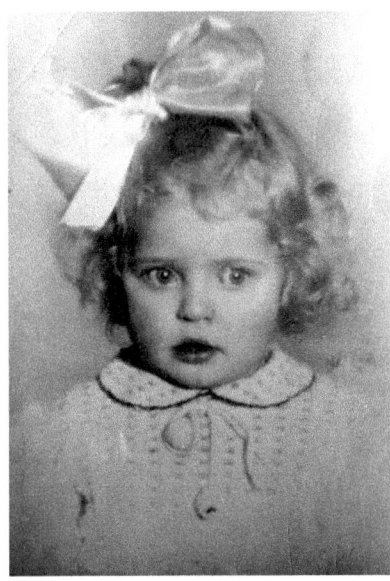

Roza (Reyzele) Yaakobson, Latvia

Chapter Notes

Introduction

1. Ysrael Gutman and Michael Berenbaum, *Anatomy of the Auschwitz Death Camp*, Bloomington: Indiana University Press, 1994, p. 10.
2. Adolf Hitler, *Mein Kampf*, Cambridge: Riverside Press, 1943, pp. 65, 150, 453, 640; William L. Shirer, *The Rise and Fall of the Third Reich*, New York: MJF Books, 1959, pp. 430–31, 964; Christopher R. Browning, *The Origins of the Final Solution*, Lincoln: University of Nebraska Press, 2004, pp. 111–37.
3. Shirer, *Rise and Fall of the Third Reich*, pp. 538–41, 851–52.
4. Peter Longerich, *Holocaust: The Nazi Persecution and Murder of the Jews*, New York: Oxford University Press, 2010, pp. 144, 192–95, 242–47, 236–37, 224, 230–31, 255; Browning, *The Origins of the Final Solution*, pp. 226, 244.
5. Longerich, *Holocaust: The Nazi Persecution and Murder of the Jews*, pp. 305–09; Rudolf Höss, *Death Dealer: The Memoirs of the SS Commandant at Auschwitz*, ed. Steven Paskuly, Amherst: Prometheus Books, 1992, pp. 374–76.
6. Longerich, *Holocaust: The Nazi Persecution and Murder of the Jews*, pp. 323, 330–35.
7. Library of Congress, "Trial of the Major War Criminals Before International Military Tribunal, Volume I," pp. 27–92. https://www.loc.gov/rr/frd/Military_Law/pdf/NT_Vol-I.pdf, accessed March 12, 2018.
8. Gutman and Berenbaum, *Anatomy*, p. 19; Danuta Czech, *Auschwitz Chronicle: 1939–1945*, New York: Henry Holt & Co., 1990, p. 17; United States Memorial Holocaust Museum, "Auschwitz," Holocaust Encyclopedia, https://www.ushmm.org/wlc/en/article.php?ModuleId=10005189, accessed March 12, 2018.
9. Library of Congress, "Trial of the Major War Criminals Before International Military Tribunal, Volume XI," pp. 396–422. https://www.loc.gov/rr/frd/Military_Law/pdf/NT_Vol-XI.pdf, accessed March 12, 2018; Whitney Harris, Interview 33930, Segments 107, 132, Visual History Archive, USC Shoah Foundation, 1997, accessed June 3, 2018.
10. Höss, *Death Dealer: The Memoirs of the SS Commandant at Auschwitz*, p. 19.
11. Rudolf Höss, "Introduction by Primo Levi," in *Commandant of Auschwitz*, London: Weidenfeld & Nicolson, 2000, pp. 165–66, 177.
12. Höss, "Introduction by Primo Levi," in *Commandant of Auschwitz*, p. 19.
13. Höss, *Commandant of Auschwitz*, pp. 176, 178, 181.

Chapter I

1. Leon Goldensohn, *The Nuremberg Interviews*, New York: Alfred A. Knopf, 2004, p. 307.
2. Franciszek Piper, "Gas Chambers and Crematoria," in *Anatomy of the Auschwitz Death Camp*, eds. Yisrael Gutman and Michael Berenbaum, Bloomington: Indiana University Press, 1994, p. 174; Deborah Dwork and Robert Jan van Pelt, *Auschwitz: 1270 to the Present*, New York: W. W. Norton & Company, 1996, pp. 338, 342.
3. Höss, *Commandant of Auschwitz*, p. 168; Saul Friedlander, *The Years of Extermination: Nazi Germany and the Jews, 1939–1945*, New York: HarperCollins, 2007, p. 649, Kindle edition; Laurence Rees,

Auschwitz: A New History, New York: BBC Books, 2005, pp. 263–64; Longerich, *Holocaust: The Nazi Persecution and Murder of the Jews*, p. 415; Piper, "Gas Chambers and Crematoria," in *Anatomy of the Auschwitz Death Camp*, p. 174; Sybille Steinbacher, *Auschwitz*, New York: HarperCollins, 2005, p. 128; Raul Hilberg, *The Destruction of the European Jews*, New York: Holmes & Meier, 1985, p. 983.

4. Friedlander, *The Years of Extermination: Nazi Germany and the Jews, 1939–1945*, pp. 647–48, Kindle edition.
5. Rees, *Auschwitz: A New History*, p. 264.
6. Höss, *Commandant of Auschwitz*, pp. 168–69.
7. *Ibid.*, p. 169.
8. *Ibid.*, pp. 169–70.
9. George Klein, Interview 12143, Visual History Archive, USC Shoah Foundation, 1988, Segment 127, accessed July 18, 2019.
10. *Ibid.*, p. 170.
11. *Ibid.*, p. 171; Thomas Harding, *Hanns and Rudolf*, New York: Simon & Schuster Paperbacks, 2013, p. 196.
12. Höss, *Commandant of Auschwitz*, pp. 171–72.
13. *Ibid.*, p. 172.
14. *Ibid.*
15. *Ibid.*, pp. 172–73; Goldensohn, *The Nuremberg Interviews*, p. 307.
16. Shirer, *The Rise and Fall of the Third Reich*, p. 1141; Höss, *Commandant of Auschwitz*, p. 173.
17. Harding, *Hanns and Rudolf*, pp. 17, 26–27, 154.
18. *Ibid.*, pp. 72–74.
19. *Ibid.*, pp. 74–83.
20. *Ibid.*, pp. 84–94, 117.
21. *Ibid.*, pp. 121–22, 127, 170.
22. *Ibid.*, pp. 171–73; Rees, *Auschwitz: A New History*, p. 265.
23. Harding, *Hanns and Rudolf*, pp. 151, 174–75.
24. *Ibid.*, pp. 177–78.
25. Höss, *Death Dealer: The Memoirs of the SS Commandant at Auschwitz*, pp. 28 n. 4, 33 n. 18, 340, 343, 354–55, 361; Pery Broad, *KZ Auschwitz*, Oświęcim: Panstwowe Muzeum Oświęcim, 1965, pp. 55–56.
26. Harding, *Hanns and Rudolf*, pp. 179, 181.
27. *Ibid.*, pp. 183–86, 189–90.
28. *Ibid.*, pp. 200–01; Höss, *Commandant of Auschwitz*, p. 173.
29. Harding, *Hanns and Rudolf*, pp. 192–95.
30. *Ibid.*, pp. 228–33.
31. *Ibid.*, pp. 202, 227–28; Höss, *Commandant of Auschwitz*, p. 173.
32. Harding, *Hanns and Rudolf*, pp. 235–37.
33. *Ibid.*, pp. 237–38.
34. *Ibid.*, p. 238.
35. *Ibid.*, pp. 238–39.
36. *Ibid.*, pp. 240–41; Höss, *Commandant of Auschwitz*, p. 173.
37. Harding, *Hanns and Rudolf*, pp. 241–42; Höss, *Commandant of Auschwitz*, p. 173.
38. Harding, *Hanns and Rudolf*, pp. 242–43; Höss, *Commandant of Auschwitz*, p. 174.
39. Harding, *Hanns and Rudolf*, pp. 243–45; Höss, *Commandant of Auschwitz*, p. 174; Goldensohn, *The Nuremberg Interviews*, p. 295.
40. Harding, *Hanns and Rudolf*, p. 245; Höss, *Commandant of Auschwitz*, p. 174; Holocaust Education & Archive Research Team, "Rudolf Höss, Commandant of Auschwitz," http://www.holocaustresearchproject.org/othercamps/hoess.html, accessed June 15, 2018.
41. Whitney Harris, Interview 33930, Segments 108, 109, Visual History Archive, USC Shoah Foundation, 1997, accessed June 3, 2018; Höss, *Commandant of Auschwitz*, p. 174.
42. Höss, *Commandant of Auschwitz*, p. 174.

Chapter II

1. Wikisource, "1911 Encyclopaedia Britannica/Baden (Germany)," https://en.wikisource.org/wiki/1911_Encyclopædia_Britannica/Baden_(Germany), accessed April 4, 2018; Höss, *Commandant of Auschwitz*, pp. 29–30; Aleksander Lasik, "Rudolph Höss: Manager of Crime," in *Anatomy of the Auschwitz Death Camp*, Bloomington: Indiana University Press, 1994, p. 289; GENi, "Franz Xaver Höss," https://www.geni.com/people/Franz-Höss/6000000076970035394, accessed April 11, 2019.
2. Höss, *Commandant of Auschwitz*, p. 30.
3. *Ibid.*, pp. 31–32; Goldensohn, *The Nuremberg Interviews*, p. 310.
4. G. M. Gilbert, *Nuremberg Diary*, New York: Da Capo Press, 1995, pp. 269–70.
5. Höss, *Commandant of Auschwitz*, pp. 32–33.
6. Gilbert, *Nuremberg Diary*, p. 269;

Robert L. Beir and Brian Josepher, *Roosevelt and the Holocaust*, New York: Skyhorse Publishing, 2013, p. 126; Mitchell G. Bard, "Virtual Jewish World: Baden, Germany," 2008, http://www.jewishvirtuallibrary.org/baden-germany-virtual-jewish-history-tour, accessed April 5, 2018.
   7. Höss, *Commandant of Auschwitz*, p. 33.
   8. R. S. Nolan, "Catholic Encyclopedia (1913)/Law of the Seal of Confession," https://en.wikisource.org/wiki/Catholic_Encyclopedia_(1913)/Law_of_the_Seal_of_Confession, accessed April 5, 2018.
   9. Höss, *Commandant of Auschwitz*, pp. 34–35.
   10. *Ibid.*, pp. 35–36.
   11. Harding, *Hanns and Rudolf*, pp. 11–13; Goldensohn, *The Nuremberg Interviews*, p. 312.
   12. Wikipedia, "Second Battle of Kut," https://en.wikipedia.org/wiki/Second_Battle_of_Kut, accessed July 28, 2019; Höss, *Commandant of Auschwitz*, pp. 36–37.
   13. Höss, *Commandant of Auschwitz*, p. 37.
   14. *Ibid.*, p. 38.
   15. *Ibid.*, pp. 38–39.
   16. *Ibid.*, pp. 39–40.
   17. *Ibid.*, pp. 39–41; Harding, *Hanns and Rudolf*, p. 16.
   18. Höss, *Commandant of Auschwitz*, pp. 41–42; Goldensohn, *The Nuremberg Interviews*, pp. 310, 312.
   19. Höss, *Commandant of Auschwitz*, p. 42.
   20. Robert G. L. Waite, *Vanguard of Nazism*, New York: W. W. Norton & Company, 1952, pp. 1–2, 30.
   21. Höss, *Commandant of Auschwitz*, p. 42; Waite, *Vanguard of Nazism*, pp. 29, 42, 58–62, 66–68.
   22. Höss, *Commandant of Auschwitz*, pp. 42–43; Waite, *Vanguard of Nazism*, pp. 105–06, 111–12; Goldensohn, *The Nuremberg Interviews*, p. 297.
   23. Höss, *Commandant of Auschwitz*, p. 43; Waite, *Vanguard of Nazism*, pp. 191–95; Goldensohn, *The Nuremberg Interviews*, p. 297.
   24. Höss, *Commandant of Auschwitz*, p. 56; Gilbert, *Nuremberg Diary*, p. 270; Waite, *Vanguard of Nazism*, pp. 196, 264–65, 281; "Library of Congress, Trial of the Major War Criminals Before International Military Tribunal, Volume XXXIII," https://www.loc.gov/rr/frd/Military_Law/pdf/NT_Vol-XXXIII.pdf, accessed April 3, 2018, p. 275; Lasik, "Rudolph Höss: Manager of Crime," in *Anatomy of the Auschwitz Death Camp*, p. 289.
   25. Waite, *Vanguard of Nazism*, pp. 166, 236–37.
   26. Höss, *Commandant of Auschwitz*, pp. 44–45; Harding, *Hanns and Rudolf*, p. 37.
   27. Höss, *Commandant of Auschwitz*, pp. 45–46; Harding, *Hanns and Rudolf*, p. 37.
   28. Höss, *Commandant of Auschwitz*, pp. 46–47.
   29. *Ibid.*, pp. 47–52.
   30. *Ibid.*, pp. 55–57.
   31. *Ibid.*, pp. 58, 61; Harding, *Hanns and Rudolf*, pp. 42–43.
   32. Höss, *Commandant of Auschwitz*, pp. 61–62.
   33. *Ibid.*, pp. 54, 62.
   34. Harding, *Hanns and Rudolf*, pp. 52–53; Manfred Deselaers, *And Your Conscience Never Haunted You?* Oświęcim: Auschwitz-Birkenau State Museum, 2017, pp. 59–60; Höss, *Commandant of Auschwitz*, p. 201.
   35. Höss, *Commandant of Auschwitz*, p. 63; Gilbert, *Nuremberg Diary*, p. 259.

Chapter III

   1. Shirer, *The Rise and Fall of the Third Reich*, pp. 25, 42, 44, 117, 119, 136, 138.
   2. *Ibid.*, pp. 137–38.
   3. *Ibid.*, pp. 166, 187, 226–27, 229.
   4. *Ibid.*, pp. 38, 120–21; Tom Segev, *Soldiers of Evil*, Jerusalem: Domino Press, 1987, p. 54.
   5. Segev, *Soldiers of Evil*, pp. 56, 73–74.
   6. *Ibid.*, pp. 80–82, 83, 87.
   7. Goldensohn, *The Nuremberg Interviews*, p. 298; Segev, *Soldiers of Evil*, p. 83; Desalaers, *And Your Conscience Never Haunted You?* p. 65; Höss, *Death Dealer: The Memoirs of the SS Commandant at Auschwitz*, p. 332, Kindle edition.
   8. Höss, *Commandant of Auschwitz*, pp. 63–65.
   9. *Ibid.*, pp. 65, 235; Segev, *Soldiers of Evil*, pp. 10, 17, 107, 118–19.
   10. Höss, *Commandant of Auschwitz*, pp. 65, 235–36; Segev, *Soldiers of Evil*, pp. 58, 95–96, 97.
   11. Höss, *Commandant of Auschwitz*, pp. 68, 79, 235–36.
   12. *Ibid.*, pp. 68, 236; Segev, *Soldiers of Evil*, pp. 94–95.

13. Höss, *Commandant of Auschwitz*, pp. 65–66.
14. *Ibid.*, pp. 66–67.
15. *Ibid.*, pp. 66, 68–69.
16. *Ibid.*, pp. 65–67.
17. *Ibid.*, pp. 69–71, 78.
18. *Ibid.*, pp. 82–83.
19. Shirer, *The Rise and Fall of the Third Reich*, pp. 518–20, 594–97.
20. Höss, *Commandant of Auschwitz*, pp. 83–84, 242; Lasik, "Rudolph Höss: Manager of Crime," in *Anatomy of the Auschwitz Death Camp*, p. 292.
21. Höss, *Commandant of Auschwitz*, pp. 84–85.
22. *Ibid.*, pp. 86–87.
23. *Ibid.*, pp. 85–86.
24. *Ibid.*, p. 105.
25. Segev, *Soldiers of Evil*, pp. 23–24, 33.
26. *Ibid.*, p. 214.

Chapter IV

1. Lasik, "Rudolph Hoess: Manager of Crime," in *Anatomy of the Auschwitz Death Camp*, p. 292; Dwork and van Pelt, *Auschwitz: 1270 to the Present*, pp. 166, 168; Steinbacher, *Auschwitz*, p. 22.
2. Goldensohn, *The Nuremberg Interviews*, p. 299; Dwork and van Pelt, *Auschwitz: 1270 to the Present*, pp. 166–68.
3. Lasik, "Rudolph Hoess: Manager of Crime," p. 292; Dwork and van Pelt, *Auschwitz: 1270 to the Present*, pp. 166–68; Höss, *Commandant of Auschwitz*, p. 103.
4. Czech, *Auschwitz Chronicle: 1939–1945*, p. 16; Steinbacher, *Auschwitz*, p. 23; Höss, *Commandant of Auschwitz*, pp. 106, 107–08.
5. Dwork and van Pelt, *Auschwitz: 1270 to the Present*, pp. 168–69; Höss, *Commandant of Auschwitz*, pp. 109–110.
6. Höss, *Commandant of Auschwitz*, pp. 76–77.
7. *Ibid.*, p. 77.
8. Dwork and van Pelt, *Auschwitz: 1270 to the Present*, pp. 169–71.
9. *Ibid.*, pp. 169–74; Höss, *Commandant of Auschwitz*, pp. 204–05.
10. Czech, *Auschwitz Chronicle: 1939–1945*, p. 43; Broad, *KZ Auschwitz*, p. 10.
11. Harding, *Hanns and Rudolf*, p. 99; Broad, *KZ Auschwitz*, pp. 53–54.
12. Dwork and van Pelt, *Auschwitz: 1270 to the Present*, pp. 175–76.
13. Broad, *KZ Auschwitz*, pp. 15, 17.
14. *Ibid.*, pp. 16–17; Hermann Langbein, *People in Auschwitz*, Chapel Hill: University of North Carolina Press, 2004, Kindle edition, p. 329; Library of Congress, "Trial of the Major War Criminals Before International Military Tribunal, Volume V," p. 653, https://www.loc.gov/rr/frd/Military_Law/pdf/NT_war-criminals_Vol-V.pdf, accessed July 18, 2019.
15. Czech, *Auschwitz Chronicle: 1939–1945*, p. 35; Dwork and van Pelt, *Auschwitz: 1270 to the Present*, p. 176.
16. Czech, *Auschwitz Chronicle: 1939–1945*, pp. 105–06; Broad, *KZ Auschwitz*, pp. 18–23.
17. Czech, *Auschwitz Chronicle: 1939–1945*, pp. 145, 153, 165, 171, 174, 176, 179, 181, 183; Broad, *KZ Auschwitz*, pp. 18–23.
18. Broad, *KZ Auschwitz*, pp. 24–29.
19. Goldensohn, *The Nuremberg Interviews*, p. 298; Broad, *KZ Auschwitz*, pp. 32–33.
20. Auschwitz-Birkenau Memorial and Museum, "The Organizational Structure of Auschwitz Concentration Camp," http://auschwitz.org/en/history/the-ss-garrison/the-organizational-structure-of-auschwitz-concentration-camp/, accessed April 14, 2018; Hilberg, *The Destruction of the European Jews*, p. 864; Franciszek Piper, "The System of Prisoner Exploitation," in *Anatomy of the Auschwitz Death Camp*, eds. Yisrael Gutman and Michael Berenbaum, Bloomington: Indiana University Press, 1994, p. 37; Aleksander Lasik, "Historical-Sociological Profile of the Auschwitz SS," in *Anatomy of the Auschwitz Death Camp*, p. 272.
21. Dwork and van Pelt, *Auschwitz: 1270 to the Present*, p. 177.
22. Dwork and van Pelt, *Auschwitz: 1270 to the Present*, p. 254; Czech, *Auschwitz Chronicle: 1939–1945*, pp. 43, 48, 50; Rees, *Auschwitz: A New History*, pp. 32, 34.
23. Dwork and van Pelt, *Auschwitz: 1270 to the Present*, p. 254; Lasik, "Rudolph Hoess: Manager of Crime," in *Anatomy of the Auschwitz Death Camp*, p. 292; Czech, *Auschwitz Chronicle: 1939–1945*, p. 50.
24. Höss, *Commandant of Auschwitz*, pp. 114–15; Goldensohn, *The Nuremberg Interviews*, p. 300; Lasik, "Rudolph Hoess: Manager of Crime," in *Anatomy of the Auschwitz Death Camp*, p. 294.
25. Höss, *Commandant of Auschwitz*, pp. 122–24; Rees, *Auschwitz: A New History*, p. 65; Czech, *Auschwitz Chronicle: 1939–1945*, pp. 94, 102; Steinbacher, *Auschwitz*, p. 90.

26. Dwork and van Pelt, *Auschwitz: 1270 to the Present*, pp. 262–65; Robert Jan van Pelt, "A Site in Search of a Mission," in *Anatomy of the Auschwitz Death Camp*, eds. Yisrael Gutman and Michael Berenbaum, Bloomington: Indiana University Press, 1994, pp. 118–26; Langbein, *People in Auschwitz*, p. 98.
27. Dwork and van Pelt, *Auschwitz: 1270 to the Present*, pp. 268–69.

Chapter V

1. Ann Tusa and John Tusa, *The Nuremberg Trial*, New York: Atheneum, 1984, p. 160; Nazi Concentration Camps—Film Shown at Nuremberg War Crimes Trial, https://www.bing.com/videos/search?q=fil m+shown+at+nuremberg+trials&view=det ail&mid=0724B20B704E1D1FD8F00724B2 0B704E1D1FD8F0&FORM=VIRE.
2. Library of Congress, "Trial of the Major War Criminals Before International Military Tribunal, Volume VI," p. 228, https://www.loc.gov/rr/frd/Military_Law/ pdf/NT_Vol-VI.pdf, accessed May 30, 2018.
3. Gilbert, *Nuremberg Diary*, p. 260; Goldensohn, *The Nuremberg Interviews*, p. 298; Höss, *Commandant of Auschwitz*, p. 20.
4. Höss, *Commandant of Auschwitz*, pp. 114, 144; Library of Congress, "Trial of the Major War Criminals Before International Military Tribunal, Volume XI," p. 403.
5. Library of Congress, "Trial of the Major War Criminals Before International Military Tribunal, Volume XI," p. 404.
6. Langbein, *People in Auschwitz*, p. 294; Höss, *Commandant of Auschwitz*, p. 178.
7. Langbein, *People in Auschwitz*, p. 295.
8. Höss, *Commandant of Auschwitz*, pp. 68, 79, 235–36.
9. Höss, *Commandant of Auschwitz*, pp. 68, 79, 115, 179, 235–36; Höss, *Death Dealer: The Memoirs of the SS Commandant at Auschwitz*, p. 100 n. 1.
10. Deselaers, *And Your Conscience Never Haunted You?* pp. 109–10.
11. *Ibid.*
12. Broad, *KZ Auschwitz*, pp. 16–17; Czech, *Auschwitz Chronicle: 1939–1945*, pp. 53, 70.
13. Höss, *Commandant of Auschwitz*, pp. 117–18; Czech, *Auschwitz Chronicle: 1939–1945*, p. 350.
14. Broad, *KZ Auschwitz*, p. 13 n. 15; Czech, *Auschwitz Chronicle: 1939–1945*, pp. 59, 67, 69, 76; Höss, *Commandant of Auschwitz*, p. 111.
15. Langbein, *People in Auschwitz*, pp. 257–58; Czech, *Auschwitz Chronicle: 1939–1945*, p. 350; Höss, *Commandant of Auschwitz*, p. 102.
16. Czech, *Auschwitz Chronicle: 1939–1945*, p. 184.
17. Filip Müller, *Eyewitness Auschwitz*, Chicago: Ivan R. Dee, 1979, pp. 1–3.
18. *Ibid.*, pp. 3–5.
19. Hermann Langbein, "The Auschwitz Underground," in *Anatomy of the Auschwitz Death Camp*, eds. Yisrael Gutman and Michael Berenbaum, Bloomington: Indiana University Press, 1994, pp. 485–502.
20. Höss, *Commandant of Auschwitz*, pp. 83, 117, 132; Rees, *Auschwitz: A New History*, p. 170.

Chapter VI

1. Rees, *Auschwitz: A New History*, p. 170.
2. Auschwitz-Birkenau Memorial and Museum, "The Unloading Ramps and Selections," http://auschwitz.org/en/history/ auschwitz-and-shoah/the-unloading-ramps-and-selections, accessed June 2, 2018.
3. Henri Landwirth, *Gift of Life*, privately published, 2009, pp. 17–18.
4. Wendy Holden, *Born Survivors*, London: HarperCollins, 2015, Kindle edition, p. 30; Elie Wiesel, *Night*, New York: Hill & Wang, 1972, pp. 22–23; Library of Congress, "Trial of the Major War Criminals Before International Military Tribunal, Volume VI," p. 205.
5. Primo Levi, *Survival in Auschwitz*, New York: Touchstone, 1996, p. 19; Dwork and van Pelt, *Auschwitz: 1270 to the Present*, p. 340; Holden, *Born Survivors*, p. 120; Victor E. Frankl, *Man's Search for Meaning*, Boston: Beacon Press, 2014, p. 11; Library of Congress, "Trial of the Major War Criminals Before International Military Tribunal, Volume VI," p. 215.
6. Holden, *Born Survivors*, pp. 69, 121; Library of Congress, "Trial of the Major War Criminals Before International Military Tribunal, Volume VI," p. 215.
7. Rees, *Auschwitz: A New History*, p. 100; Auschwitz-Birkenau Memorial and Museum, "The Unloading Ramps and Selections"; Höss, *Commandant of Auschwitz*, p. 189.
8. Library of Congress, "Trial of the

Major War Criminals Before International Military Tribunal, Volume XI," p. 400.
9. Goldensohn, *The Nuremberg Interviews*, p. 302.
10. Helena Kubica, "Children," in *Anatomy of the Auschwitz Death Camp*, eds. Yisrael Gutman and Michael Berenbaum, Bloomington: Indiana University Press, 1994, p. 414; Wiesel, *Night*, pp. 31-32.
11. Levi, *Survival in Auschwitz*, p. 22; Andrzej Strzelecki, "The Plunder of Victims and Their Corpses," in *Anatomy of the Auschwitz Death Camp*, eds. Yisrael Gutman and Michael Berenbaum, Bloomington: Indiana University Press, 1994, p. 247.
12. Levi, *Survival in Auschwitz*, p. 23.
13. *Ibid.*, pp. 23-24.
14. *Ibid.*, pp. 24-25.
15. *Ibid.*, pp. 25-27.
16. *Ibid.*, pp. 26-27.
17. Holden, *Born Survivors*, pp. 121-22.
18. *Ibid.*, pp. 122-24, 153.
19. *Ibid.*, pp. 124-26.
20. *Ibid.*, p. 126; Library of Congress, "Trial of the Major War Criminals Before International Military Tribunal, Volume VI," pp. 145, 206.
21. Kazimierz Smolen, *Auschwitz, 1940-1945*, Albuquerque: Route 66 Publishing, 1995, pp. 42-43; Steinbacher, *Auschwitz*, pp. 31-32; Langbein, *People in Auschwitz*, pp. 13-14.
22. Smolen, *Auschwitz, 1940-1945*, pp. 45-46; Steinbacher, *Auschwitz*, p. 33; Langbein, *People in Auschwitz*, p. 90.
23. Smolen, *Auschwitz, 1940-1945*, p. 46; Library of Congress, "Trial of the Major War Criminals Before International Military Tribunal, Volume VI," pp. 210, 219.
24. Höss, *Commandant of Auschwitz*, pp. 115, 178-79; Langbein, *People in Auschwitz*, p. 46.

Chapter VII

1. Holden, *Born Survivors*, p. 137; Smolen, *Auschwitz, 1940-1945*, pp. 48-49; Kitty Hart, *Return to Auschwitz*, New York: American Book-Stratford Press, 1982, p. 102; Library of Congress, "Trial of the Major War Criminals Before International Military Tribunal, Volume VI," pp. 206-07.
2. Library of Congress, "Trial of the Major War Criminals Before International Military Tribunal, Volume VI," pp. 207-08; Czech, *Auschwitz Chronicle: 1939-1945*, p. 324.
3. Lasik, "Historical-Sociological Profile of the Auschwitz SS," in *Anatomy of the Auschwitz Death Camp*, pp. 274, 284-86; Rees, *Auschwitz: A New History*, p. 295; Czech, *Auschwitz Chronicle: 1939-1945*, p. 164.
4. Lasik, "Historical-Sociological Profile of the Auschwitz SS," in *Anatomy of the Auschwitz Death Camp*, pp. 284-86.
5. Danuta Czech, "The Auschwitz Prison Administration," in *Anatomy of the Auschwitz Death Camp*, eds. Yisrael Gutman and Michael Berenbaum, Bloomington: Indiana University Press, 1994, pp. 363-64.
6. *Ibid.*, p. 364.
7. *Ibid.*, p. 364; Langbein, *People in Auschwitz*, pp. 13, 144; Rees, *Auschwitz: A New History*, p. 22.
8. Höss, *Commandant of Auschwitz*, pp. 115-16.
9. *Ibid.*
10. Langbein, *People in Auschwitz*, p. 146; Höss, *Commandant of Auschwitz*, p. 116.
11. Höss, *Commandant of Auschwitz*, pp. 115-16.
12. Deselaers, *And Your Conscience Never Haunted You?* pp. 148-49; Langbein, *People in Auschwitz*, p. 302; Höss, *Commandant of Auschwitz*, pp. 115-16, 144.
13. Czech, *Auschwitz Chronicle: 1939-1945*, p. 224; Höss, *Commandant of Auschwitz*, p. 115.
14. Höss, *Death Dealer: The Memoirs of the SS Commandant at Auschwitz*, pp. 278-79.
15. Primo Levi, *Auschwitz Report*, London: Verso, 2006, p. 44; Frankl, *Man's Search for Meaning*, p. 28; Smolen, *Auschwitz, 1940-1945*, p. 60; Library of Congress, "Trial of the Major War Criminals Before International Military Tribunal, Volume XXXIII," pp. 275-79.
16. Smolen, *Auschwitz, 1940-1945*, p. 61; Langbein, *People in Auschwitz*, p. 17.
17. Levi, *Survival in Auschwitz*, pp. 69, 78-79.
18. Library of Congress, "Trial of the Major War Criminals Before International Military Tribunal, Volume VI," pp. 208-09.
19. Czech, *Auschwitz Chronicle: 1939-1945*, p. 150.
20. Library of Congress, "Trial of the Major War Criminals Before International Military Tribunal, Volume VI," p. 209.
21. *Ibid.*, pp. 209-10.
22. Czech, *Auschwitz Chronicle: 1939-*

Notes—Chapter VII

1945, p. 304; Irena Strzelecka, "Hospitals," in *Anatomy of the Auschwitz Death Camp*, eds. Yisrael Gutman and Michael Berenbaum, Bloomington: Indiana University Press, 1994, pp. 385–87, 390; Library of Congress, "Trial of the Major War Criminals Before International Military Tribunal, Volume VI," p. 210.

23. "Hippocratic oath," *Encyclopaedia Britannica*, 2017, https://www.britannica.com/topic/Hippocratic-oath, accessed June 8, 2018.

24. Library of Congress, "Trial of the Major War Criminals Before International Military Tribunal, Volume XXXIII," pp. 275–79; Library of Congress, "Law Reports of Trials of War Criminals, Vol. VII," p. 11.

25. Robert Jay Lifton and Amy Hackett, "Nazi Doctors," in *Anatomy of the Auschwitz Death Camp*, eds. Yisrael Gutman and Michael Berenbaum, Bloomington: Indiana University Press, 1994, pp. 303–310; Czech, *Auschwitz Chronicle: 1939-1945*, pp. 386, 414.

26. Library of Congress, "Law Reports of Trials of War Criminals, Vol. VII," pp. 15–16.

27. Helena Kubica, "The Crimes of Josef Mengele," in *Anatomy of the Auschwitz Death Camp*, eds. Yisrael Gutman and Michael Berenbaum, Bloomington: Indiana University Press, 1994, pp. 320–27; Czech, *Auschwitz Chronicle: 1939-1945*, p. 244.

28. Steinbacher, *Auschwitz*, pp. 51–52; Levi, *Survival in Auschwitz*, p. 35.

29. Steinbacher, *Auschwitz*, pp. 53, 56–58.

30. Ibid., pp. 51–54, 61; Shmuel Krakowski, "The Satellite Camps," in *Anatomy of the Auschwitz Death Camp*, eds. Yisrael Gutman and Michael Berenbaum, Bloomington: Indiana University Press, 1994, p. 54.

31. Irene Strzelecka, "Women," in *Anatomy of the Auschwitz Death Camp*, eds. Yisrael Gutman and Michael Berenbaum, Bloomington: Indiana University Press, 1994, pp. 395–96; Steinbacher, *Auschwitz*, pp. 91–95.

32. Strzelecka, "Women," in *Anatomy of the Auschwitz Death Camp*, pp. 395–96; Steinbacher, *Auschwitz*, pp. 91–95; Höss, *Commandant of Auschwitz*, pp. 137–38; Library of Congress, "Trial of the Major War Criminals Before International Military Tribunal, Volume VI," p. 207; Czech, *Auschwitz Chronicle: 1939-1945*, p. 211.

33. Library of Congress, "Trial of the Major War Criminals Before International Military Tribunal, Volume VI," p. 212; Kubica, "Children," in *Anatomy of the Auschwitz Death Camp*, pp. 417, 421.

34. Nili Keren, "The Family Camp," in *Anatomy of the Auschwitz Death Camp*, eds. Yisrael Gutman and Michael Berenbaum, Bloomington: Indiana University Press, 1994, pp. 428–29.

35. Yehuda Bauer, "Gypsies," in *Anatomy of the Auschwitz Death Camp*, eds. Yisrael Gutman and Michael Berenbaum, Bloomington: Indiana University Press, 1994, pp. 441–50; Czech, *Auschwitz Chronicle: 1939-1945*, p. 338.

36. Langbein, *People in Auschwitz*, pp. 91–92, 94; Levi, *Survival in Auschwitz*, p. 88; Frankl, *Man's Search for Meaning*, p. 18; Czech, "The Auschwitz Prison Administration," in *Anatomy of the Auschwitz Death Camp*, p. 371.

37. Langbein, *People in Auschwitz*, pp. 106–08.

38. Wiesel, *Night*, pp. 71–72; Holden, *Born Survivors*, p. 138; Langbein, *People in Auschwitz*, pp. 108, 109, 111; Höss, *Death Dealer: The Memoirs of the SS Commandant at Auschwitz*, p. 323.

39. Hart, *Return to Auschwitz*, pp. 82–83.

40. Johann Paul Kremer, "Diary," in *KZ Auschwitz Seen by the SS*, New York: Howard Fertig, 1994, p. 215 n. 51.

41. Ester Sendrowicz, Interview 22539, Visual History Archive, USC Shoah Foundation, 1996, Segments 88–89, 91–92, accessed July 31, 2019.

42. Czech, "The Auschwitz Prison Administration," in *Anatomy of the Auschwitz Death Camp*, pp. 367–68; Langbein, *People in Auschwitz*, pp. 125, 310.

43. Czech, "The Auschwitz Prison Administration," in *Anatomy of the Auschwitz Death Camp*, pp. 367–68.

44. Ibid., p. 368; Langbein, *People in Auschwitz*, p. 123.

45. Frankl, *Man's Search for Meaning*, p. 65.

46. Höss, *Commandant of Auschwitz*, pp. 141–42.

47. Library of Congress, "Trial of the Major War Criminals Before International Military Tribunal, Volume VI," p. 208.

48. Steinbacher, *Auschwitz*, pp. 33–34; Czech, *Auschwitz Chronicle: 1939-1945*, pp. 136–37, 143, 164, 279; Krakowski, "The Satellite Camps," in *Anatomy of the Auschwitz Death Camp*, p. 55; Broad, *KZ Auschwitz*, p. 24.

49. Dwork and van Pelt, *Auschwitz: 1270 to the Present*, p. 317.
50. Smolen, *Auschwitz, 1940–1945*, pp. 83–84.
51. Broad, *KZ Auschwitz*, p. 42; Höss, *Commandant of Auschwitz*, p. 135 n. 1.
52. Broad, *KZ Auschwitz*, pp. 42–44; Höss, *Commandant of Auschwitz*, p. 135.
53. Broad, *KZ Auschwitz*, pp. 43–45; Czech, *Auschwitz Chronicle: 1939–1945*, pp. 249, 256–57.
54. Czech, *Auschwitz Chronicle: 1939–1945*, pp. 256–57; Library of Congress, "Trial of the Major War Criminals Before International Military Tribunal, Volume XI," p. 410.
55. Hart, *Return to Auschwitz*, pp. 97–100; Holden, *Born Survivors*, p. 157.
56. Broad, *KZ Auschwitz*, pp. 13–15 n. 21; Czech, *Auschwitz Chronicle: 1939–1945*, p. 200; Smolen, *Auschwitz, 1940–1945*, p. 21.
57. Czech, *Auschwitz Chronicle: 1939–1945*, pp. 129–31.
58. Thomas Harding, "Hiding in N. Virginia, A Daughter of Auschwitz," *Washington Post*, September 7, 2013, https://www.washingtonpost.com/lifestyle/magazine/hiding-in-n-virginia-a-daughter-of-auschwitz/2013/09/06/1314d648-04fd-11e3-a07f-49ddc7417125_story.html?noredirect=on&utm_term=.31eaf13074c6, accessed June 9, 2018.
59. Höss, *Commandant of Auschwitz*, pp. 156–57.
60. Höss, *Commandant of Auschwitz*, p. 75.
61. Levi, *Survival in Auschwitz*, pp. 40–41, 92.

Chapter VIII

1. Longerich, *Holocaust: The Nazi Persecution and Murder of the Jews*, pp. 135–42; Lifton and Hackett, "Nazi Doctors," in *Anatomy of the Auschwitz Death Camp*, p. 302.
2. *Ibid.*, pp. 277–78.
3. *Ibid.*, p. 144, 192–95, 242–47, 236–37, 224, 230–31, 255; Browning, *The Origins of the Final Solution*, pp. 226, 244.
4. Longerich, *Holocaust: The Nazi Persecution and Murder of the Jews*, p. 279; Rees, *Auschwitz: A New History*, pp. 51–52.
5. Longerich, *Holocaust: The Nazi Persecution and Murder of the Jews*, pp. 278–80; Lifton and Hackett, "Nazi Doctors," in *Anatomy of the Auschwitz Death Camp*, p. 302;

Piper, "Gas Chambers and Crematoria," in *Anatomy of the Auschwitz Death Camp*, p. 160; Rees, *Auschwitz: A New History*, pp. 109, 147, 150–51.
6. Library of Congress, "Trial of the Major War Criminals Before International Military Tribunal, Volume XXXIII," p. 275; Höss, *Commandant of Auschwitz*, pp. 145, 190.
7. Czech, *Auschwitz Chronicle: 1939–1945*, p. 76; Library of Congress, "Trial of the Major War Criminals Before International Military Tribunal, Volume XI," p. 398; Library of Congress, "Trial of the Major War Criminals Before International Military Tribunal, Volume XXXIII," p. 277.
8. Shirer, *The Rise and Fall of the Third Reich*, p. 964; Longerich, *Holocaust: The Nazi Persecution and Murder of the Jews*, p. 289.
9. Jewish Virtual Library, "The Einsatzgruppen: Heydrich's Instructions to Einsatzgruppen Chiefs (September 21, 1939)," http://www.jewishvirtuallibrary.org/heydrich-s-instructions-to-einsatzgruppen-chiefs-september-1939-2, accessed April 11, 2018; Czech, *Auschwitz Chronicle: 1939–1945*, p. 73.
10. Jewish Virtual Library, "The 'Final Solution': Göring Commission to Heydrich," https://www.jewishvirtuallibrary.org/gring-commission-to-heydrich, accessed April 11, 2018.
11. Höss, *Commandant of Auschwitz*, pp. 183–85; Czech, *Auschwitz Chronicle: 1939–1945*, p. 78.
12. Whitney R. Harris, *Tyranny on Trial*, Dallas: Southern Methodist University Press, 1954, p. 312.
13. Höss, *Commandant of Auschwitz*, pp. 183–85; Czech, *Auschwitz Chronicle: 1939–1945*, p. 78; Dwork and van Pelt, *Auschwitz: 1270 to the Present*, p. 304.
14. Strzelecka, "Hospitals," in *Anatomy of the Auschwitz Death Camp*, p. 389; Steinbacher, *Auschwitz*, pp. 87–88; Czech, *Auschwitz Chronicle: 1939–1945*, pp. 77–78, 84.
15. Czech, *Auschwitz Chronicle: 1939–1945*, pp. 85–87, 90.
16. Höss, *Commandant of Auschwitz*, pp. 146–47.
17. *Ibid.*
18. *Ibid.*; Dwork and van Pelt, *Auschwitz: 1270 to the Present*, pp. 292–93; Jean-Claude Pressac with Robert-Jan Van Pelt, "The Machinery of Mass Murder at Auschwitz," in *Anatomy of the Auschwitz Death Camp*, eds. Yisrael Gutman and Michael Beren-

baum, Bloomington: Indiana University Press, 1994, pp. 209, 215.
19. Höss, *Commandant of Auschwitz*, p. 148 n. 3; Steinbacher, *Auschwitz*, p. 89; Longerich, *Holocaust: The Nazi Persecution and Murder of the Jews*, pp. 305–09; Höss, *Death Dealer: The Memoirs of the SS Commandant at Auschwitz*, pp. 374–76; Czech, *Auschwitz Chronicle: 1939-1945*, p. 135; Dwork and van Pelt, *Auschwitz: 1270 to the Present*, p. 326.
20. Broad, *KZ Auschwitz*, pp. 54–59; Czech, *Auschwitz Chronicle: 1939-1945*, p. 135.
21. Czech, *Auschwitz Chronicle: 1939-1945*, p. 146; Piper, "Gas Chambers and Crematoria," in *Anatomy of the Auschwitz Death Camp*, p. 161; Dwork and van Pelt, *Auschwitz: 1270 to the Present*, pp. 302, 305; Goldensohn, *The Nuremberg Interviews*, p. 302.
22. Höss, *Commandant of Auschwitz*, p. 148.
23. Dwork and van Pelt, *Auschwitz: 1270 to the Present*, p. 304.
24. Piper, "Gas Chambers and Crematoria," in *Anatomy of the Auschwitz Death Camp*, pp. 161–62.
25. Ibid.
26. Czech, *Auschwitz Chronicle: 1939-1945*, p. 218; Gilbert, *Nuremberg Diary*, p. 250; Piper, "Gas Chambers and Crematoria," in *Anatomy of the Auschwitz Death Camp*, pp. 166–67; Dwork and van Pelt, *Auschwitz: 1270 to the Present*, p. 321.
27. Piper, "Gas Chambers and Crematoria," in *Anatomy of the Auschwitz Death Camp*, p. 166.
28. Piper, "Gas Chambers and Crematoria," in *Anatomy of the Auschwitz Death Camp*, pp. 166–67, 170.
29. Ibid.
30. Gilbert, *Nuremberg Diary*, pp. 249–50; Piper, "Gas Chambers and Crematoria," in *Anatomy of the Auschwitz Death Camp*, pp. 166, 168, 171, 173; Shlomo Venezia, *Inside the Gas Chambers*, Cambridge, Polity Press, 2009, pp. 72–73; Höss, *Commandant of Auschwitz*, p. 199..
31. Goldensohn, *The Nuremberg Interviews*, pp. 303–04; Dwork and van Pelt, *Auschwitz: 1270 to the Present*, pp. 329–32; Czech, *Auschwitz Chronicle: 1939-1945*, pp. 358, 364–65, 429; Piper, "Gas Chambers and Crematoria," in *Anatomy of the Auschwitz Death Camp*, pp. 165–66, 173; Steinbacher, *Auschwitz*, p. 98.
32. Holocaust Education & Archive Research Team, "Rudolf Höss, Commandant of Auschwitz"; Goldensohn, *The Nuremberg Interviews*, pp. 300–01.
33. Library of Congress, "Trial of the Major War Criminals Before International Military Tribunal, Volume XXXIII," pp. 275–79; Dwork and van Pelt, *Auschwitz: 1270 to the Present*, pp. 336–37.
34. Venezia, *Inside the Gas Chambers*, Cambridge: Polity Press, 2009, pp. 74, 76–79; Czech, *Auschwitz Chronicle: 1939-1945*, pp. 162, 191–92.
35. Piper, "Gas Chambers and Crematoria," in *Anatomy of the Auschwitz Death Camp*, pp. 162, 170; Goldensohn, *The Nuremberg Interviews*, p. 302; Venezia, *Inside the Gas Chambers*, p. 58; Höss, *Commandant of Auschwitz*, p. 197.
36. Piper, "Gas Chambers and Crematoria," in *Anatomy of the Auschwitz Death Camp*, p. 170; Kremer, "Diary," in *KZ Auschwitz Seen by the SS*, p. 214.
37. Czech, *Auschwitz Chronicle: 1939-1945*, p. 146; Höss, *Commandant of Auschwitz*, p. 148; Miklos Nyiszli, *Auschwitz: A Doctor's Eyewitness Account*, New York: Arcade Publishing, 1960, Kindle edition, location 623.
38. Hart, *Return to Auschwitz*, pp. 82–83.
39. Steinbacher, *Auschwitz*, pp. 22, 60; Piper, "Gas Chambers and Crematoria," in *Anatomy of the Auschwitz Death Camp*, p. 162.
40. Müller, *Eyewitness Auschwitz*, pp. 49–50.
41. Höss, *Commandant of Auschwitz*, pp. 187–88, 208; Czech, *Auschwitz Chronicle: 1939-1945*, pp. 198–99.
42. Höss, *Commandant of Auschwitz*, p. 188; Czech, *Auschwitz Chronicle: 1939-1945*, pp. 238–39.
43. Höss, *Commandant of Auschwitz*, p. 188.
44. Ibid., p. 187; Czech, *Auschwitz Chronicle: 1939-1945*, pp. 242, 275; Steinbacher, *Auschwitz*, pp. 97–98; Langbein, *People in Auschwitz*, p. 191; Strzelecki, "The Plunder of Victims and Their Corpses," in *Anatomy of the Auschwitz Death Camp*, p. 261.
45. Dwork and van Pelt, *Auschwitz: 1270 to the Present*, pp. 320–21; Broad, *KZ Auschwitz*, pp. 49–50; Czech, *Auschwitz Chronicle: 1939-1945*, pp. 277–78.
46. Höss, *Commandant of Auschwitz*, pp. 190–91.
47. Höss, *Death Dealer: The Memoirs of the SS Commandant at Auschwitz*, p. 355;

Czech, *Auschwitz Chronicle: 1939-1945*, p. 513; Müller, *Eyewitness Auschwitz*, pp. 83–85.

48. Höss, *Death Dealer: The Memoirs of the SS Commandant at Auschwitz*, p. 355; Müller, *Eyewitness Auschwitz*, p. 87.

49. Höss, *Death Dealer: The Memoirs of the SS Commandant at Auschwitz*, pp. 355–56; Aleksander Lasik, "Postwar Prosecution of the Auschwitz SS," in *Anatomy of the Auschwitz Death Camp*, eds. Yisrael Gutman and Michael Berenbaum, Bloomington: Indiana University Press, 1994, p. 598; Müller, *Eyewitness Auschwitz*, pp. 88–89.

50. Höss, *Commandant of Auschwitz*, pp. 155–56; Harding, "Hiding in N. Virginia, A Daughter of Auschwitz," *Washington Post*, September 7, 2013.

51. Höss, *Death Dealer: The Memoirs of the SS Commandant at Auschwitz*, p. 21; Gilbert, *Nuremberg Diary*, p. 259.

52. Höss, *Commandant of Auschwitz*, pp. 149–50.

53. Ibid., pp. 154–55.

54. Ibid., pp. 150, 154.

55. Ibid., pp. 149–50, 181; Kubica, "Children," in *Anatomy of the Auschwitz Death Camp*, pp. 417, 421.

56. Goldensohn, *The Nuremberg Interviews*, p. 303.

57. Kremer, "Diary," in *KZ Auschwitz Seen by the SS*, p. 214 n. 50; Dwork and van Pelt, *Auschwitz: 1270 to the Present*, p. 351; Langbein, *People in Auschwitz*, p. 191; Smolen, *Auschwitz, 1940-1945*, p. 33; Piper, "Gas Chambers and Crematoria," in *Anatomy of the Auschwitz Death Camp*, p. 170.

58. Höss, *Commandant of Auschwitz*, p. 198.

59. Langbein, *People in Auschwitz*, p. 191; Piper, "Gas Chambers and Crematoria," in *Anatomy of the Auschwitz Death Camp*, p. 170; Venezia, *Inside the Gas Chambers*, pp. 64–65.

60. Dwork and van Pelt, *Auschwitz: 1270 to the Present*, p. 351; Nyiszli, *Auschwitz: A Doctor's Eyewitness Account*, Kindle edition, location 684, 690.

61. Nyiszli, *Auschwitz: A Doctor's Eyewitness Account*, Kindle edition, location 684–90; Czech, *Auschwitz Chronicle: 1939-1945*, p. 284.

62. Piper, "Gas Chambers and Crematoria," in *Anatomy of the Auschwitz Death Camp*, pp. 163, 170–71; Czech, *Auschwitz Chronicle: 1939-1945*, p. 212; Steinbacher, *Auschwitz*, p. 128.

63. Nyiszli, *Auschwitz: A Doctor's Eyewitness Account*, Kindle edition, location 690–705; Venezia, *Inside the Gas Chambers*, pp. 63–64.

64. Venezia, *Inside the Gas Chambers*, pp. 106–07.

65. Nyiszli, *Auschwitz: A Doctor's Eyewitness Account*, Kindle edition, location 846–66, 1455–74.

66. Dwork and van Pelt, *Auschwitz: 1270 to the Present*, p. 326; Piper, "Gas Chambers and Crematoria," in *Anatomy of the Auschwitz Death Camp*, p. 160; Venezia, *Inside the Gas Chambers*, pp. 101–02; Höss, *Commandant of Auschwitz*, p. 199.

67. Venezia, *Inside the Gas Chambers*, pp. 102–03.

68. Müller, *Eyewitness Auschwitz*, p. 17.

69. Höss, *Commandant of Auschwitz*, p. 151.

70. Rees, *Auschwitz: A New History*, p. 220.

71. Friedlander, *The Years of Extermination: Nazi Germany and the Jews, 1939-1945*, pp. 613–14.

72. Rees, *Auschwitz: A New History*, p. 224; Steinbacher, *Auschwitz*, pp. 59–60; Lasik, "Rudolph Hoess: Manager of Crime," in *Anatomy of the Auschwitz Death Camp*, p. 295.

73. Langbein, *People in Auschwitz*, p. 48; Rees, *Auschwitz: A New History*, pp. 224, 228; Dwork and van Pelt, *Auschwitz: 1270 to the Present*, p. 338.

74. Friedlander, *The Years of Extermination: Nazi Germany and the Jews, 1939-1945*, pp. 614–15, 618; Dwork and van Pelt, *Auschwitz: 1270 to the Present*, pp. 338, 342; Rees, *Auschwitz: A New History*, p. 234; Czech, *Auschwitz Chronicle: 1939-1945*, p. 627; Hilberg, *The Destruction of the European Jews*, p. 978; Höss, *Death Dealer: The Memoirs of the SS Commandant at Auschwitz*, p. 360.

75. Müller, *Eyewitness Auschwitz*, pp. 98–99.

76. Czech, *Auschwitz Chronicle: 1939-1945*, p. 622; Nyiszli, *Auschwitz: A Doctor's Eyewitness Account*, Kindle edition, location 1052–59.

77. Nyiszli, *Auschwitz: A Doctor's Eyewitness Account*, Kindle edition, location 1059–66.

78. Langbein, *People in Auschwitz*, p. 414; Höss, *Death Dealer: The Memoirs of the SS Commandant at Auschwitz*, p. 350; Steinbacher, *Auschwitz*, p. 110; Lasik, "Rudolph

Hoess: Manager of Crime," in *Anatomy of the Auschwitz Death Camp*, p. 295; Deselaers, *And Your Conscience Never Haunted You?* p. 173; Müller, *Eyewitness Auschwitz*, p. 142.
79. Höss, *Commandant of Auschwitz*, p. 126; Bauer, "Gypsies," in *Anatomy of the Auschwitz Death Camp*, p. 449; Czech, *Auschwitz Chronicle: 1939-1945*, p. 626.
80. Höss, *Commandant of Auschwitz*, p. 200.
81. Müller, *Eyewitness Auschwitz*, pp. 108-09.
82. *Ibid.*, pp. 111-12.
83. *Ibid.*, pp. 112-14.
84. *Ibid.*, pp. 114-15, 118-19.
85. Nyiszli, *Auschwitz: A Doctor's Eyewitness Account*, Kindle edition, location 1345-1356.
86. *Ibid.*, location 1359-76.
87. *Ibid.*, location 1382-84, 1408-13.

Chapter IX

1. Strzelecki, "The Plunder of Victims and Their Corpses," in *Anatomy of the Auschwitz Death Camp*, pp. 247-49; Broad, *KZ Auschwitz*, p. 86; Höss, *Commandant of Auschwitz*, p. 194.
2. Strzelecki, "The Plunder of Victims and Their Corpses," in *Anatomy of the Auschwitz Death Camp*, pp. 246, 249-50.
3. *Ibid.*, pp. 250-51.
4. *Ibid.*, pp. 251-53; Langbein, *People in Auschwitz*, p. 137.
5. Strzelecki, "The Plunder of Victims and Their Corpses," in *Anatomy of the Auschwitz Death Camp*, pp. 253-54.
6. Jewish Virtual Library, "Himmler's Posen Speech 'Extermination,'" http://www.jewishvirtuallibrary.org/himmler-s-posen-speech-quot-extermination-quot, accessed June 12, 2018.
7. Strzelecki, "The Plunder of Victims and Their Corpses," in *Anatomy of the Auschwitz Death Camp*, pp. 256-57; Langbein, *People in Auschwitz*, p. 136.
8. Langbein, *People in Auschwitz*, p. 311; Stanislaw Dubiel, "Deposition of Stanislaw Dubiel," in *KZ Auschwitz Seen by the SS*, New York, Howard Fertig, 1994, 289.
9. Dubiel, "Deposition of Stanislaw Dubiel" in *KZ Auschwitz Seen by the SS*, pp. 289-90.
10. *Ibid.*
11. Höss, *Commandant of Auschwitz*, pp. 194-96.
12. Strzelecki, "The Plunder of Victims and Their Corpses," in *Anatomy of the Auschwitz Death Camp*, pp. 257-58; Lasik, "Rudolph Hoess: Manager of Crime," in *Anatomy of the Auschwitz Death Camp*, p. 294.
13. Harding, *Hanns and Rudolf*, p. 157; Library of Congress, "Trial of the Major War Criminals Before International Military Tribunal, Volume XX," pp. 493, 503-07, https://www.loc.gov/rr/frd/Military_Law/pdf/NT_Vol-XX.pdf, accessed June 23, 2018.
14. Strzelecki, "The Plunder of Victims and Their Corpses," in *Anatomy of the Auschwitz Death Camp*, p. 258; Broad, *KZ Auschwitz*, pp. 88-89; Library of Congress, "Trial of the Major War Criminals Before International Military Tribunal, Volume XX," pp. 480-81, 507.
15. Deselaers, *And Your Conscience Never Haunted You?* pp. 190-94; Rees, *Auschwitz: A New History*, pp. 191-93.
16. Höss, *Commandant of Auschwitz*, p. 157; Steinbacher, *Auschwitz*, pp. 59-60.
17. Czech, *Auschwitz Chronicle: 1939-1945*, pp. 140, 144; Höss, *Commandant of Auschwitz*, p. 158; Lasik, "Rudolph Hoess: Manager of Crime," in *Anatomy of the Auschwitz Death Camp*, pp. 294-95; Harding, *Hanns and Rudolf*, p. 159.
18. Höss, *Commandant of Auschwitz*, pp. 244-47.
19. *Ibid.*, pp. 157-59.
20. *Ibid.*, pp. 161-62.
21. *Ibid.*
22. Segev, *Soldiers of Evil*, pp. 170-71.
23. Höss, *Commandant of Auschwitz*, p. 163.
24. *Ibid.*, pp. 163-64.

Chapter X

1. Tusa and Tusa, *The Nuremberg Trial*, p. 29; Whitney Harris, Interview 33930, Segment 108, Visual History Archive, USC Shoah Foundation, 1997, accessed June 3, 2018.
2. Harris, Interview 33930, Segments 108, 109; Höss, *Commandant of Auschwitz*, pp. 174-75.
3. Harris, Interview 33930, Segments 125-27.
4. Höss, *Commandant of Auschwitz*, p. 174; Library of Congress, Trial of the Major War Criminals Before International Military Tribunal, Volume XI, pp. 398-99, 401-02, 406, 414.

5. Tusa and Tusa, *The Nuremberg Trial*, p. 319; Library of Congress, Trial of the Major War Criminals Before International Military Tribunal, Volume XI, pp. 397–98, 400–01.
6. Library of Congress, Trial of the Major War Criminals Before International Military Tribunal, Volume XI, pp. 414–15.
7. Tusa and Tusa, *The Nuremberg Trial*, p. 320; Library of Congress, Trial of the Major War Criminals Before International Military Tribunal, Volume XI, pp. 416–17.
8. "Interrogations, Summaries of Interrogations, and Related Records, 1945–1946", Hoess, Rudolf, April 5, 1946, Record Group 238, National Archives and Records Administration, October 15, 2019, https://catalog.archives.gov/id/57323382, pp. 8-10.
9. Library of Congress, Trial of the Major War Criminals Before International Military Tribunal, Volume XI, p. 417.
10. Harris, Interview 33930, Segments 107, 132; Tusa and Tusa, *The Nuremberg Trial*, pp. 160–61.
11. Harris, Interview 33930, Segment 126; Tusa and Tusa, *The Nuremberg Trial*, pp. 319–20.
12. "Interrogations, Summaries of Interrogations, and Related Records, 1945–1946", Hoess, Rudolf, April 16, 1946, Record Group 238, National Archives and Records Administration, October 15, 2019, https://catalog.archives.gov/id/57323382, pp. 1-14.
13. Höss, *Commandant of Auschwitz*, p. 175; The National Archives of the UK: War Crimes, FO 371/57649, http://discovery.nationalarchives.gov.uk/recordcopy/RC1509119-08866349-0e17-4b71-bef3-c7b49365310f, accessed April 25, 2018.
14. Höss, *Commandant of Auschwitz*, p. 175.
15. *Ibid.*, pp. 175–76.
16. Harding, *Hanns and Rudolf*, pp. 262–63; Deselaers, "*And Your Conscience Never Haunted You?*," p. 208.
17. Höss, *Commandant of Auschwitz*, p. 77.
18. Joseph Tenenbaum, *Auschwitz In Retrospect: The Self-Portrait of Rudolf Hoess, Commander of Auschwitz*, Pickle Partners Publishing, 2015, Kindle Edition, 535–43.
19. Library of Congress, Law Reports of Trials of War Criminals, Vol VII, pp. 11–12.
20. Library of Congress, Trial of the Major War Criminals Before International Military Tribunal, Volume II, p. 30. https://www.loc.gov/rr/frd/Military_Law/pdf/NT_Vol-II.pdf, accessed May 20, 2018; Deselaers, "*And Your Conscience Never Haunted You?*," pp. 214–15.
21. Library of Congress, Law Reports of Trials of War Criminals, Vol VII, pp. 13–16.
22. *Ibid.*, p. 17.
23. Deselaers, "*And Your Conscience Never Haunted You?*," p. 215.
24. *Ibid.*, 216; Library of Congress, Law Reports of Trials of War Criminals, Vol VII, p. 17.
25. Deselaers, "*And Your Conscience Never Haunted You?*," p. 216; Lasik, "Rudolph Hoess: Manager of Crime" in *Anatomy of the Auschwitz Death Camp*, p. 297; Library of Congress, Law Reports of Trials of War Criminals, Vol VII, p. 18.

Chapter XI

1. Höss, *Commandant of Auschwitz*, pp. 115, 178–79.
2. *Ibid.*, pp. 176, 181; Höss, *Death Dealer: The Memoirs of the SS Commandant at Auschwitz*, pp. 189–93.
3. Höss, *Commandant of Auschwitz*, p. 181.
4. Dwork and van Pelt, *Auschwitz: 1270 to the Present*, pp. 168–69; Höss, *Commandant of Auschwitz*, pp. 109–110, 134.
5. Höss, *Commandant of Auschwitz*, p. 163.
6. *Ibid.*, p. 178.
7. Langbein, *People in Auschwitz*, p. 146.
8. Höss, *Commandant of Auschwitz*, p. 115; Langbein, *People in Auschwitz*, pp. 302, 329.
9. Sarah Joskowitz, Interview 47504, Visual History Archive, USC Shoah Foundation, 1998, Segment 101, accessed July 1, 2018; Mike Vogel, Interview 40285, Visual History Archive, USC Shoah Foundation, 1998, Segment 26, accessed July 1, 2018; Czech, *Auschwitz Chronicle: 1939–1945*, pp. 622–23.
10. Deselaers, *And Your Conscience Never Haunted You?* pp. 148–49.
11. *Ibid.*
12. Segev, *Soldiers of Evil*, pp. 31–32.
13. Höss, *Commandant of Auschwitz*, pp. 141, 178–79.
14. *Ibid.*, pp. 86, 144.
15. *Ibid.*, pp. 69, 73, 80.
16. Langbein, *People in Auschwitz*, pp. 312, 400.
17. Höss, *Commandant of Auschwitz*, pp. 144–45.

18. Harding, *Hanns and Rudolf*, pp. 146–47; Deselaers, *And Your Conscience Never Haunted You?* p. 119; Höss, *Commandant of Auschwitz*, pp. 142, 144.
19. Langbein, *People in Auschwitz*, p. 41.
20. Langbein, *People in Auschwitz*, pp. 45, 47, 307.
21. Czech, *Auschwitz Chronicle: 1939–1945*, pp. 544–45, 549, 553–54.
22. Langbein, *People in Auschwitz*, pp. 317–318.
23. Höss, *Commandant of Auschwitz*, p. 82.
24. Ibid., pp. 144–45.
25. Ibid., pp. 153–54.
26. Broad, *KZ Auschwitz*, pp. 66–67; Lasik, "Historical-Sociological Profile of the Auschwitz SS," in *Anatomy of the Auschwitz Death Camp*, p. 286; Langbein, *People in Auschwitz*, p. 287.
27. Höss, *Commandant of Auschwitz*, pp. 21, 84–85, 153, 155.
28. Ibid., pp. 131, 144.
29. Gilbert, *Nuremberg Diary*, pp. 260, 267–68.
30. Höss, *Commandant of Auschwitz*, pp. 82, 131; Gilbert, *Nuremberg Diary*, p. 269; Langbein, *People in Auschwitz*, p. 314.
31. Höss, *Commandant of Auschwitz*, pp. 144, 178.
32. Gilbert, *Nuremberg Diary*, pp. 259–60.
33. Höss, *Commandant of Auschwitz*, pp. 165–66, 171–73.
34. Ibid., p. 190; Library of Congress, "Trial of the Major War Criminals Before International Military Tribunal, Volume XI," p. 398.
35. Library of Congress, "Trial of the Major War Criminals Before International Military Tribunal, Volume XXII," pp. 514–17, https://www.loc.gov/rr/frd/Military_Law/pdf/NT_Vol-XXII.pdf, accessed April 3, 2018.
36. Rees, *Auschwitz: A New History*, p. 224; Höss, *Commandant of Auschwitz*, p. 156; Langbein, *People in Auschwitz*, p. 48.
37. Höss, *Commandant of Auschwitz*, p. 154.
38. Gilbert, *Nuremberg Diary*, pp. 249–50.
39. Ibid., pp. 250–51.
40. Ibid., p. 260.
41. Goldensohn, *The Nuremberg Interviews*, p. 298.
42. Ibid., p. 308.
43. Ibid., p. 310, 315.
44. Ibid.
45. Höss, *Commandant of Auschwitz*, p. 154; Goldensohn, *The Nuremberg Interviews*, p. 309.
46. Gilbert, *Nuremberg Diary*, p. 258; Höss, *Commandant of Auschwitz*, pp. 156, 181; Goldensohn, *The Nuremberg Interviews*, p. 309.
47. Höss, *Commandant of Auschwitz*, p. 181; Deselaers, *And Your Conscience Never Haunted You?* p. 209.
48. Höss, *Commandant of Auschwitz*, pp. 180–81.
49. Frankl, *Man's Search for Meaning*, p. 80.

Chapter XII

1. Deselaers, *And Your Conscience Never Haunted You?* pp. 209–11; Prof. Dr. Stanislaw Batawia, *Rudolf Höss, kommendant obozu w Oswiecimiu* [Rudolf Höss, Commander of the Auschwitz Camp], Warsaw: 1951, pp. 13f, 26f.
2. Batawia, *Rudolf Höss, kommendant obozu w Oswiecimiu* [Rudolf Höss, Commander of the Auschwitz Camp], p. 57.
3. Gilbert, *Nuremberg Diary*, p. 259.
4. Höss, *Commandant of Auschwitz*, p. 180.
5. Höss, *Death Dealer: The Memoirs of the SS Commandant at Auschwitz*, pp. 193–95.
6. Ibid., pp. 189–93.
7. Deselaers, *And Your Conscience Never Haunted You?* p. 220.
8. Ibid., pp. 220–22.
9. Ibid., p. 224.
10. United States Memorial Holocaust Museum, "Auschwitz," Holocaust Encyclopedia, https://www.ushmm.org/wlc/en/article.php?ModuleId=10005189, accessed March 12, 2018; Segev, *Soldiers of Evil*, p. 211; Deselaers, *And Your Conscience Never Haunted You?* pp. 223–24.
11. Höss, *Death Dealer: The Memoirs of the SS Commandant at Auschwitz*, p. 196; Harding, *Hanns and Rudolf*, pp. 272–73; Deselaers, *And Your Conscience Never Haunted You?* p. 225.
12. Höss, *Death Dealer: The Memoirs of the SS Commandant at Auschwitz*, pp. 196–97; Harding, *Hanns and Rudolf*, pp. 273–74; Frankl, *Man's Search for Meaning*, p. 9; Laurence Rees, "Auschwitz: Inside the Nazi State," http://www.pbs.org/auschwitz/40-45/liberation/1945b.html, accessed March 12, 2018.

Chapter XIII

1. GENi, "Lore Winternitz," https://www.geni.com/people/Lore-Winternitz/6000000023469964316, accessed March 15, 2019; GENi, "Stepan Michael Winternitz," https://www.geni.com/people/Stepan-Winternitz/6000000023470028315, accessed March 15, 2019; Holocaust.cz, "Lore Winternitzova," https://www.holocaust.cz/en/database-of-victims/victim/134874-lore-winternitzova, accessed March 15, 2019; MyHeritage, "Lore Winternitzova," https://www.myheritage.com/matchingresult-eebf9ed15302670fbad523c4ec1cda53?authrn=partner_Geni&trp=match_button_profile#smart_matches.

2. John Jay Hughes, "A Mass Murderer Repents: The Case of Rudolf Hoess, Commandant of Auschwitz," Archbishop Gerety Lecture at Seton Hall University, South Orange, New Jersey, March 25, 1998.

3. Richard Sonnenfeldt, Interview 46858, Visual History Archive, USC Shoah Foundation, 1996, Segment 190, accessed July 31, 2019.

4. Höss, *Commandant of Auschwitz*, p. 25.

5. William Styron, *Sophie's Choice*, New York: Open Road Integrated Media, 2010, Kindle edition, pp. 528–29, 560.

6. Hart, *Return to Auschwitz*, pp. 171–72.

7. Deselaers, *And Your Conscience Never Haunted You?* p. 380.

8. Segev, *Soldiers of Evil*, pp. 9, 218.

Appendix I

1. Holocaust Education & Archive Research Team, "Rudolf Höss, Commandant of Auschwitz," http://www.holocaustresearchproject.org/othercamps/hoess.html, accessed June 15, 2018.

Appendix II

1. Library of Congress, "Trial of the Major War Criminals Before International Military Tribunal, Volume XXXIII," pp. 275–79, https://www.loc.gov/rr/frd/Military_Law/pdf/NT_Vol-XXXIII.pdf, accessed April 3, 2018.

Bibliography

Auschwitz-Birkenau Memorial and Museum. "The Organizational Structure of Auschwitz Concentration Camp." http://auschwitz.org/en/history/the-ss-garrison/the-organizational-structure-of-auschwitz-concentration-camp/. Accessed April 14, 2018.
Auschwitz-Birkenau Memorial and Museum. "The Unloading Ramps and Selections." http://auschwitz.org/en/history/auschwitz-and-shoah/the-unloading-ramps-and-selections. Accessed June 2, 2018.
Bard, Mitchell G. "Virtual Jewish World: Baden, Germany." Jewish Virtual Library, 2008. http://www.jewishvirtuallibrary.org/baden-germany-virtual-jewish-history-tour. Accessed April 5, 2018.
Batawia, Prof. Dr. Stanislaw. *Rudolf Höss, kommendant obozu w Oswiecimiu* [Rudolf Höss, Commander of the Auschwitz Camp].Warsaw: 1951.
Bauer, Yehuda. "Gypsies," in *Anatomy of the Auschwitz Death Camp*. Eds. Yisrael Gutman and Michael Berenbaum. Bloomington: Indiana University Press, 1994.
Beir, Robert L., and Brian Josepher. *Roosevelt and the Holocaust*. New York: Skyhorse Publishing, 2013.
Broad, Pery. *KZ Auschwitz*. Oświęcim: Panstwowe Muzeum Oświęcim, 1965.
Browning, Christopher R. *The Origins of the Final Solution*. Lincoln: University of Nebraska Press, 2004.
Czech, Danuta. *Auschwitz Chronicle: 1939–1945*. New York: Henry Holt & Co., 1990.
Czech, Danuta. "The Auschwitz Prison Administration," in *Anatomy of the Auschwitz Death Camp*. Eds. Yisrael Gutman and Michael Berenbaum. Bloomington: Indiana University Press, 1994.
Deselaers, Manfred. *And Your Conscience Never Haunted You?* Oświęcim: Auschwitz-Birkenau State Museum, 2017.
Dubiel, Stanislaw. "Deposition of Stanislaw Dubiel," in *KZ Auschwitz Seen by the SS*. New York: Howard Fertig, 1994.
Dwork, Deborah, and Robert Jan van Pelt. *Auschwitz: 1270 to the Present*. New York: W. W. Norton & Company, 1996.
Encyclopaedia Britannica. "Hippocratic Oath." 2017. https://www.britannica.com/topic/Hippocratic-oath. Accessed June 8, 2018.
Frankl, Viktor E. *Man's Search for Meaning*. Boston: Beacon Press, 2014.
Friedlander, Saul. *The Years of Extermination: Nazi Germany and the Jews, 1939–1945*. New York: HarperCollins, 2007. Kindle Edition.
GENi. "Franz Xaver Höss." https://www.geni.com/people/Franz-Höss/6000000076970035394. Accessed April 11, 2019.
GENi. "Lore Winternitz." https://www.geni.com/people/Lore-Winternitz/600000023469964316. Accessed March 15, 2019.
GENi. "Stepan Michael Winternitz." https://www.geni.com/people/Stepan-Winternitz/6000000023470028315. Accessed March 15, 2019.
Gilbert, G. M. *Nuremberg Diary*. New York: Da Capo Press, 1995.
Goldensohn, Leon. *The Nuremberg Interviews*. New York: Alfred A. Knopf, 2004.

Gutman, Ysrael, and Michael Berenbaum, eds. *Anatomy of the Auschwitz Death Camp.* Bloomington: Indiana University Press, 1994.
Harding, Thomas. *Hanns and Rudolf.* New York: Simon & Schuster Paperbacks, 2013.
Harding, Thomas. "Hiding in N. Virginia, A Daughter of Auschwitz." *Washington Post*, September 7, 2013. https://www.washingtonpost.com/lifestyle/magazine/hiding-in-n-virginia-a-daughter-of-auschwitz/2013/09/06/1314d648-04fd-11e3-a07f-49ddc7417125_story.html?noredirect=on&utm_term=.31eaf13074c6. Accessed June 9, 2018.
Harris, Whitney. Interview 33930, Visual History Archive, USC Shoah Foundation, 1997. Accessed June 3, 2018.
Harris, Whitney R. *Tyranny on Trial.* Dallas: Southern Methodist University Press, 1954.
Hart, Kitty. *Return to Auschwitz.* New York: American Book-Stratford Press, 1982.
Hilberg, Raul. *The Destruction of the European Jews.* New York: Holmes & Meier, 1985.
Hitler, Adolf. *Mein Kampf.* Cambridge: Riverside Press, 1943.
Holden, Wendy. *Born Survivors.* London: HarperCollins, 2015.
Holocaust Education & Archive Research Team. "Rudolf Höss, Commandant of Auschwitz." http://www.holocaustresearchproject.org/othercamps/hoess.html. Accessed June 15, 2018.
Holocaust.cz. "Lore Winternitzova." https://www.holocaust.cz/en/database-of-victims/victim/134874-lore-winternitzova. Accessed March 15, 2019.
Höss, Rudolf. *Death Dealer: The Memoirs of the SS Commandant at Auschwitz.* Ed. Steven Paskuly. Amherst: Prometheus Books, 1992. Kindle Edition.
Höss, Rudolf. "Introduction by Primo Levi," in *Commandant of Auschwitz.* London: Weidenfeld & Nicolson, 2000.
Hughes, John Jay. "A Mass Murderer Repents: The Case of Rudolf Hoess, Commandant of Auschwitz." Archbishop Gerety Lecture at Seton Hall University, South Orange, New Jersey. March 25, 1998.
"Interrogations, Summaries of Interrogations, and Related Records, 1945–1946", Hoess, Rudolf, April 5, 1946, Record Group 238, National Archives and Records Administration, October 15, 2019, https://catalog.archives.gov/id/57323382.
Jewish Virtual Library. "The Einsatzgruppen: Heydrich's Instructions to Einsatzgruppen Chiefs (September 21, 1939)." http://www.jewishvirtuallibrary.org/heydrich-s-instructions-to-einsatzgruppen-chiefs-september-1939-2. Accessed April 11, 2018.
Jewish Virtual Library. "The 'Final Solution': Göring Commission to Heydrich." https://www.jewishvirtuallibrary.org/gring-commission-to-heydrich. Accessed April 11, 2018.
Jewish Virtual Library. "Himmler's Posen Speech—'Extermination.'" http://www.jewishvirtuallibrary.org/himmler-s-posen-speech-quot-extermination-quot. Accessed June 12, 2018.
Jewish Virtual Library. "Rudolf Höss: 1900–1947." http://www.jewishvirtuallibrary.org/rudolf-h-ouml-ss. Accessed May 22, 2018.
Joskowitz, Sarah. Interview 47504, Visual History Archive, USC Shoah Foundation, 1998. Accessed July 1, 2018.
Keren, Nili. "The Family Camp," in *Anatomy of the Auschwitz Death Camp.* Eds. Yisrael Gutman and Michael Berenbaum. Bloomington: Indiana University Press, 1994.
Kor, Eva. Interview 1917, Visual History Archive, USC Shoah Foundation, 1995. Accessed March 23, 2018.
Krakowski, Shmuel. "The Satellite Camps," in *Anatomy of the Auschwitz Death Camp.* Eds. Yisrael Gutman and Michael Berenbaum. Bloomington: Indiana University Press, 1994.
Kremer, Johann Paul. "Diary," in *KZ Auschwitz Seen by the SS.* New York: Howard Fertig, 1994.
Kubica, Helena. "Children," in *Anatomy of the Auschwitz Death Camp.* Eds. Yisrael Gutman and Michael Berenbaum. Bloomington: Indiana University Press, 1994.
Kubica, Helena. "The Crimes of Josef Mengele," in *Anatomy of the Auschwitz Death Camp.* Eds. Yisrael Gutman and Michael Berenbaum. Bloomington: Indiana University Press, 1994.
Landwirth, Henri. *Gift of Life.* Privately published, 2009.
Langbein, Hermann. "The Auschwitz Underground," in *Anatomy of the Auschwitz Death Camp.* Eds. Yisrael Gutman and Michael Berenbaum. Bloomington: Indiana University Press, 1994.
Langbein, Hermann. *People in Auschwitz.* Chapel Hill: University of North Carolina Press, 2004. Kindle Edition.

Lasik, Aleksander. "Historical-Sociological Profile of the Auschwitz SS," in *Anatomy of the Auschwitz Death Camp*. Eds. Yisrael Gutman and Michael Berenbaum. Bloomington: Indiana University Press, 1994.
Lasik, Aleksander. "Postwar Prosecution of the Auschwitz SS," in *Anatomy of the Auschwitz Death Camp*. Eds. Yisrael Gutman and Michael Berenbaum. Bloomington: Indiana University Press, 1994.
Lasik, Aleksander. "Rudolph Hoess: Manager of Crime," in *Anatomy of the Auschwitz Death Camp*. Eds. Yisrael Gutman and Michael Berenbaum. Bloomington: Indiana University Press, 1994.
Levi, Primo. *Auschwitz Report*. London: Verso, 2006.
Levi, Primo. *Survival in Auschwitz*. New York: Touchstone, 1996.
Library of Congress. "Trial of the Major War Criminals Before International Military Tribunal, Volume I." https://www.loc.gov/rr/frd/Military_Law/pdf/NT_Vol-I.pdf. Accessed March 12, 2018.
Library of Congress. "Trial of the Major War Criminals Before International Military Tribunal, Volume II." https://www.loc.gov/rr/frd/Military_Law/pdf/NT_Vol-II.pdf. Accessed May 20, 2018.
Library of Congress. "Trial of the Major War Criminals Before International Military Tribunal, Volume V." https://www.loc.gov/rr/frd/Military_Law/pdf/NT_war-criminals_Vol-V.pdf. Accessed April 3, 2018.
Library of Congress. "Trial of the Major War Criminals Before International Military Tribunal, Volume VI." https://www.loc.gov/rr/frd/Military_Law/pdf/NT_Vol-VI.pdf. Accessed May 30, 2018.
Library of Congress. "Trial of the Major War Criminals Before International Military Tribunal, Volume XI." https://www.loc.gov/rr/frd/Military_Law/pdf/NT_Vol-XI.pdf. Accessed March 12, 2018.
Library of Congress. "Trial of the Major War Criminals Before International Military Tribunal, Volume XX." https://www.loc.gov/rr/frd/Military_Law/pdf/NT_Vol-XX.pdf. Accessed June 23, 2018.
Library of Congress. "Trial of the Major War Criminals Before International Military Tribunal, Volume XXII." https://www.loc.gov/rr/frd/Military_Law/pdf/NT_Vol-XXII.pdf. Accessed April 3, 2018.
Library of Congress. "Trial of the Major War Criminals Before International Military Tribunal, Volume XXXIII." https://www.loc.gov/rr/frd/Military_Law/pdf/NT_Vol-XXXIII.pdf. Accessed April 3, 2018.
Library of Congress. "Trial of the Major War Criminals Before International Military Tribunal, Volume XXXV." https://www.loc.gov/rr/frd/Military_Law/pdf/NT_Vol-XXXV.pdf. Accessed April 4, 2018.
Library of Congress. "Law Reports of Trials of War Criminals, Vol. VII." https://www.loc.gov/rr/frd/Military_Law/pdf/Law-Reports_Vol-7.pdf. Accessed March 12, 2018.
Lifton, Robert Jay, and Amy Hackett. "Nazi Doctors," in *Anatomy of the Auschwitz Death Camp*. Eds. Yisrael Gutman and Michael Berenbaum. Bloomington: Indiana University Press, 1994.
Longerich, Peter. *Holocaust: The Nazi Persecution and Murder of the Jews*. New York: Oxford University Press, 2010.
Müller, Filip. *Eyewitness Auschwitz*. Chicago: Ivan R. Dee, 1979.
The National Archives. "War Crimes, FO 371/57649." http://discovery.nationalarchives.gov.uk/recordcopy/RC1509119-08866349-0e17-4b71-bef3-c7b49365310f. Accessed April 25, 2018.
Nazi Concentration Camps—Film Shown at Nuremberg War Crimes Trial. https://www.bing.com/videos/search?q=film+shown+at+nuremberg+trials&view=detail&mid=0724B20B704E1D1FD8F00724B20B704E1D1FD8F0&FORM=VIRE.
Nolan, R. S. "Catholic Encyclopedia (1913)/Law of the Seal of Confession." https://en.wikisource.org/wiki/Catholic_Encyclopedia_(1913)/Law_of_the_Seal_of_Confession. Accessed April 5, 2018.
Nyiszli, Miklos. *Auschwitz: A Doctor's Eyewitness Account*. New York: Arcade Publishing, 1960. Kindle Edition.
Piper, Franciszek. "Gas Chambers and Crematoria," in *Anatomy of the Auschwitz Death Camp*.

Eds. Yisrael Gutman and Michael Berenbaum. Bloomington: Indiana University Press, 1994.
Piper, Franciszek. "The System of Prisoner Exploitation," in *Anatomy of the Auschwitz Death Camp*. Eds. Yisrael Gutman and Michael Berenbaum. Bloomington: Indiana University Press, 1994.
Pressac, Jean-Claude, with Robert Jan van Pelt. "The Machinery of Mass Murder at Auschwitz," in *Anatomy of the Auschwitz Death Camp*. Eds. Yisrael Gutman and Michael Berenbaum. Bloomington: Indiana University Press, 1994.
Rees, Laurence. *Auschwitz: A New History*. New York: BBC Books, 2005.
Rees, Laurence. "Liberation & Revenge." Auschwitz: Inside the Nazi State. http://www.pbs.org/auschwitz/40-45/liberation/1945b.html.
"Second Battle of Kut." https://en.wikipedia.org/wiki/Second_Battle_of_Kut. Accessed July 28, 2019.
Segev, Tom. *Soldiers of Evil*. Jerusalem: Domino Press, 1987.
Sendrowicz, Ester. Interview 22539, Visual History Archive, USC Shoah Foundation, 1996. Accessed July 31, 2019.
Shirer, William L. *The Rise and Fall of the Third Reich*. New York: MJF Books, 1959.
Smolen, Kazimierz. *Auschwitz, 1940–1945*. Albuquerque: Route 66 Publishing, 1995.
Sonnenfeldt, Richard. Interview 46858, Visual History Archive, USC Shoah Foundation, 1996. Accessed July 31, 2019.
Steinbacher, Sybille. *Auschwitz*. New York: HarperCollins, 2005.
Strzelecka, Irena. "Hospitals," in *Anatomy of the Auschwitz Death Camp*. Eds. Yisrael Gutman and Michael Berenbaum. Bloomington: Indiana University Press, 1994.
Strzelecka, Irena. "Women," in *Anatomy of the Auschwitz Death Camp*. Eds. Yisrael Gutman and Michael Berenbaum. Bloomington: Indiana University Press, 1994.
Strzelecki, Andrzej. "The Plunder of Victims and Their Corpses," in *Anatomy of the Auschwitz Death Camp*. Eds. Yisrael Gutman and Michael Berenbaum. Bloomington: Indiana University Press, 1994.
Styron, William. *Sophie's Choice*. New York: Open Road Integrated Media, 2010. Kindle Edition.
Tenenbaum, Joseph. *Auschwitz In Retrospect: The Self-Portrait of Rudolf Hoess, Commander of Auschwitz*. United Kingdom: Pickle Partners Publishing, 2015. Kindle Edition.
Tusa, Ann, and John Tusa. *The Nuremberg Trial*. New York: Atheneum, 1984.
United States Memorial Holocaust Museum. "Introduction to the Holocaust." Holocaust Encyclopedia. https://www.ushmm.org/wlc/en/article.php?ModuleId=10005189. Accessed March 12, 2018.
van Pelt, Robert Jan. "A Site in Search of a Mission," in *Anatomy of the Auschwitz Death Camp*. Eds. Yisrael Gutman and Michael Berenbaum. Bloomington: Indiana University Press, 1994.
Venezia, Shlomo. *Inside the Gas Chambers*. Cambridge: Polity Press, 2009.
Vogel, Mike. Interview 40285, Visual History Archive, USC Shoah Foundation, 1998. Accessed July 1, 2018.
Waite, Robert G. L. *Vanguard of Nazism*. New York: W.W. Norton & Company, 1952.
Wiesel, Elie. *Night*. New York: Hill & Wang, 1972.

Index

Numbers in **_bold italics_** indicate pages with illustrations

Aktion 14f13 program 22
Aktion Höss 142
Aktion 1005 130
Alexander, Alfred 20
Alexander, Hanns Hermann 19–20, 22–23, 28; arrest of Rudolf Höss 25–26; assigned to war crimes investigation team 21; change of name 21; Dunkirk 20; enlistment in RAF 20; family emigration from Germany 20; Hedwig Höss interrogation 24–25; Hössler interrogation 21–22
Alexander, Henny 20
Alte Judenrampe 74; see also trains
Amen, John Harlan 158, 159
Amtsgruppe DI 13, 153, 156, 171, 200; Höss appointment to 141, 154
Anatomy of the Auschwitz Death Camp 142
And Your Conscience Never Haunted You? 196
anti-Semitism 3, 6, 20, 141, 180–181, 182, 198
ARBEIT MACHT FREI 49, 163; Höss explanation of 49–**_50_**
Artaman League 5, 37, 40, 51
Aumeier, Hans 22, 55–56, 57, 120
Auschwitz 1, 2, 4, 8, 9, 10, 11, 48, 155, 156, 159, 160, 161, 162, 163, 164, 165, 166, 167, 169, 170, 171, 172, 174, 175, 176, 178, 182, 187, 189, 195, 196, 199, 200, 201, 229; change in purpose 51; construction by inmates 51; date created 49; destruction of 13; evacuation 14, 156; Final Solution 112; Höss report 48; initial problems 49; initial purpose 48; liberation by Soviets 14; organizational structure 58–59; *see also* Auschwitz-Birkenau; Auschwitz I; Auschwitz II; Auschwitz III; Birkenau; Oswiecim
Auschwitz: A Doctor's Eyewitness Account 138
Auschwitz: A New History 183

Auschwitz-Birkenau **_63_**, 89, 141, **_143_**, 152, 156, 163; *see also* Auschwitz II; Birkenau
Auschwitz I 4, 14, 22, 38, 49, **_50_**, **_59_**, 74, 96, 106, 111, 124, 141, 153, 176, 183, 188; blocks 52; crematorium 22, 38, 55, 56, 57, 59, **_60_**, 106, 115, 116, 118–119, 120, 124, 139, 152, 196; first transport 51, 117–120; gas chamber 116–**_117_**; map **_54_**; security **_52_**; *see also* Stammlager
Auschwitz II 4, 14, **_62_**, **_76_**, **_77_**, **_78_**, **_80_**, **_122_**, **_123_**, **_125_**, **_126_**, **_127_**, **_128_**, **_131_**, **_132_**, **_143_**, 153; barracks capacity 63–64; camp capacity 63; construction by Russian POWs 62–63; decision to build 60–62; latrine capacity **_64_**; map **_61_**; remnants after destruction **_14_**; *see also* Auschwitz-Birkenau; Birkenau
Auschwitz III 4, 153; *see also* Monowitz

Babi Yar 111, 130
Bach-Zelewski, Erich von dem 48
Baden-Baden 20, 28, 198; *Kristallnacht* 30; *see also* childhood
Baer, Richard 16, **_95_**, **_107_**, **_108_**, 141
bales of hair **_15_**
Baranowski, Hermann 44, 46–47
barracks 26, 31, **_62_**, 69, 85, 87, 90, 97, 101, 102, 103, 104, 118, 121, 124, 127, 152, 164; Canada 149; capacity **_63_**, 92; Polish Army 1, 48, 49, 154; undressing room 14, 100, 120; wash barracks 64
Batawia, Dr. Stanislaw 188–189, 195, 203
Bergen-Belsen 22, 23, 49, 66, 132, 171, 187; conditions 21, 156; destination of Auschwitz inmates 21
Birkenau 14, 23, 60–61, 62, 63–64, 74, 77, 78, 84, 92, 96–97, 101, 103, 111, 114, 120, 124, 130, 132, 142, 149, 153, 183, 199; *see also* Auschwitz-Birkenau; Auschwitz II

237

238　　　　　　　　　　　　　　　Index

Bischoff, Karl 63–65, 92
Blobel, Paul 130
block elders 69, 73, 87, 88, 89, 92, 100, 172; *see also* prisoner functionaries
Block 10 53, 54, 94, 176, 196
Block 11 52–56, 59, 71, 87, 115, 116, 152, 153, 196; courtyard executions 2, 57–58, **59**, 70, 105, 172, 177, 199; standing cells 172, 176; *see also* Death Wall
Block 25 (Auschwitz-Birkenau) 86, 92, 100, 102
Bormann, Martin 35, 44, 154
British captivity 1, **26**–27, 157; Camp Tomato 26, 169; statement of March 15, 1946 (Appendix I) 10, 169
Broad, Pery 52, 53, 55, 58, 70, 103–104, 118, 131–132, 148, 179–180
Brzezinka 60; *see also* Birkenau
Budy massacre 103–104; Höss cover-up 104, 171–172, 175
Buna factory 59–60, 80, 95–96
Bunker I 22, 124, 129, 139; capacity 120; *see also* provisional installations
Bunker II 124, 126, 129, 139, 142; capacity 120; destruction 14–15; *see also* Bunker V; provisional installations
Bunker V 142; *see also* Bunker II
Burger, Wilhelm Max 23
burning of bodies 13, 22, 55, 107, 133, 135, 139, 157, 160, 168, 186; ash burial site 132; capacity 59, 122, 123, 184; "express work" 142–143; in pits 13, 14, 27, 76, 121, 123, 124, 129, 130, **131**, 142, 143, 144; stench 76, 128, 129, 132, 161, 179, 183

Canada I and II 149, 150, 151; *see also* property of Jews
carbon monoxide 8, 22, 111, 114, 116, 120; efficiency 124, 160
Catholic Church 28, 29, 181, 195; Höss disillusionment with 30–31, 32, 33, 35, 41; readmission to 195
cattle cars 7, 75, **76**, 118, 185; *see also* trains
child victims 13, 74, 75–76, 79, 90, 94–95, 107, 110, 111, 112, 124, **125, 126, 127, 128**, 132, 137, 142, 201; Höss and 116, 134–135, 159, 160, 179, 186, 195, 200; Appendix III
childhood 28; loveless 2, 29; outbreak of World War I 31; wartime love affair 32–33; *see also* Baden-Baden; Mannheim
children (Höss) 24, 38, 106, 107, 134, 151, 154, 178, 182, 196; final letter to 189–191, 194, 202
Clauberg, Carl 94, 196
Commandant of Auschwitz 67, 180, 200
concentration camp 1, 2, 4, 8, 13, 18, 21, 23, 26, 40, 41, 42, 44, 45, 48, 49, 50, 51, 53, 58, 66, 67, 68, 69, 73, 89, 96, 98, 102, 108, 110, 112, 118, 132, 149, 154, 158, 159, 161, 164–165, 166, 169, 171, 173, 174, 175, 176, 183, 187, 189; Buchenwald 66; Gross-Rosen 16–17; Majdanek 141; Mauthausen 66, 158; Natzweiler 203; Nordhausen 66; Ohrdruf 66; Plaszow 47, 163; Ravensbruck 17, 67, 97, 153; Stutthof 155–156; Theresienstadt 97–98, 187, 198
conviction and imprisonment for Walter Kadow murder 5, 35–36; psychological impact 36; release 36–37
corruption 149; Grabner 150, 152; Höss 150–152, 153; SS guards 152
crematorium II 74, 97, 121, **122**, 133, 142, 146; construction 121; cremation capacity 123; design 121; destruction **14**; dissection room 122, 137; killing capacity 122, 160; ovens **123**
crematorium III 74, 121, 133, 142; construction 121; cremation capacity 123; design 121; destruction 14; gold melting room 122–123; killing capacity 122, 160
crematorium IV 14, 121, 123
crematorium V 14–15, 121, 123, 142
Criminal Police 51, 59, 152
Cross, William Victor 24, 25
Cyprian, Dr. Tadeusz 166, 167, 187, 189
Cyrankiewicz, Joseph 177

Dachau 9, 26, 41, 49, 66, 187; assessment of prisoners 44; assignment to 5, 41; block leader 43; flogging 43; promotions 41–42, 43–44
Death March 16–17
Death Wall 54–55, **59**, 87, 105, 152, 172, 176, 177, 199; description of death at 55–57, 59; *see also* Block 11
Death's Head Formations 42–43, 45; *see also* Eicke, Theodor
Deselaers, Father Manfred 196, 202
disease and sanitation 21, 48, 52, 63, 65, 83, 90, 92, 93, 94, 97, 98, 104, 106, 110, 129, 155, 156, 157, 159
Doenitz, Karl 157, 161
dogs, use of 75, 102, 126, 143, 145, 174
Dubiel, Stanislaw 150–151

Eichmann, Adolf 7, 8, 13, 26, 130, 142, 144, 155, 159, 163, 186; Auschwitz visit 114, 115, 116, 120; Hungarian Jews 141; trial 199
Eicke, Theodor 18, 41, 44, 47, 50, 58, 73, 155, 172, 176, 200; assessment of Höss 43, 108, 175; compared to Höss 68–69, 71; death 18; hate indoctrination 42, 45–46; *see also* Death's Head Formations
Eimer, Dr. Alfred 166

Einsatzgruppen 6, 111, 113
Eisfeld, Walter 48
Emmerich, Wilhelm 133
"enemies of the State" 1, 5, 42, 46, 68, 110, 112, 165, 189, 195; *see also* Jews
Ertl, Fritz 63
escape 22, 56, 73, 86, 103, 129, 154, 174, 177; Höss punishment for 70–71, 172; SS reward for stopping 86, 105
execution 168, 188, 196–*197*; apology to Polish people 10, 170, 199, 202; final statement 195
extermination camps 1, 11, 13, 40, 127, 157, 172, 191, 195; Belzec 8, 26, 74, 111, 112, 113; Chelmno 8, 22, 74, 111, 130; Sobibor 8, 26, 74, 111, 112, 113; Treblinka 8, 26, 74, 111, 112, 113, 123, 124, 157, 159–160, 161

family camps 97; extermination 98, 145; *see also* Gypsies
Final Solution 1, 2, 9, 13, 15, 26, 29, 38, 73, 74, 112–113, 114, 115, 134, 141, 144, 152, 153, 155, 157, 159, 161, 170, 175, 186, 196, 199, 200, 201; Höss view of 89, 178, 180; as "secret Reich matter" 7, 158, 183; Wannsee Conference 113, 117; *see also* Holocaust
Flensburg 18, 19, 23, 24, 182
food 3, 16–17, 21, 75, 89, 96, 139, 148, 150–151, 165, 171, 174; daily ration 90–91; deprivation 53, 67, 73, 83, 85, 102; hunger 8, 58, 91, 105; mess tins 91–92; "organizing" 91, 149
Fox, Captain 21–22
Frank, Hans 157, 161, 162
Frankl, Viktor 102, 187, 196
Freikorps 5, 33, 37, 44; Höss service in 33–35, 48, 187; Nazi prelude 35
Fritzsch, Karl 49, 70–71, 169; influence of Höss 71, 172; Zyklon B experiment 115
Führer 5, 16, 18, 29, 112, 152, 154, 159, 178, 182, 201, 203; *see also* Hitler, Adolf
Funktionschäftling 72, 87, 172

gas chambers 2, 4, 8, 9, 10, 21, 22, 23, 38, 67, 74, 77–78, 79, *80*, 82, 84, 86, 90, 92, 94, 95, 96, 99–101, 102, 106, 114, 116, *122*, 123, *127*, *128*, 129, 130, 145, 148, 149, 151, 152, 155, 157, 160, 162, 164, 166, 167, 184, 189, 198, 199, 200, 201; compared to Treblinka 124; deception 27, 76, 118–119, 120–121, 124, *125*–*126*, 160; design 121; destruction 13, 14, 15; effect on SS 136, 179–180; family camp 98; first transport 51, *117*–120; Höss presence 134–135, 136–137, 186; improvement for Hungarian Jews 142; manner of death 136–137; miracle 146–147; percentage of arrivals 111, 112; removal of hair 138; removal of jewelry and gold fillings 138; shooting of prisoners 125–126, 139, 143–144; *see also* Bunkers; crematorium II; crematorium III; crematorium IV; crematorium V
Genn, Lt. Col. Leo 21–23
German Red Cross 95
Gestapo 45, 51, 53, 56, 58–59, 93, 114, 133, 158
ghettoes 6, 75, 129, 142, 159–160, 187
Gilbert, G.M. 29–30, 38, 122, 134, 158, 180, 181, 182, 186, 189, 199, 203; assessment of Höss 184–185
Glücks, Richard 48, 49, 58, 105, 155, 163; Auschwitz escapes 71; fugitive 18–19, 23–24; relationship with Höss 154
Goebbels, Joseph 67, 112; Höss influenced by 30, 180, 181; propaganda 113; suicide 8, 18, 157
gold and jewelry extraction 27, 82, 123, 138, 160, 165; *see also* gas chambers
Goldensohn, Leon 26, 48, 78–79, 123, 134, 136, 158, 184, 186, 189, 199, 203; assessment of Höss 185
Göring, Hermann 1, 8, 34, 60, 112, 157, 161, 162, 165, 200; memo on Final Solution 113
Göth, Amon 47, 163
Grabner, Maximilian 55–57, 59, 100, 104; arrest for murder 152–153; comparison to Höss 53–54, 70, 172; corruption 86, 150, 152; gas chamber 118–119
Grawitz, Ernst-Robert 95
Grese, Irma 23, 175
Grönke, Erich 150, 151
Gypsies 8, 41, 44, 74, 83, 94, 110, 161; execution 98, 144; number killed 8; *see also* family camps

Haas, Adolf 156, 171
Hantz, Stanislaw 197
Harris, Whitney R. 1, 9, 27, 160–161, 199; Höss interrogation 157, 158, 198
Hart, Kitty 85, 104–105, 202; on additional selections 100; on exterminations 128
Hartjenstein, Friedrich 141, 153
Hassebroeck, Johannes 40
Hensel, Fritz 24, 194, 196
Hess, Rudolf 157
Heydrich, Reinhard 6, 7, 9, 44, 111, 112, 117, 148, 158; memo to *Einsatzgruppen* 113
Himmler, Heinrich 2, 5, 18, 37, 41, 45, 46, 58, *61*, 67, 94, 106, 107, 149, 153, 154, 163, 164, 168, 171, 175, 182, 184, 187, 188, 191, 198, 200, 201, 203; on Auschwitz escapes 71, 105; Auschwitz visits 60, 103, 129; award to Höss 62; capture and suicide 8, 19, 23, 157; on corruption 86, 149, 152; creation of Auschwitz 49, 51, 59; and ex-

240 Index

termination 110, 111, 112, 113, 114, 134, 155, 158, 170, 178, 180, 181, 183, 185, 186; final order 19; on kapos 87; negotiation with Allies 15; 1941 meeting with Höss 1, 7, 26, 112–115, 159; Operation Himmler 44; order to destroy gas chambers and crematoria 13–14; order to evacuate camps 16, 17; Posen speech 150; on prisoner treatment 89–90, 173–174; promotion of Höss 130, 176; "special treatment" 118; SS chief 40

Hitler, Adolf 3, 16, 29, 37, 42, 44, 45, 46, 48, 69, 107, 110, 135, 141, 154, 162, 165, 167, 168, 170, 181, 185, 187, 188, 189, 200, 201, 202, 203; awards to Höss 62, 144; Beer Hall putsch 35, 39; chancellorship and presidency 20, 39–40, 41; Final Solution 1, 2, 9, 15, 26, 112, 114, 148, 152, 161, 164, 175, 178, 179, 186; *Mein Kampf* 5, 30, 67, 112, 180; Reichstag speech 6, 112–113; soldiers' oath to 40; suicide 8, 18, 157, 182; *see also* Führer

Hodys, Eleanor 153

Holocaust 3, 23, 27, 114, 161, 180, 199; *see also* Final Solution

homosexuals 8, 41, 44, 83, 161

Hoppe, Paul Werner 155; gassing advice from Höss 155–156

Horthy, Miklos 141

Höss, Franz Xaver 28, 30; death 31; influence on Höss 28–29

Höss, Hedwig 5, 18, 19, 41, 43, 44, 106, 154, 182; corruption 150–151; final letter to 170, 189, 191–195, 202; on gassing 134; on Hodys 153; interrogation of 24–25; marriage 37–38

Höss, Klaus 18, 19, 23, 24–25, 38, 106, 192, 194, 203; final letter to 190

Höss, Lina 28; death 33

Höss, Margarete 28–29, 33

Höss, Maria Luise 28–29, 33

Höss villa 38, 101, 106, 150, 154, 183, 188, 196

Hössler, Franz 101, 130, 131; gas chamber 118–119, 133; interrogation by Lt. Alexander 21–22; trial and execution 23

Hungarian Jews 4, 22, 23, 27, 74, 137, *143*, 144, 149, 150; Aktion Höss 142; deportation 142; Höss return to Auschwitz 141–142, 173, 183; number gassed 13, 142, 159, 184, 198; *see also* Jews

Huttig, Hans 203

I.G. Farben 59–60, 115; slave labor 95–96

Inspectorate of Concentration Camps 13, 18, 23–24, 43, 47, 49, 58, 141, 148, 154, 173, 183

Jehovah's Witnesses 8, 41, 44, 83, 162

Jews 3, 5, 7, 9, 13, 15–16, 22, 41, 44, 56, 60, 74, 87, 100, 103, 105, 120, 136, 145, 148, 151, 152, 157, 158, 161, 165, 166, 177, 179, 184, 187, 188, 200, 201, 202; Aktion 1005 130; *Einsatzgruppen* 110–111, 113; "enemies of the State" 1, 42, 46, 68, 112, 189, 195; family camp 97–98; Final Solution 1, 2, 73, 90, 112–114, 117, 134, 150, 159, 167, 178, 181; first transport to Auschwitz 27, 114, 116, 118–119; in Germany 20, 25; Höss view 29, 67, 69, 135, 164, 170, 182, 185, 196, 199; *Kristallnacht* 30; medical experimentation 94; number killed 8; resistance 132–133; selection *78*, *80*, *125*, *126*, *127*, *128*; slave labor 95, 96; "special treatment" 110, 118, 128; Treblinka 124; *untermensch* 64, 135, 196; yellow star 83; *see also* Hungarian Jews

Joskowitz, Sarah 172–173

Kadow, Walter murder 35–36, 44

Kaltenbrunner, Ernst 9, 158, 161

Kammler, Hans 120

kapos 69, 75, 79, 81, 82, 85, 86–87, 88, 103, 163, 172; Höss use of 73, 89; *see also* prisoner functionaries

Kattowitz 54, 58

Kauffmann, Kurt 158–159

Keitel, Wilhelm 157, 162

Kielar, Wieslaw 53

Klein, Fritz 22, 23, 100

Klein, George 17

kommandos 69, 85, 96, 100, 101, 138, 147, 148–149, 172

Kramer, Josef 49, *108*, 141; appointment to Bergen-Belsen 156; interrogation of 23; trial and execution 23

Krankeman, Ernst 87, 88, 103, 172

Kremer, Johann Paul 94, 100–101, 127, 136, 150

Kristallnacht 5, 20, 30

Landwirth, Henri 75

Lang, Franz (Höss alias) 8, 19, 23; arrest 25; Gottrupel 23–25

Langbein, Hermann 53, 68, 176–177, 180; comparison of Höss to Grabner 172; influence of Höss 172; on kapos 87, 88; on Musselmänner 99

Langefeldt, Frau 97

Lasik, Aleksander 141

latrines *64*–65, 92, 97

Lawrence, Geoffrey 165

Levi, Primo 2, 10, 67, 79–81, 90–91, 96, 108–109, 180, 200

Liebehenschel, Arthur 84, 141–142, 153, 154,

183; compared to Höss 176; efforts to stop prisoner abuse 176–177; execution 177
Lohn, Father Wladyslaw 195, 196
Lolling, Enno 23
Loritz, Hans 44, 46–47, 49
Löwenbein, Priska 81, 100
Ludendorff, Erich Friedrich Wilhelm 34, 37
Lüneberg war crimes trial 23

Mandl, Maria 101
Mannheim 28, 32, 33; *Kristallnacht* 30; *see also* childhood
Man's Search for Meaning 187
mass graves 21, 120, 123, 129–130, 135, 139; removal of bodies 130–132
Maurer, Gerhard 18, 19, 23, 24, 163
medical care 67, 92–93, 104, 137, 171, 174; infirmary 92–93; SS doctors 92, 138, 199
medical experiments 3, 93–95, 106, 157, 165, 166, 196, 199; cancer research 167; castration 94, 166; Höss complicity in 27, 93–94, 157; sterilization 94, 166
Meisel, Yankel 103
memoirs 9, 10, 31, 49, 67, 71, 144, 155, 156, 158, 163, 169, 175, 199; criminality 170, 182–183; on Final Solution 178, 180, 181, 183; on Jewish property 151–152; on Jews 180–182; on killing 130, 133–135, 136–137; on living conditions 170–171; obedience 178; officer and soldier 9, 178, 182, 183; on prisoner abuse 68, 88, 90, 169, 171, 174; on slave labor 155; stifling emotions 135–136, 140, 178–179; unwilling and unknowing cog 2, 164, 170, 187
Mengele, Josef 3, **95, 108,** 122, 137; experiments on dwarves and twins 94–95; selections 77, 81, 82
Mildner, Rudolf 58
mobile vans 8, 111, 114, 130
Moll, Otto 143–144, 179; award from Hitler 144; cruelty 143–144; execution of 144; Höss assessment of 144; Höss confrontation 162
Monowitz 4, 14, 68, 80, 96, 141, 153; *see also* Auschwitz III
Morgen, Konrad 152–153, 154; Final Solution 152; investigation into corruption 152
Muhsfeldt, Erich 139, 147
Müller, Filip 140, 142, 144; on brutality 71–72, 87; mass graves 129; suicide attempt 145–146
Müller, Heinrich 114, 158
Musselmänner 98–99, 143; *see also* prisoner abuse and mistreatment
The Myth of the 20th Century 180

Nathan, Anka 82, 105
National Socialist German Workers' Party (NSDAP) 35, 164, 167, 181; ascendancy to power 39–40; joinder by Höss 35, 37; *see also* Nazis
Naujocks, Alfred Helmut 44–45
Nazis 3, 9, 10, 13, 14, 15, 18, 19, 20, 21, 24, 29, 30, 42, 47, 48, 56, 57, 68, 75, 76, 81, 88, 97, 98, 105, 129, 134, 138, 139, 141, 148, 149, 168, 180, 185, 195, 198, 200, 201, 203; criminality 22, 27, 157, 162, 163, 165, 182–183; Freikorps as forerunner 37; Jewish property 150; joinder by Höss 35; killing by work and murder 73, 74, 79, 95, 110, 111, 112–113, 125, 161; racial purity 40, 181; Soviet POWs 62–63, 64; SS doctors 92, 93–94, 107, 127, 138, 199; use of concentration camps 4, 41, 47, 51–52, 66–67, 108, 124, 154, 156, 164, 169, 189, 199; *see also* National Socialist German Workers' Party (NSDAP)
Night of the Long Knives 42
Nuremberg trial 8, 23, 157, 165, 198; courtroom film 66, 161; Höss affidavit of April 5, 1946 (Appendix II) 9, 10, 27, 90, 93, 112, 124, 158, 159–160, 161, 169; Höss testimony 1, 9, 10, 27, 66, 68, 77, 90, 104, 112, 134, 158–159, 161, 169, 170, 171, 183; Tribunal 66, 67, 158, 159–160, 161, 183
The Nuremberg Trial 161
Nyiszli, Miklos 137, 138, 139, 143, 146–147

Operation Barbarossa 64, 110, 113
Operation Himmler 44–45
Operation Reinhard(t) 148, 151; *see also* property of Jews
Oranienburg 23, 141, 154
orchestras 76, 101–102, 103
"organize" 49, 68, 91, 149, 171
Oswiecim 1, 4, 5, 48, 74, 196; *see also* Auschwitz

Palitzsch, Gerhard 49, 69, 72, 87, 120, 169; corruption 152; executioner 54–55, 57; influenced by Höss 70, 172
penal company 22, 55, 103, 173
People in Auschwitz 54, 68, 177, 180
Perl, Gisella 64–65
phenol injection 63, 93, 94, 100, 104, 114, 127, 165, 171, 199
Pohl, Oswald 1, 16, 54, 58, 120, 150, 154, 155, 156, 163; Auschwitz improvement 51; slave labor 51
Polish prisoners (Poles) 1, 48, 51, 53, 54, 56, 57–58, 64, 70, 71, 73, 87, 101, 105–106, 120, 161, 163, 165, 170, 172, 192; apology to 195, 196; number killed 8

Polish trial (Höss) 2, 162, **166**; admissions 167, 199–200; cooperation 163–164; defense 167; demeanor at trial 167; evidence 166–167; Indictment 164–165; Polish custody **162**–163, 203; Tribunal 165, 166, 167, 168, 200; verdict 167

Political Department 51, 52, 53, 58–59, 70, 86, 100, 104, 118, 150, 152, 172, 177, 179

prisoner abuse and mistreatment 51, 87, 171, 179; arriving females 81–82; arriving males 79–81; conditions for women 97; Höss awareness of 83–84; Höss denial of responsibility for 68–69, 89, 90, 162, 172; Höss failure to alleviate 89. 108, 169, 175, 176, 177–178; pregnancy 79, 82, 97; random violence 102–103; records of 105–106; suicide 105; tattoo 82–83; use of dogs 102, 126, 143, 145, 174; *see also* Musselmänner

prisoner functionaries 69, 75, 84, 103, 169, 175; abuse by 3, 71, 104, 171, 172, 174, 176, 178; "greens" 87, 172; Höss influence and use of 70, 73, 86–89, 171; nationality 87; privileges 87; *see also* block elders and kapos

property of Jews 75, 148–149; Höss corruption 150–151; kommandos 148–149; re-use of 149–150; SS pilfering 150; warehouses 148–149; *see also* Canada; Operation Reinhard(t)

provisional installations **77**; *see also* Bunker I; Bunker II

Quackernack, Walter 133
quarantine 48, 52, 83–84

Rajewski, Ludwik 83
Rees, Laurence 183
Das Reich 180
Reich Main Administration and Economic Office (WVHA) 51
Reich Main Security Office (RSHA) 6, 9, 58–59, 111, 113, 148, 155, 158; denial of extermination order 152–153
Reinecke, Günther 153
Reminiscences of an SS Man 55
Renaud, Germaine 85
resistance 42, 58, 68, 73, 100; Bergen-Belsen transport 132–133
Return to Auschwitz 100, 202
Röhm, Ernst 42
roll call 51, 57, 69–70, 82, 85, 92, 98, 99, 100, 101; Höss and 69–70, 172, 173
Rose, Alma 101
Rosenberg, Alfred 180, 181
Rossbach, Gerhard 34–35
Rumbula Forest 111

Sachsenhausen 9, 10, 26, 44, 49, 54, 154, 180; executions 45, 46, 175, 180; Höss assignment to 5, 44; Höss cruelty 69–70, 172, 175; Höss view of inmates 107; personnel taken to Auschwitz 72, 73, 87, 88, 103; promotion 44

St. Michaelisdonn 18, 24
Sauna 81
Schillhorn, Hans 175
Schillinger, Josef 133
Schlage, Bruno 73
Schlageter, Albert Leo 35
Schmauser, Heinrich 17
Schumann, Horst 94, 196
Schurz, Hans 59
Schutzstaffel (SS) 40; Chief Medical Office 160; courts 152–153; Höss joinder 41; insignia 46; lack of pity 42; racial purity 40; separation from family and religion 40–41; SS man 41, 46, 99, 103, 143, 150, 163, 188, 189, 200; tattoo 41; uniform 40; *see also* Death's Head Formations
Schwarz, Heinrich 141, 153
Segev, Tom 40, 42, 47, 203
Sehn, Jan 9, 163, 187
selection 21, 22, 76, **77**, **78**, 79, **80**, 83, 94, 97, 112, 124–**125**, **126**, **127**, **128**–129, 133; additional selections 96, 99–101, 102–103, 105; arrival 75–76; Höss familiarity with 27, **77**–79, 101, 134–135, 160
Sendrowicz, Ester 101
Sicherheitsdienst (SD) 53
slave labor 4, 14, 16, 48, 51, 60, 64, 74, 111, 159, 164; armaments 154; Buna 95–96; conditions 3, 8, 96; deaths 96, 155
Smolen, Kazimierz 69
Soldiers of Evil 40–41, 42, 47, 203
Sonderkommando 133, 136, 144, 160, 179; aid to infirm 125, 126; aid to SS shooting 143–144; body removal 127, 129, 138, 146–147; cremation 130, 142–143; family among victims 137, 138–139; Höss view of 139, 140; killing of 127, 128, 145; life as 139–141; *see also* Special Detachment
Sonnenfeldt, Richard 200
Sonnenstein Euthanasia Center 22, 120
Sophie's Choice 201
Soviet POWs 8, 64, 102, 105–106, 161, 188; use to build Auschwitz 62–63; Zyklon B tested on 115–116
Soviet Union 6, 8, 64, 111, 113, 141, 157, 182
Special Detachment 125, 127, 130, 134; *see also* Sonderkommando
Speer, Albert 1, 157, 165
Spritzer, Jenny 177
SS Economic-Administrative Main Office

13, 58, 154; regulation on prisoner treatment 173–174; *see also* WVHA
SS guards 43, 81, 125, 131, 133, 137, 175; corruption 152; dogs 102; mistreatment by 3, 68, 103–104; number 86; reward for stopping escape 86, 105; willing participation in Final Solution 179
Stalin, Joseph 6, 136
Stammlager 49, *52*, *59*, 60, 74, 94, 97, 101, 117, 120, 121, 130; *see also* Auschwitz I
Staszkiewicz, Barbara 70
Staszkiewicz, Bronislaw 70
Steinlauf 108–109
Sturmabteilung (SA) (Brownshirts) 20, 30, 35, 40
Styron, William 201
Sylt Naval Intelligence School 19, 23

T4 program 110
Tenenbaum, Joseph 164
Third Reich 1, 3, 4, 6, 18, 29, 35, 40, 44, 58, 74, 89, 107, 143, 164, 165, 170, 178, 183, 187, 189, 195, 199, 200, 203
Thomsen, Frau 18
Topf & Sons 59, 143
Totenbuch 105, 170, 177
Totenkopf 41
trains 74, 90, 101, 114, 124, 129, 133, 163; on Death March 17; Hungarian Jews 142, 183–184; ramps 74, 124; selection at platform 27, 76, 93, 94, 107, 117, 128, 148, 151; unloading 75, 78, 152, 179, 185, 202; *see also* Alte Judenrampe; cattle cars
Treblinka 8, 26, 74, 111, 112, 113, 123, 159; Auschwitz as improvement 124, 157, 160, 161; Höss visit 124; *see also* extermination camps
Tusa, Ann 161
Tusa, John 161
21st Baden Regiment of Dragoons 31

untermensch 64, 135, 196, 199, 201
Upper Silesia 16, 27, 34, 48, 114

Vacek 71–73, 87, 88, 172
Vaillant-Couturier, Marie Claude 66–67, 76, 85, 92, 93, 97, 102

Valentin, Dr. Erwin 177
Vanguard of Nazism 35
Venezia, Leon 138–139
Venezia, Shlomo 126, 137, 138, 139–140
Vistula and Sola rivers 48, 106, 123, 130
Vogel, Mike 173
Volkenrath, Elizabeth 22, 23
von Herff, Maximillian 176, 183
von Hindenburg, Paul 40
Vrba, Rudolf 103

Wadowice 168, 195, 196
Waite, Robert G.L. 35
Waitz, Robert 68
Wannsee Conference 7, 113, 117; *see also* Final Solution
Wehrmacht 6, 111, 113, 141
Weimar Republic 34
Weisenthal, Simon 3
Wiesel, Elie 79
Winkel 83
Winternitz, Lore 198; Appendix III
Winternitz, Rudolf 198; Appendix III
Winternitz, Stepan Michael 198; Appendix III
Wirth, Christian 152
Wirths, Eduard 22, 94, 100
World War I 2, 6, 9, 15, 20, 31, 34, 37, 39, 41, 45, 112, 187; German surrender 33; Höss service in 5, 31–33
World War II 3, 4, 5, 10, 15, 117, 141, 200; attack on Poland 6, 20, 45; incitement by Germany 44–45
WVHA 13, 16, 17, 47, 51, 54, 58, 71, 89, 94, 120, 141, 150, 153, 154, 155, 195; *see also* SS Economic-Administrative Main Office and Reich Main Administration and Economic Office

Yana 145–146

Zaremba, Father Tomasz 196
Zyklon B 27, 117, 118, 125, 127, 137, 145, 155, 157, 188; delivery 122; experiment with 7, *115*; Höss satisfaction with 116; killing time 124, 136, 160; manufacturer 115

www.ingramcontent.com/pod-product-compliance
Ingram Content Group UK Ltd.
Pitfield, Milton Keynes, MK11 3LW, UK
UKHW041938140426
5217IPUK00014B/553